Grade 10

CHRIST AND CULTURE

CANADIAN CONFERENCE
OF CATHOLIC BISHOPS

CHRIST AND CULTURE

Section I: Christ and culture – Foundations

Unit 1
To be human is…?

Unit 2
Who has culture?

Unit 3
The God question

Section II: Christ in our culture

Unit 4
Relating to oneself: Who am I?

Unit 5
Relating to the other: The voice of the other in me

Unit 6
Relating to civil society: Living together in solidarity

Unit 7
Relating to the Church: We are the Church

Unit 8
Relating to the world: Disciples and witnesses

Section III: Celebrating Christ in our culture

Unit 9
Celebrating Christ in our culture

Canadian Conference of Catholic Bishops
Conférence des évêques catholiques du Canada

Dear Students,

Composing this text often moved me and the writing team to prayer. What I wish most to share with you is my own prayer to God, who is always present and active in our lives and in our culture.

Almighty God, out there millions of galaxies decorate the cosmos, while deep within the human body, thousands of genes contribute to the unique identity of every person. Millions are the signs of the majesty, beauty and depth of your creation.

We praise you as we marvel and wonder at the handiwork of your creation.

Lord Jesus, your death and resurrection reveal the power of God's love. Your promises reveal our destiny. Your teaching reveals the truth. Your word reveals the freedom, forgiveness and fidelity of God. In you, the Word made flesh, we celebrate the sign of salvation for all the nations.

We praise you and we give you thanks for the gift of redemption.

Holy Spirit, our consolation, advocate and guide, your gifts carry us beyond our limits. Your indwelling makes us one body. Your power transforms
   ordinary water into new life,
   bread and wine into the foretaste of eternal life,
   olive oil into the scent of wonder and healing,
   human words into the melody of divine forgiveness and mercy.

We praise you as we celebrate the mystery of God's kingdom in our daily lives.

I hope that this Grade 10 program moves you to prayer and to a deeper understanding of the mystery of life and love in Christ Jesus.

Sincerely yours,

+ Richard Grecco

Most Rev. Richard Grecco, Th.D.
Auxiliary Bishop of London

Section I
Christ and culture – Foundations

Section aim:

to name the principles that guide Catholics in understanding their role in shaping culture

Unit 1   To be human is...?

Aim: to understand what it means to be human from a Catholic perspective

What does it mean to be human?

You probably have no doubt that you are human. You may, from time to time, have some doubts about your teachers, or family members, or friends. But you likely have no doubt at all that you yourself are fully and completely a human being.

Then why begin this religion course with the question, "What does it mean to be human?" The answer seems obvious. We can just hold up a mirror to ourselves and say, "This is what it means to be human." However, look at the collection of newspaper headlines on the next page. Do they raise any questions for you about what human beings are?

People have been trying to answer this question over the ages. Take the science of anthropology, for example. It looks for answers about the origins, development and customs of humankind. Anthropology is generally used as a starting point for studies of culture, because culture is a product of human activity.

This course is about Christ and culture. In this first theme, you will explore what it means to be human from the perspective of your own experience, and from the experience of the Catholic community.

Focus your learning

- **Aware and Informed**
  What is it that makes me a human being?

- **Practical and Active**
  How can I make my life more human?

- **Creative and Grateful**
  How can I respond to the goodness of creation?

Key terms

human

person

anthropology

freedom

creation

culture

Catechism of the Catholic Church

Firefighter Sacrifices Own Life to Save Unconscious Victim

Student Stabbed in Front of Classmates

Homeless Woman Freezes to Death at Busy Downtown Intersection

Local Students Collect Funds for Youth Shelter

Medical Breakthrough in Cancer Research

St. Pat's Hoopsters Shoot for Gold in Provincial Tournament

Newborn Found Alive in Nightclub Dumpster

Peacekeepers Return to Heroes' Welcome

Teen Receives Governor General's Award for Bravery

What do you think?

When you read headlines like these, or when you watch the evening news on TV, what do you think about the world we live in? What do you think about your fellow human beings?

Imagine that you are an alien from another galaxy sent to Planet Earth to scout out the potential for intergalactic cooperation among intelligent life forms. You have been given the mission to draw up a character profile of a human being. This profile will help the other aliens to understand what it means to be a human. Which sources of information would you use to gather data and to make judgments? How would you verify your findings? What would you report to your fellow aliens back on the mother ship?

Creation

What does anthropology say about humans?

God created the world in all its richness, diversity and order. *Everything that exists owes its existence to God the Creator.* (See *Catechism of the Catholic Church*, #337-338.) The Christian faith respects scientific research for the explanation it tries to give of the process by which the cosmos appeared in time. But Christian faith goes further: in the birth of the universe, faith sees and celebrates the work of the creating God.

Anthropology is the science that studies the origin, development and customs of human beings. Physical anthropology deals with physiological and anatomical evolution, and classification of the human species. Cultural anthropology deals with the social development, practices and beliefs of human beings. These are the types of questions that anthropologists might ask about what it means to be human:

- What is a human being? How are humans different from other living creatures?
- Where did we come from? How did we originate and evolve?
- How do we as humans work, think, feel, communicate, celebrate, fashion objects and reshape the world?
- How do we order our lives with our fellow human beings?
- How do we deal with the unknown?

Anthropologists use many methods for seeking answers to their questions: they study and classify fossils and artifacts, and they observe and analyze the behaviours, languages, and other characteristics of specific cultural groups. Developments in the field of genetics are giving anthropologists new tools for understanding the human puzzle.

human:

noun – a person; adjective – of or characteristic of a person or persons; having the nature or form of a person; akin to *homo*, a man, and *humus*, soil.

(Webster's Dictionary)

What a piece of work is man! How noble in reason! how infinite in faculties! in form and moving, how express and admirable! in action how like an angel! in apprehension, how like a god! the beauty of the world! the paragon of animals!

(William Shakespeare)

Human freedom

God created us as intelligent beings, conferring on us the dignity of persons who can initiate and control our own actions. Freedom is the power, rooted in reason and will, to act or not to act, to do this or that. It is the power to act deliberately on our own responsibility. By free will, we shape our own lives. (See *Catechism of the Catholic Church*, #1730, 1731.)

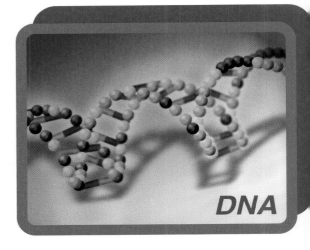
DNA

Genetic research is opening the door to new insights into what makes us the way we are. Science does a very good job at exploring questions about the basic structures of things and how they work. Through science, we are finding new types of questions to ask. However, science can examine only what it can classify and measure and quantify. The human person is so much more than a measurable biological entity. To understand what it is to be human, we must go beyond science. The Christian Scriptures and tradition contain several thousand years of reflection on what it means to be human. These reflections help us understand who we are.

A writer called "the Yahwist"

We don't know him – or, possibly, her very well. He lived in the tenth century before Christ. He has been called the Yahwist because of the name he uses for the LORD God. Around 950 BC, he wrote an account of how the LORD God had created the first human beings. Obviously, it was not an eyewitness account. He wrote it as someone who was an intimate of God. He had observed the lives of those whom God had blessed. Although these men and women were not perfect, and at times, quite nasty to one another, he saw beyond their sometimes-nasty ways. Some say he used as his model what he saw of honour, dignity and power in the lives of kings. The writer saw this same dignity and power in every man and every woman. But he had to look deeply. His times were not that much different from our time. He saw a beautiful truth about the interaction between God and humans. This inter-change, he felt, was God's truth about human beings. We find a similar way of presenting human beings in the Book of Ezekiel:

> Thus says the LORD God:
> "You were the signet of perfection,
> full of wisdom and perfect in beauty.
> You were in Eden, the garden of God;
> every precious stone was your
>   covering ...
> worked in gold were your settings and
>   your engravings.
> On the day that you were created
> they were prepared." (28.12-13)

the time of king David

Psalms are written around the same time

What does the Bible say about humans?

What did the Yahwist want to pass on to us about human beings through his writings? What word-picture of the human does he draw? In chapter 2 of Genesis, he paints a picture of humans as God intended them to be, without their faults and their sometimes-nasty ways. The story of Genesis is not a story of an original couple, but a story of every man and woman. It tells of a time when there is not yet a Chosen People, when there are not yet Jews, Muslims and Christians. It reveals a truth for every man and woman on the earth. In this chapter of the Book of Genesis, human beings are presented in their pristine beauty and goodness. In the next chapter, the Yahwist writes how this order is overturned when humans are seduced to go their own way. Here are a few of the traits of humans as we find them in Genesis 2.4b-24:

1

Humans are a creation of God: Human beings are the outcome of the desire of God. God formed us. God gave us life, our desire for one another, our relation to animals, our moral life, and our ability to speak. At the heart of all reality is the gift of God. Whatever we are is a gift of God.

2

Humans are a mixture of earth and divine breath: See with what care and love the LORD God forms the human being out of the earth. And see how God breathes into the human being the breath of life. Humans are clay and divine breath, earthy and divine, finite and infinite. Part of us is drawn to the earth, and part to what lies beyond us. We are more than our bodily selves: we are an incarnation (embodiment) of the divine.

→

3 Humans are good: Creation is an exchange of goodness. God is good and declares the creature good. There is in the creature an image of God, something of the inner love of God. Of all creatures, only humans enter into dialogue with God. Our goodness lies in our ability to respond to God's goodness. Humans are at core response-able. It is no wonder, therefore, that we pray so naturally to God.

4 Humans are male and female: To be human is to be either female or male. Together, as male and female, we are the image of God. The one is not more an image of God than the other is. What the man exclaims in Genesis 2.23, "This at last is bone of my bones and flesh of my flesh," is equally true for the woman. As Eve says when she gives birth to Cain, "I have produced a man with the help of the Lord." (Genesis 4.1) The human is essentially related to the other. In the Genesis story, before their disobedience, the man and the woman feel no shame in their nakedness because they have no barriers between them. They are in communion with each other before their sin causes division.

The dignity of the human person

Our dignity as human persons is rooted in our creation in the image and likeness of God. This dignity finds its fulfillment in our daily sharing God's own happiness and holiness. It is essential that we freely direct ourselves to this happiness. By our own deliberate actions, we are free to choose the good promised by God. God has created a desire for the good in all of us. This is attested to by moral conscience. We contribute to our own interior growth. All of our experiences, feelings, passions and actions become a means of this growth. With the help of God's grace, we grow in virtue and avoid sin. And if we sin, we entrust ourselves to the mercy of our Father in heaven.

(See *Catechism of the Catholic Church*, #1700.)

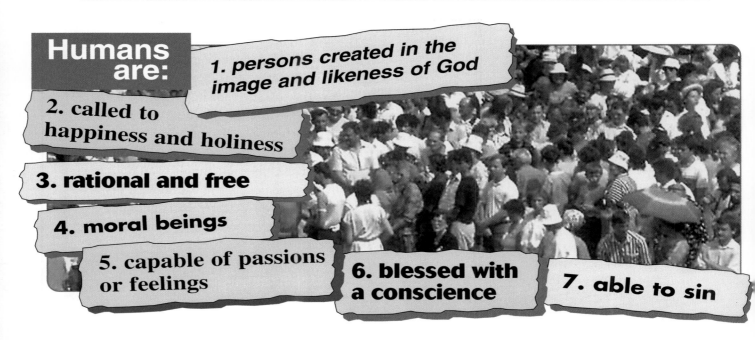

Humans are:

1. persons created in the image and likeness of God

2. called to happiness and holiness

3. rational and free

4. moral beings

5. capable of passions or feelings

6. blessed with a conscience

7. able to sin

This monument on Parliament Hill in Ottawa stands in tribute to the "Famous Five" who fought for the recognition of women as persons.

Women are persons!

The Persons Case of 1929 was a landmark victory in the struggle of Canadian women for equality. For years, groups had requested that a woman be appointed to the Senate, naming Judge Emily Murphy as their candidate. Three consecutive Prime Ministers were advised that women could not be appointed to the Senate on the basis that they were not "qualified Persons" according to Section 24 of the British North America Act, 1867, and therefore ineligible to serve in the Senate.

In 1927, Judge Murphy invited four Alberta women's leaders – Henrietta Muir Edwards, Louise McKinney, Nellie McClung and Irene Parlby – to join her and petition the Government for clarification under Section 24. When the Supreme Court ruled in 1928 that women were not qualified for the Senate, they appealed to the highest court in the British Empire, the Privy Council of Great Britain. On October 18, 1929, the Privy Council reversed the Supreme Court decision.

Thereafter, women were eligible for appointment to the Senate, although none of the Famous Five became senators. These determined women paved the way for women to participate equally with men in public life.

We are created as persons

The basic right of personhood is given in creation. Our society has recognized that men, women and children, healthy or infirm, are persons, and has granted them legal status. Our society still has not recognized all humans as persons, however. The unborn child is not recognized, from a legal standpoint, as a person. In some societies, slaves are denied the status of person. In wartime, we sometimes regard human beings on the opposing side of a conflict not as persons, but as "the enemy." Catholics believe that all human beings are persons by virtue of their being created in God's image and likeness.

Amazing!

A woman visiting Canada stood for a long time looking at the monument to the Famous Five. She read the inscription on the plaque, turned to the Canadian women standing beside her, and said one word that conveyed so much about her experience in her own country: "Amazing!"

This is the official compendium of Catholic teaching. The *Catechism* looks at the four major areas of Catholic life:

1. The profession of faith: all of the major beliefs of our faith tradition;

2. The celebration of the Christian mystery: the sacramental life of the Church;

3. Life in Christ: how Jesus intended for us to live in our relationships with others;

4. Christian prayer: how to pray as Jesus did.

The *Catechism* is referred to throughout this program. It is a rich source of information on our Catholic faith and way of life.

The human vocation: Life in God's Spirit

1. Humans are created in the image and likeness of God
Of all visible creatures, only humans can know and love the Creator. Only we are called to share, by knowledge and love, in God's own life. (See *Catechism*, #355-56.)

2. Humans are called to happiness and holiness
God has placed the desire for happiness in the human heart in order to draw all people to the One, who alone can fulfill this desire. True happiness, which we can find only in God, is the goal of our existence. God calls us to be holy, so that our desire for happiness may be fulfilled. (See *Catechism*, #1718, 1719.)

3. Humans are rational and free
By reason, we can understand the order of things established by the Creator. By free will, we can direct ourselves to our true good. (See *Catechism*, #1704, 1731, 1733, 1734.)

4. Humans are moral beings
Freedom is what makes us different from animals. Humans can act with freedom; animals cannot. Because we intend to do certain things, our actions are moral: they are either good or evil. (See *Catechism*, #1749, 1750, 1755.)

5. Humans have passions or feelings
Feelings or passions incline us to act or not to act. They are part of human nature. They are a sort of passageway between our senses – touch, sight, hearing and feeling – and our mind. In themselves, feelings are neither morally good nor morally evil. (See *Catechism*, #1763-1767.)

6. Humans are blessed with a conscience
Moral conscience is present at the heart of every person. It is like a voice that tells us, at the appropriate moment, to do good and to avoid evil. (See *Catechism*, #1795-1802.)

7. Humans are able to sin
As intelligent and free creatures, we can choose good or evil. When we fail to love God and neighbour, this is what the Scriptures call sin. Sin is an offence against reason, truth and right conscience. It is an offence against God. (See *Catechism*, #311, 1849, 1850, 1869.)

Psalm 8

O LORD, our Sovereign,
how majestic is your name in all the earth!

When I look at your heavens, the work of your fingers,
the moon and the stars that you have established;
what are human beings that you are mindful of them,
mortals that you care for them?

Yet you have made them a little lower than God,
and crowned them with glory and honour.
You have given them dominion over the works of your hands;
you have put all things under their feet,
all sheep and oxen, and also the beasts of the field,
the birds of the air, and the fish of the sea,
whatever passes along the paths of the seas.

O LORD, our Sovereign,
how majestic is your name in all the earth!

Principle #1

To be human is to be a person, created in the image and likeness of God.

To be human, the Scriptures say, is to be a mixture of clay and of God's breath. We are of clay because our bodies are fragile, mortal and linked to the earth for food and sustenance. We are of God because the human spirit reaches for God – for truth, goodness, beauty, order and creativity. Humans are a trace, an image of God. Our place in creation is a special vocation.

Theme 2

Why do we need one another?

Being left alone can be great, for a little while. Even when we are alone, we need the security of knowing that we belong with someone else. We need to know that we have someone to go to when we have had enough solitude.

Being completely alone is something we dread. In fact, one of the most brutal punishments that our society imposes within our prisons is solitary confinement. Physical punishments can break the body, but isolation breaks the human spirit. We all know something of the pain of isolation whenever we are excluded by others for whatever reason. We all want to be included and valued as members of the group.

God created us as social beings. God planted within us the desire for relationships that are fulfilling. In this theme, you will examine the relational nature of human beings and explore the implications of our communal nature.

Focus your learning

- **Aware and Informed**
  Why do we need one another?

- **Practical and Active**
  What steps can I take to improve my relationships?

- **Creative and Grateful**
  How do my relationships become a source of blessing?

Key terms

community   vocation

communion   talents

solidarity   encyclical

Trinity

Flower, Mister?

By Kay Hoernig

He hurried through the milling crowd with his briefcase, his hat and his "excuse-me's" – the impeccable success. His expensive outfit that had everything matching down to his shoelaces cried of success. His countenance bore the languid, bored expression of a discoverer who decided he has discovered everything there is to discover. Wrinkles had begun to appear around his mouth, but they were not laugh wrinkles. Security had taken the adventurous sparkle out of his eyes. Routine had given him a pale skin tone.

Right now he was rushing past the people in order to get to his nook in the world – his office desk – on time. He was in such a hurry, in fact, that he barely heard the old woman's "Flower, mister?" before he brushed past her into the building. He made it to the office exactly in time. And his day went as scheduled.

The next day he was again in the bustle of people-traffic, but now he was on time. Turning the last corner, he saw the old woman. "What a repulsive sight!" he thought. "Why do they allow such a thing in front of my building?" He quickened his step, stared straight ahead, and rushed past her without acknowledging her "Flower, mister?" He made it to his office exactly on time. And his day went as scheduled. But he thought about the toothless old woman several times.

The following day he approached the last corner before his building and stopped. "Could I go around her?" he wondered. He knew he couldn't. He waited for a crowd of people to come by so he could sneak by her among them. Then he straightened his shoulders and a determined look came to his face. "This is my country, too," he silently yelled at her. He boldly marched around the corner toward the office building, but his step slowed as he neared the old woman.

Her tattered clothes made him guiltily conscious of his own extravagant suit. Her shriveled, bent body proclaimed a life of hard work. The odour of old age that she carried with her made him want to turn and run in the opposite direction. But his conscience wouldn't let him. "Flower, mister?" she nearsightedly squinted at him. He stuck his hand in his pocket. "How much are they?" he asked, in a hurry to get it over with. She handed him one, along with a toothless smile. He pitched some coins at her, grabbed the flower, and ran into the building, to safety.

He was tempted to throw the flower out the window, but he had paid too much for it to do that. So he stuck it in a cup of water and put it on a high shelf. Looking at its prettiness made him remember the old woman's repulsive ugliness. He made it to the office a little late. And his day was full of frustrating changes and emergencies.

By the next day his anger had turned to pity. To be reduced to almost begging in the streets must be a horrible state of life. He was lucky. This time, after her "Flower, mister?" he laid down a five-dollar bill on top of her flowers. The wind promptly picked it up and started chasing it away. The old woman didn't even look at it. He ran after the money, captured it, and brought it back to her. She had followed him with her puzzled eyes, but on his return she held out a flower and a smile and said, "Flower, mister?" He handed her the money while accepting the flower, but she just smiled at him and made no move toward the bill.

Then he was angry at her again. He abruptly turned away and left. How dare she have so little regard for money, especially when she's so needy! But he was bewildered, too. He stuck this flower into the cup with the other one and tried to forget the incident. He had no idea what time he came in that morning or what happened the rest of the day. His mind was too occupied with thinking.

All weekend he wondered about the occurrences of the past week. What had happened? Why had the old woman picked on him as her victim? Why had the people changed so much? Slowly it dawned on him that maybe the change was within himself. He did a lot of thinking that weekend, more than he had done for the last 20 years.

Monday morning she was standing there again. He quietly

walked up to her. "Flower, mister?" she queried. He accepted the flower, belligerently daring her to ask for payment. She didn't. Now he was really confused and walked into his office. He took down the cup of flowers. After changing the water, he added this last one to the bunch and set the cup on his desk.

All day he wondered about that old woman. Then he started noticing things. The people in the building were acting differently toward him. The older businessmen looked at the flowers disapprovingly; the younger ones became flustered. The secretaries talked to him cheerfully instead of with the usual forced interest. His visitors that day seemed easier to get along with. He was startled when he glanced at the clock and realized he only had 10 minutes more to work.

The next morning he approached the corner with an unsure step. Yes, the old woman was still there. For the first time he really looked at her. In the folds of her skin lay the dirt and stains from tending her own flowers. He noticed especially the laugh wrinkles around her mouth and her peaceful expression. Why hadn't he seen these things before?

He walked up to her. "Flower, mister?" she asked. He gently took it from her fingers and humbly said, "Thank you." Her smile widened and a grateful look sprang up into her eyes. "You're welcome," she answered.

All that week he looked forward to each morning when he could see her again. Funny thing about those flowers; they lasted an awfully long time. By now he had a bouquet on his desk. And the office and work seemed a lot more cheerful. Why had the old woman picked on him? He didn't know, but he hated to remember what it was like before she did. The weekend came all too soon, and he was sorry: he wouldn't see her for two days. But he did something special that weekend.

Monday morning he started off to work with a spring in his step and a merry "good morning" for all on his lips. The people he passed looked at him in wonderment. Was he crazy? Could be! But somehow they envied his craziness.

He shyly drew near to the old woman and put his hands behind his back. "Flower?" she smiled at him. He brought out the bouquet of daisies from behind his back and handed them to her. Her face lit up with the radiance of joy.

Maybe because the flowers were plain and simple, wild and free. Or perhaps because they signified the hard work and open country of farms. Or maybe she saw the dirt and stain under his fingernails that came from picking the flowers himself.

He left her standing there cherishing the bouquet; but he took with him part of her radiance. And he also had a bouquet.

Be in Touch – Your Child Needs You

Do you touch your baby enough?

Just at a time when researchers are discovering more and more emotional as well as medical benefits from touch, they are also finding that young children are getting touched less than ever.

"Babies are spending too much time in infant seats," says brain development researcher Lise Eliot of Chicago Medical School.

Psychologist Tiffany Field, the nation's leading touch researcher, tells parents to use the portable seats sparingly, especially for babies younger than six months, and to not abandon front- or back-pack baby carriers. "Most infants prefer to be in contact with you, to smell and feel you," she says. It's a matter of emotional security as well as sensory stimulation.

The benefits of touch began to surface about a decade ago when Field found that preemies (babies born prematurely) were more likely to thrive if they had skin-to-skin contact with mom or dad. Data shows advantages to all babies from touch.

Touch is often what is missing in children diagnosed with failure to thrive. "They aren't growing or developing, but they are not physically ill in any way that is recognizable," says Eliot. "Usually tender loving care brings them around."

Touch is critical because it is the only sense that accomplishes three things babies need: It provides a sense of security and safety through cuddling, engages them with the human world, and begins the process of back and forth communication.

(from PsycPORT News Story "Be in Touch with Baby's Physical, Emotional Health" November 3, 2000)

What do you think?

Hundreds of children with severe disabilities lie neglected in hospital beds around the world. There is silence. Not one of them is crying. What do you think are the possible reasons for this behaviour?

For the birds

Scientists have learned great things about relationships from the birds!

– When geese fly south for the winter, they fly in a V formation.

– Together they can fly 71% farther than they could if they were to fly alone.

– Each goose supports the geese behind it by causing an updraft that actually assists the birds flying behind and slightly above it.

– If the lead goose gets tired, it simply drops off to a position further back in the V and allows another goose to take the lead.

– Each goose honks to support the rest of the geese in the V formation.

– If a goose tries to go it alone, it quickly finds out that it is much more difficult and rejoins the rest of the flock.

– If a goose gets sick and cannot continue the flight, a couple of geese will stay with it until it can rejoin the flock or has died.

– Together they accomplish more. Speaking in human terms: by encouraging each other, sharing the leadership, and caring for the weaker members of the group, they achieve their goal.

Now, what about you?

• Describe a situation where being part of a group was to your advantage.

• Describe how the members of the group supported each other.

• What did you achieve as a group that you would not have achieved alone?

• How have you ever contributed to a group and helped the others in it?

Five principles of humanity

In 1964, Jean Vanier, the son of a former Governor General of Canada, made his home with adults with intellectual disabilities, and so began the first L'Arche (meaning "The Ark") community. To this day, he has taken these persons for his family. Hundreds of these L'Arche communities have been established around the world. Living in community has taught Jean Vanier much about human nature. Here are five principles for becoming human that he would share with us:

Principle #1   All humans are sacred, whatever their culture, race, or religion, whatever their capacities or incapacities, and whatever their weaknesses or strengths may be. Each of us needs help to become all that we might be.

Principle #2   Our world and our individual lives are in the process of evolving. It is a question of loving all the essential values of the past and reflecting on how they are to be lived in the new. These values include openness, love, wholeness, unity, peace, the human potential for healing and redemption, and, most important, the necessity of forgiveness.

Principle #3   Maturity comes through working with others, through dialogue, and through a sense of belonging and a searching together.

Principle #4   Human beings need to be encouraged to make choices, and to become responsible for their own lives and for the lives of others.

Principle #5   In order to make such choices, we need to reflect and to seek truth and meaning. To be human means to remain connected to our humanness and to reality, to choose to move toward connectedness. To be human is to accept ourselves just as we are, with our own history, and to accept others as they are.

Excerpt from *Becoming Human*, copyright © 1998 by Jean Vanier and the CBC. Reprinted by permission of House of Anansi Press.

The *Catechism of the Catholic Church* and the human community

The vocation of humanity is to show forth the image of God. It is a calling to be transformed into the image of Christ. This vocation takes a personal form, since each of us is called to enter into the divine beatitude. This calling also concerns the human community as a whole.

(See *Catechism of the Catholic Church*, #1877.)

Don't Be Fooled by Me

Don't be fooled by me.
Don't be fooled by the masks I wear.

For I wear a thousand masks, and none of them is me.
I give the impression that I am secure.

Confidence is my name and coolness my game.
But don't believe me.

Beneath lies the real me – in confusion and fear and aloneness.

But I don't tell you this, because I'm afraid to.
I am afraid that you will think less of me,
that you'll laugh at me.

I'm afraid that deep down I'm nothing and I'm no good.

Yet only you can call me into aliveness –
each time you're kind and encouraging,
each time you try to understand because you care.

Who am I? you may wonder.
I am someone you know very well.

I am every man, woman, and child you meet.

(Anonymous)

Meeting with young people in St. John's, Newfoundland, on 12 September, 1984, Pope John Paul II said, "I am here to proclaim the presence of Jesus in your lives and the power of his love working in your hearts. Because of this presence and this power you can do great things."

Catholicism and community

Pope John Paul II, throughout his years as leader of the Church, has spoken a message of mission and hope to young people everywhere. When he was visiting Canada in 1984, he told young people that Jesus embodies God's love for us. He told how Jesus reveals to us that we, too, can commit ourselves to live in love. "With Jesus," said Pope John Paul, "you will love life." With Christ's example and with his Spirit present in your hearts, find the courage to abandon the things that undermine and destroy your identity. Find a path worthy of who you are. In every generation, Christ awakens among the young the sense that they "are called to play a special part in shaping and building a better world…. In solidarity with your brothers and sisters of different nations and races and cultures, it is possible for you to change the world and to shape a better future for all." In this future, the human dignity of each and every person will be respected.

The Pope's reference to solidarity underlines our belief as Catholics that human beings are social beings. The story of creation affirms that it is →

"The person is for the community and the community is for the person."

(Jacques Maritain)

"Each individual has dignity and value in and of themselves, but becomes fully a person only through relationships and community."

(Thomas Groome)

"Communion is the to-and-fro of love. It is the trust that comes from the intuitive knowledge that we are safe in the hands of another and that we can be open and vulnerable, one to another."

(Jean Vanier)

"It is a feature of the human person that [he or she] can achieve true and full humanity only by means of culture, that is through the cultivation of the goods and values of nature."

(Pastoral Constitution on the Church in the Modern World, #53)

not good for a man or a woman to be alone. We need one another for help and support. We also need others so that we can develop our ability to work together and interact socially. Above all, we need to love and to be loved.

The call that we have received from God, according to the Bible, is to show forth the image of God. We are called to do this not only on a personal level, but also as communities. Our human communities are called to mirror the divine community of persons – the Trinity. The need to live in community and in society comes to us therefore from God; it is inscribed in our nature. It is part of our vocation – our call.

How do we define community and society? The *Catechism of the Catholic Church* describes society as a group of persons bound together by a sense of unity that goes beyond each one of them. A society is an assembly that is at once visible and spiritual. As such, it endures through time: it gathers up the past and prepares for the future. By means of society, I am established as an "heir." I receive certain "talents" that enrich my identity and that I must develop. I owe loyalty to the communities of which I am a part. I owe respect to those in authority who have charge over the common good.

(See *Catechism of the Catholic Church*, #1880.)

Did you know?

Encyclicals are official pastoral letters written by the Pope for the entire people of God. They give advice or shed light on issues that need to be better understood in the light of the teaching of the Church.

In his encyclical *Pacem in terris*, Pope John XXIII had this to say about society: "Human society must primarily be considered something pertaining to the spiritual. Through it, in the bright light of truth, [people] should share their knowledge, be able to exercise their rights and fulfill their obligations, be inspired to seek spiritual values, mutually derive pleasure from the beautiful of whatever order it be; always be readily disposed to pass on to others the best of their own cultural heritage; and eagerly strive to make their own the spiritual achievements of others" (#36).

Reality check   *Relationships gone wrong*

Youth violent crime

The rate of youths charged with violent crime in 1998 was 77% higher than a decade before. In this same 10-year period, the rate of violent crime among female youths more than doubled (+127%), compared with an increase of 65% among male youths.

Young people tend to victimize others who are about the same age and who they already know. Six in 10 victims of violent crime were acquaintances of the accused young person.

(*Statistics Canada*, **The Daily,** *Catalogue 11-001, July 6, 1999*)

Peers play a strong role

Clearly, friends and associates have a big influence on an adolescent's actions. In a 1996–97 study, one adolescent in seven (15%) reported belonging to a group that "did risky things." Girls were as likely as boys to be part of such a group. Youths who considered themselves part of such a group were much more likely to say they were involved in disorderly conduct, that they had skipped school at least once, that they attached low importance to school marks, and that they had started smoking. They were also much more likely to say they had stolen things and had been in fights three or more times.

Most (84%) of the adolescents who said they smoked also said they had three or more friends who smoked. By contrast, only one-quarter of non-smoking adolescents (26%) reported having three or more friends who smoked.

Teen suicide

In 1996–97, almost 7% – or about 44,000 – of 12- and 13-year-olds said that they had seriously considered suicide in the past 12 months. Almost twice as many girls (8.4%) as boys (4.6%) reported serious suicidal thoughts in the past 12 months.

Adolescents who said they were having a difficult relationship with one or both of their parents were 5.5 times more likely to have seriously considered suicide.

(*Statistics Canada*, **The Daily,** *Catalogue 11-001, July 6, 1999*)

"Belonging is important for our growth to independence; even further, it is important for our growth to inner freedom and maturity. There is an innate need in our hearts to identify with a group, both for protection and for security, to discover and affirm our identity, and to use the group to prove our worthiness and goodness."

Jean Vanier (from Becoming Human, *p. 35)*

For your eyes only
Reflecting on your relationships

Take a quiet moment to reflect on the relationships in your life today.
Answer any of these questions in your journal or notebook. Be honest with yourself.

1. Who are the important people in my life right now?
2. How do I show people that I like them?
3. Am I afraid of getting close to people?
4. Can I be myself with my friends?
5. Do I feel comfortable in sharing my true feelings in my relationships?
6. Do I have too many people in my life right now?
7. Do I consider God an important part of my life?
8. Do I think about what Jesus would do in circumstances that I find myself in?
9. Do I take responsibility for my relationships?
10. What relationships would I want to change right now? Why?
11. Am I lonely?
12. Do I wait for others to start up a friendship?
13. Which relationship needs the most attention right now?
14. How do I best show my love for others?
15. Do I let myself be loved?

Something to think about

How do you feel about what you have written?

What have you learned about yourself?

What advice might God give you about your relationships?

Principle #2

To be human is to be a person in relationship with others and to live in communities.

From the beginning God created humans as male and female so that each is "bone of my bones and flesh of my flesh." At our very core, we exist for the other. That is why we live in communities. I cannot be myself without others. As male and female, we are image and likeness of God. At heart, we are social beings. However, our relationships and communities are constantly threatened by what people do to one another.

Theme 3

Are we good?

A survey of Canadian young people shows that nearly half accept violence as a normal part of their lives.* What do you think? Do you think that violence within families or between gangs, ethnic groups and nations is a normal thing? Should we just accept violence and deal with it in a way that will ensure that, as a bottom line, we or our loved ones don't get hurt?

If violence is so prevalent in our world, how can we say that we, as human beings, are good? And violence at the hands of people is just one aspect of our lives. What about the suffering caused by the violence of nature in earthquakes and floods and tornadoes? What about the horror of incurable disease? What about economic injustice? How, in the midst of all this turmoil, can we believe the Bible when it proclaims that creation is good? In this theme, we will begin to explore this very difficult question.

*The survey was conducted by the Centre de recherche sur l'opinion publique (C.R.O.P) in 2000.

Focus your learning

- **Aware and Informed**
  How is the proclamation of the Bible that "creation is good" true?

- **Practical and Active**
  How do we respond to life's difficulties?

- **Creative and Grateful**
  How can we trust that goodness will prevail?

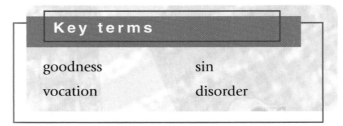

"God is the beginning, the middle, and the end of every good."
(St. Mark the Ascetic)

"What is good in itself glorifies God because it reflects God."
(Flannery O'Connor)

Key terms

goodness	sin
vocation	disorder

God's Grandeur

The world is charged with the grandeur of God.
It will flame out, like shining from shook foil;
It gathers to a greatness, like the ooze of oil
Crushed. Why do men then now not reck his rod?
Generations have trod, have trod, have trod;
And all is seared with trade; bleared, smeared with toil;
And wears man's smudge and shares man's smell: the soil
Is bare now, nor can foot feel, being shod.

And for all this, nature is never spent;
There lives the dearest freshness deep down things;
And though the last lights off the black West went
Oh, morning, at the brown brink eastward, springs –
Because the Holy Ghost over the bent
World broods with warm breast and with ah! bright wings.

(Gerard Manley Hopkins)

(*Reck* means "to have regard for; mind; heed")

1. Why does Hopkins feel that the earth is charged with God's grandeur?
2. Despite the many generations of humans who have abused the earth, God continues to show God's-self in nature. Give examples of how the earth is continually renewed.

Genesis 1.26-31

Then God said, "Let us make humankind in our image, according to our likeness; and let them have dominion over the fish of the sea, and over the birds of the air, and over the cattle, and over all the wild animals of the earth, and over every creeping thing that creeps upon the earth."

So God created humankind in his image, in the image of God he created them; male and female he created them.

God blessed them, and God said to them, "Be fruitful and multiply, and fill the earth and subdue it; and have dominion over the fish of the sea and over the birds of the air and over every living thing that moves upon the earth." God said, "See, I have given you every plant yielding seed that is upon the face of all the earth, and every tree with seed in its fruit; you shall have them for food. And to every beast of the earth, and to every bird of the air, and to everything that creeps on the earth, everything that has the breath of life, I have given every green plant for food." And it was so. God saw everything that he had made, and indeed, it was very good. And there was evening and there was morning, the sixth day.

goodness:

God is the source of all that is good. Human beings, by their nature and *vocation*, are directed toward the good. Coming from God, and going toward God, human beings live fully human lives only if they freely live in communion with God. *Goodness*, then, is the result of being "connected" with God, as branches to a vine. (See the Gospel according to John 15.1-17.)

Did you know...

...that there are two stories of creation in the Bible? (Genesis 1.1–2.4 and Genesis 2.4-25) These stories are quite different from one another, yet both reveal the truth about our origins: We come from God and are created in God's love. Science can help us to understand how the universe evolved. But only Divine Revelation tells us that we come from God, and are created for eternal life with God.

Meeting the Leper

Francis remembered the first victory of his new heart. All his life long he had panicked when he met lepers. And then one day on the road below Assisi, he did one of those surprising things that only the power of Jesus' Spirit could explain. He reached out and touched a leper, a man the very sight of whom nauseated him. He felt his knees playing tricks on him, and he was afraid he would not make it to the leper standing humbly before him. The odour of rotting flesh attacked all his senses as if he were smelling with his eyes and ears as well. Tears began to slide down his cheeks because he thought he wouldn't be able to do it; and as he began to lose his composure, he had to literally leap at the man before him. Trembling, he threw his arms around the leper's neck and kissed his cheek. Then like the feeling he remembered when he first began to walk, he was happy and confident; he stood erect and calm and loved this man in his arms. He wanted to hold him tighter but that would only be to satisfy himself now; and he was afraid to lose this new-found freedom. He dropped his arms and smiled at the leper, and the man's eyes twinkled back their recognition that Francis had received more than he had given. In the silence of their gazing, neither man dropped his eyes, and Francis marveled that a leper's eyes were hypnotically beautiful.

"Meeting the Leper," from *Francis: The Journey and the Dream*, by Murray Bodo, O.F.M., copyright 1988. Used by permission of St. Anthony Messenger Press, 1615 Republic St., Cincinnati, OH 45210; 800-488-0488. All rights reserved.

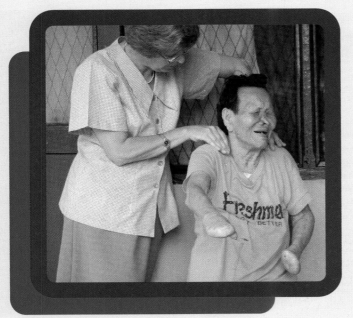

Mother Teresa, the Wino and Me

Robert F. Baldwin

Now abideth faith, hope, charity, these three; but the greatest of these is charity. (1 Corinthians 13.13)

I will never forget the day I met Mother Teresa. More than that, I will never forget what she taught me about loving other people, especially the poor.

She wasn't nearly as famous in the late seventies as she is now, but she already had hundreds of thousands of admirers around the world. I was the editor of a Catholic newspaper in Rhode Island and when I heard she would be speaking in Boston I decided to go.

I arrived at the auditorium early to get a good seat, but I discovered that I'd already been granted a seat in the press section. As I waited for the lecture to begin, I passed the time by chatting with another reporter, who turned out to be like Mother Teresa, a native of Albania. As we were talking, a priest walked over and said to my companion, "Mother Teresa would be happy to meet you right now."

With uncharacteristic boldness, I rose to my feet and tagged along. So did a handful of other reporters. We were ushered into a room where a little old lady wrapped in a blue-and-white sari was chatting with the Cardinal Humberto Medeiros, then archbishop of Boston.

I couldn't believe how tiny she was. But what I remember most is her smiling, wrinkled face and the way she bowed to me, as if I were royalty, when I was introduced.

She greeted everyone that way. I thought that if Jesus Christ walked into the room, she would greet him in exactly the same manner. The way she did it conveyed a message that said, "You are holy."

But meeting her wasn't as memorable as what she taught me about loving people. Until that day, I had always thought of charity as simply being nice to people. For Mother Teresa it was much more.

During her talk, she told us how she and the members of her order, the Missionaries of Charity, seek to recognize Christ in the poorest of the poor.

She told a story of how one of the sisters had spent an entire day bathing the wounds of a dying beggar who was brought to them from the streets of Calcutta. Mother Teresa's voice dropped to a whisper as she told the hushed auditorium that, in reality, the nun had been bathing the wounds of Jesus.

She insisted that Christ tests the love of his followers by hiding in grotesque disguises to see if we can still see him.

A few nights later, I was leaving my office after dark when a drunk accosted me. He was dirty and ragged and smelled bad.

"Did the bus leave yet?" he asked.

The only bus that ever stopped on that corner was a van that carried street people to a soup kitchen.

"You've missed it," I told him. Then I thought about Mother Teresa. I didn't exactly buy the idea that this old bum was God in disguise, but I could see a person in front of me who needed a meal. The soup kitchen wasn't very far out of my way.

"C'mon, I'll drive you," I said, hoping that he wouldn't throw up in the car.

He looked surprised, delighted and a little stunned. He studied me with bleary eyes. His next words floated to me on the smell of cheap wine and they seemed to confirm everything Mother Teresa had taught me.

"Say," he said, "you must know me."

(excerpt from *The United Church Observer*, September 2000)

By Tempest Torn

By *John Bird*

One minute, as the tornado raged around their little rented cabin in the Green Acres park on Pine Lake, in south-central Alberta, Rev. Jamie Holtom was holding his two-year-old son Lucas tight in his arms. "I was telling him everything was going to be okay," recalls Jamie. Then, the cabin seemed to explode under the force of the 300 km/h winds – and "he was gone."

Now Jamie and Katrina Holtom are living the nightmare beyond all understanding that haunts every loving parent – the tragic death of a beloved child.

"Katrina and I don't blame this on God," says Jamie, "but we don't have any explanations either. All we have are a lot of questions...."

The tornado that killed Lucas ripped through the Green Acres park on July 14 while the Holtom family was vacationing there with friends. Jamie, Katrina and their five-week-old daughter, Leah, sustained only minor injuries.

The Holtoms had been traveling in Alberta with a mission team of mostly young people from North Bramalea (Ont.) United, where Jamie ministers. Jamie had organized the trip in conjunction with St. Paul's United in Edmonton to participate in a Habitat for Humanity house-building project.

In their grief, Jamie and Katrina have found themselves falling back →

through times of grief and have proclaimed that promise. Now I will live with that hope till the day I die."

"We can't bear this alone," Jamie and Katrina told their colleagues at North Bramalea as they prepared to journey back to their home and friends. "We need to know you share this load with us."

As soon as word of the death spread through the congregation, people began to gather at the church, said church secretary Anne Robertson. By the time she arrived a prayer vigil had already spontaneously formed. Up to 40 people gathered at the front of the sanctuary, "under the cross. They were holding hands," she recalls, with each one taking a turn in the circle to offer a prayer. "They were stunned. They wanted to be together. They wanted to help."

On Sunday, [Senior Pastor Rev.] Greene told his congregation that "we have experienced Christ's love, so today we gather to prepare ourselves to be the body of Christ to Jamie, Katrina and Leah, whom we also love. We need to walk with our brother and sister in the difficult days to come. We do that, knowing God walks this path with us." Then he and many volunteers from the congregation put in

countless hours grieving with the family, helping them deal with the media, and preparing for the funeral the following Wednesday.

Eight hundred people – more than twice what the church can hold – attended.

With his shock of bright red hair, his outgoing personality and his love of music – from singing, to clapping to banging on drums and the piano – Lucas had won the hearts of the North Bramalea congregation.

So, difficult as it may have been, much of the funeral became a celebration of Lucas' short life.

"How privileged I have been … to experience your words, your love, your kisses, your hugs," his mother Katrina said in a letter to Lucas read during the service by a family friend. "I would give anything to have you run into my arms right now."

A week after the funeral, Jamie and Katrina found themselves back in Alberta. They wanted to revisit the site of their tragic loss once again, before it was bulldozed over. While looking over the site, they both found themselves gazing at "a beautiful rainbow in the distance."

It's possible to make too much of these things, Jamie says self-consciously, but "for us it was a sign of God's promise, a promise we rely on, that in Christ we are going to be together again one day."

on God's love, and the consolations of their faith. "That is a huge source of strength and hope for us. We try to stick together, Katrina and I. We read Scripture and pray, and we try to get through one more day."

He recalls how, the morning before the storm, they had happened to read Romans 8.39: "I am sure that nothing can separate us from God's love – not life or death, not angels or spirits, not the present or the future, and not powers above or powers below. Nothing in all creation can separate us from God's love for us in Christ Jesus our Lord."

"That's our hope for Lucas," says Jamie now, thinking especially of the last few seconds of their young son's life, after he was torn from his father's arms by the howling winds. "As a minister, I have brought many people

Questions for discussion

- How do we try to protect ourselves from natural disasters? Is there anything we can do to "master" them? Are some of these disasters due to human negligence? What does a disaster like this say about the earth and its goodness?
- What does it say about God and God's faithfulness to us? Is there any trace of God in the story?
- What do you think of the response to the tragedy? What response would you give in similar circumstances?

Sin is the breach of the relationship that God established with creation. It means to bring a fault or *disorder* into creation, maiming the work of God. We experience it as a power that entices or tempts us to act against good order. The *Catechism* defines it as "an utterance, a deed or a desire contrary to the eternal law."

(See *Catechism of the Catholic Church*, #1849-1851.)

Tempted!

(See Genesis 3.1-13.)

Ah, that serpent is crafty all right. He knows how to go after the jugular. The poisonous creature knows the weakness of the man and woman. No one likes to admit that in the secret of his or her heart there lies the desire to be like God. The serpent tempts Adam and Eve with visions of power. The serpent knows the age-old prejudice against God. "It is just like God," it hisses, "to not allow you to do anything. God will always keep you in check and make your life difficult with all sorts of commandments. Go ahead, eat and you will have knowledge. You will be powerful like God. You will know good and evil."

Tempted by power! Tempted to go it alone! Tempted to break out of the relationship. And that's what they get. Yes, their eyes are opened. But what do they see? Not that they are like God, as the serpent promised. Instead they see that they are naked. They have been naked all along in the story, but they never noticed it. They had nothing to hide from each other. Now they are suddenly strangers to each other. They look at each other through the eyes of a stranger and feel naked. So they sew fig leaves and make loincloths to cover themselves. But they are also ashamed before God. When they hear the sound of God walking in the garden, they hide among the trees. The woman and the man have not only become strangers to each other; they are now also strangers to God. They flee from God's presence.

Once this desire for power takes over, everything changes. Everyone and everything becomes a stranger: men and women, humans and animals, humans and the earth. Everywhere the desire for power rules. Whenever we make gods of ourselves, we lose our humanity. It should not surprise us that, whenever we flee from God and try to go it alone, God calls to us: "Adam, where are you?"

Did you know...

...that Adam and Eve didn't eat an apple? The story simply says that they ate the fruit of the tree that was forbidden.

Tragedy in Taber

Andrew Purvis – Time Magazine

Just eight days after the horrifying school massacre in Littleton, Colorado, Taber staggered under the enormity of the first fatal school shooting in Canada in more than two decades. Absolutely no one thought it possible that a 14-year-old former student at W.R. Myers High School, weighed down with adolescent resentments and a sawed-off .22-cal. rifle, would shoot two 17-year-old boys he hardly knew…. With Jason Lang dead and Shane Christmas severely wounded at the hands of an assailant too young to get a driver's licence…, there was [an] overriding reaction… of numb disbelief….

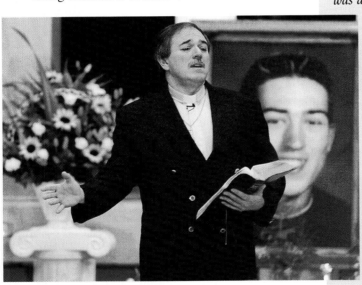

Questions for reflection

1. What is your reaction to Rev. Lang's act of forgiveness?

2. How can our anger towards others and refusal to forgive "imprison" us?

3. Do you think that Rev. Lang may have been tempted to blame God? Why or why not?

4. What do you think Rev. Lang means by, "I used to pray and ask the Lord to give me strength. My prayer is now that Jesus will be my strength"? What is the difference?

My Dear Young People,

On April 28, 1999, the life of our family was irrevocably changed when our seventeen-year-old son Jason was shot and killed in W.R. Myers High School in Taber, Alberta, by a fourteen-year-old boy. I had become a Christian some twenty-one years earlier, and that one fact would be the only reason I would survive such a devastating, unbelievable and unexpected turn of events.

I learned early on as a young Christian that even though I placed my faith in Jesus, that did not mean that I was somehow protected from the evil in this world. When they told me and my wife, Diane, that "Jason didn't make it," I was angry. I didn't direct my anger at God or even the boy who did the shooting. I was angry that the life of a young, caring boy, who himself hated bullying, and who had a good heart, was dead.

My anger, however, was turned to sadness very quickly. How could a young person come to such a terrible place in life where he would kill someone because he was angry? The shooting of our son was a random choice; the shooter did not know who Jason was.

At the Memorial Service for Jason, held five days after his death, I asked people to join me in prayer. I prayed and forgave the young man who had done the shooting, and I asked our community of Taber to do the same. I didn't spend time thinking about whether I should forgive or not. My wife and I did not discuss it; this was simply our reaction as Christians. I can honestly tell you that I take no credit for being able to express forgiveness; this was the Grace of Jesus in our hearts that made it possible. It is also important to understand what forgiveness means. Forgiveness means freedom. Most often, when people cannot forgive, they end up in a place of anger, and that anger, if left unresolved, festers into bitterness. People who come to that place are in a prison, trapped by the powerful anger within them that rules their lives.

When Jesus gave our family the grace to forgive, He set us free from that prison. My family and I will miss Jason for the rest of our lives, even though we know, because he was a Christian, that he is with the Lord now. But I am so thankful I won't have to live in anger and bitterness.

Life will always contain challenges. For me, I know that there is only one way that I will be able to carry on through whatever happens. I can say it best this way: I used to pray and ask the Lord to give me strength. My prayer is now that Jesus will be my strength. The difference is that now I realize that I am just one weak person, and what I need is Jesus, and the Holy Spirit active in my life, to carry me through.

With the Amazing Love of Jesus,

Rev. Dale Lang

Principle #3

To be human is to be essentially good, despite the capacity for disorder and sin.

The Book of Genesis details how the Word of God causes the heavens and the earth to be formed. It concludes the description of the work of each day by marvelling that it was good. We live in a good and friendly universe. It nurtures and supports us. Although this good creation is rent by failure, fragility, disorder, pain and sin, these faults, both in nature and in the human person, do not undo the goodness of creation.

Unit 1 review

In this unit, you explored what it means to be human from a Catholic perspective.

Aware and informed

What is it about me that makes me a human being?

To be human is to be:

- a person created in the image and likeness of God
- called to happiness and holiness
- rational and free
- moral
- capable of passions or feelings
- blessed with a conscience
- able to sin

Why do we need one another?

To be human is to be a person in relationship with others and to live in communities. From the beginning God created humans as male and female so that each is "bone of my bones and flesh of my flesh." At our very core, we exist for the other. That is why we live in communities. I cannot be myself without others. As male and female, we are image and likeness of God. At heart, we are social beings. However, our relationships and communities are constantly threatened by what people do to one another.

How is the proclamation of the Bible that "creation is good" true?

To be human is to be essentially good, despite the capacity for disorder and sin. The Book of Genesis details how the Word of God causes the heavens and the earth to be formed. It concludes the description of the work of each day by marvelling that it was good. We live in a good and friendly universe. It nurtures and supports us. Although this good creation is rent by failure, fragility, disorder, pain and sin, these faults, both in nature and in the human person, do not undo the goodness of creation.

Practical and Active

How can I make my life more human?

Our dignity as human persons is rooted in our creation in the image and likeness of God. This dignity finds its fulfillment in our daily sharing God's own happiness and holiness. We do so through our free actions, choosing the good by following our conscience. With the help of God's grace, we grow in virtue and avoid sin. And if we sin, we entrust ourselves to the mercy of our Father in heaven.

What steps can I take to improve my relationships?

Jean Vanier suggests that "*communion* is the to-and-fro of love. It is the trust that comes from the intuitive knowledge that we are safe in the hands of another and that we can be open and vulnerable, one to another." We can improve our relationships by being careful with one another, respecting one another, being honest and trustworthy with one another.

How do we respond to life's difficulties?

Rev. Dale Lang offered us some good advice on dealing with difficulties in life. In his letter to us he wrote, "Life will always contain challenges. For me, I know that there is only one way that I will be able to carry on through whatever happens. I can say it best this way: I used to pray and ask the Lord to give me strength. My prayer is now that Jesus will be my strength. The difference is that now I realize that I am just one weak person, and what I need is Jesus, and the Holy Spirit active in my life, to carry me through."

Creative and Grateful

Only you can answer these questions. The answer is found in your relationship with God.

How can I respond to the goodness of creation?

How do my relationships become a source of blessing?

How can I trust that goodness will prevail?

Unit 2

Who has culture?

Aim: to examine the dynamic nature of culture as a context for meaning

Theme 4

What is culture?

We sometimes hear people say that "so-and-so has culture," meaning that this person knows something about music or art, or knows how to dress in style, or how to behave in formal situations. In fact, all of us "have culture." We "have it" because culture is almost like the air we breathe; we live in it without really noticing it, until we stop to take a good look.

That's what this theme is about – taking a good look at the culture within which we live. Like the air we breathe, culture sustains us in our everyday lives. It gives our lives beauty and order. But also like the air we breathe, when it is polluted, it can harm us. So where can we start to explore culture? Just like exploring air – start anywhere! Wherever you look, you will find some element of culture.

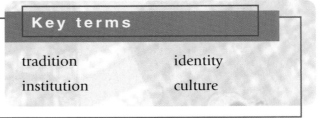

Focus your learning

- **Aware and Informed**
  How would you define "culture"?

- **Practical and Active**
  How can I become more aware of how culture affects me?

- **Creative and Grateful**
  How does culture enrich my life?

Key terms

tradition	identity
institution	culture

What do you think?

What elements of culture can you identify in these puzzle pieces?

Do all of these pieces belong to a discussion about culture? Why or why not?

Do some of these puzzle pieces tell us more about our culture than others? How?

The images on this puzzle don't all fit together, but the pieces do. How is culture like this puzzle?

Exploring culture

We can explore culture in many ways. The following diagram is one way of getting a first look at culture. It is built around three elements of culture. These elements are not the whole story of culture, but they are a good start. The most basic element of culture is human action. In the first web, we place all the things that we humans do between our rising in the morning and our going to bed at night. These actions are the basic building blocks of culture. In the second web, we take one of these actions, for example "eating," and write down all the words and actions that are associated with eating. In the third web, we get closest to the notion of culture. There we identify how we perform these actions in our family, in our Church, in our school, in Canada, and so on. All these actions form a system or set of meanings that sets us apart from others. They are what makes our culture unique.

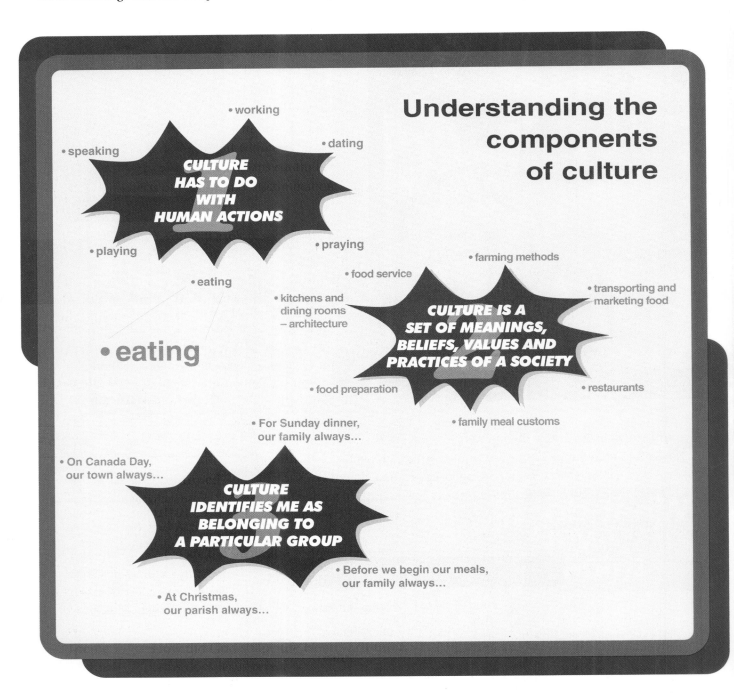

Who's got culture?

We usually think of artists, painters, concert pianists, poets and writers as having culture. They are very important to the life of any culture, but they are only one part of culture. Culture is literally everything; it pervades all we do, how we think, how we speak, how we act, how we dress, how we eat, what games we play, what songs we sing, and so on.

When something is close to us, it is difficult to define it. The same thing is true of culture. Clyde Kluckhohn, an American anthropologist, found more than 160 different definitions of culture. We don't need to know all of them. It is enough to have a definition that works for us. Let's begin by identifying seven traits of culture. Then we will give our definition of culture.

1. Humans create culture

Culture distinguishes us from the rest of nature. Plants don't have it. Animals don't have it. Culture's origin is not genetic or biological. Only humans have it.

2. Culture consists of ways of doing things

Culture is not about the fact *that* we eat, or communicate, or pray, but about *how* we eat, *how* we communicate, *how* we pray. To pray is to adopt a certain form of prayer. To speak is to speak a language, such as English. Culture is about the form. Culture is about the meaning given to doing things. It is a set of meanings or beliefs about how things should be done. Culture is a set of values about the things we do every day, such as driving cars, opening doors, going to the movies, and so on.

3. Culture is public

Culture is not about how *I* do things; it is about how *we* as a group or a community or a people do things. It is not private; it is public. Canadians do things in a certain way; Roman Catholics hold certain beliefs and values; our schools do things in a certain way.

4. Culture arises from tradition

Many of our ways of doing things we inherited from our parents or ancestors. We call these ways *traditions*. Some of these ways go back hundreds, sometimes thousands of years. The way we celebrate Christmas, the way we greet each other, the way we choose governments, the way the Catholic Church is structured – all these traditions were started by people before we were born. Other ways of doing things, such as surfing the Internet, are more recent.

For Catholics, "Tradition" has another important meaning: "What Christ entrusted to the apostles, they in turn handed on by their preaching and writing, under the inspiration of the Holy Spirit, to all generations, until Christ returns in glory" (*Catechism of the Catholic Church*, #96). Tradition in this sense is the handing on of the living gospel through the apostolic succession of bishops, the chief teachers in the Church.

5. Culture is made up of rule-governed actions

Because so many of these ways of doing things come from tradition, we feel that we have a certain duty to keep them. They function like rules. Most of these rules seem natural to us, and we don't question them. That is why traditions change slowly. Many of the rules parents set are rules that they learned when they were young. Young people tend to test or to break the rules set by tradition, only to discover that they have set new rules for action. If there were no rules, there would be chaos.

→

6. Culture becomes established in institutions

Over time, these ways of doing things become established and society reaches a consensus about them. We begin to see that these ways of doing things are linked together to form a "system" of doing things. We sometimes call these "systems" *institutions*. For example, what we do in the family we call the institution of the family. This includes everything from marriage, to the ways we live and eat together. The way we relate to God (the way we worship, relate to others and celebrate the sacraments, and the kinds of churches we build or church services we attend) we call the institution of the Church.

7. Culture gives us our identity

The ways we do things are the source of our cultural *identity*. They set us apart from other cultures. The way the family is structured and does things in Canada is different from the way families operate in other societies. The way that the Coastal peoples of British Columbia live and relate to one another and the earth is different from that of the Mi'kmaq of Nova Scotia. The way that we worship and give witness to our faith and structure the Church creates our Catholic identity. In the same way, our sets of meanings, values and beliefs as Canadians give us our Canadian identity.

How then do we define culture? Putting all of the above traits into one definition is hard. But in this program, we use the following understanding:

> **Culture is the set of meanings, beliefs, values and rules for living shared by groups and societies as the source of their identity.**

Media search on youth culture

The media have a big impact on young people. In your class, do a quick survey of the number of hours per week that young people spend on average doing the following:

- watching television
- viewing movies
- listening to music
- using the Internet
- playing computer games

Which of the media, in your opinion, most influences youth culture (radio, music, television, Internet, magazines, newspapers, movies, others)? To which do you give the most time?

Ask yourself the following questions:

- How does this medium reflect and influence youth culture?
- What appeals most to you about this medium?
- How does this medium have an impact on how you behave, dress, eat, date, spend time, etc.?
- Who sponsors this medium? What influence would the sponsor like to have upon you?
- How free are we to reject or accept the values, beliefs and meanings of the medium?
- What pressure do you experience to follow the trends, the language, the codes of conduct of the medium?

Dialogue between cultures for a civilization of love and peace

Dialogue between cultures, a privileged means for building the civilization of love, is based upon the recognition that there are values which are common to all cultures *because they are rooted in the nature of the person. These values express humanity's most authentic and distinctive features. Leaving aside ideological prejudices and selfish interests, it is necessary to foster people's awareness of these shared values, in order to nurture that intrinsically universal cultural "soil" which makes for fruitful and constructive dialogue.*

(Pope John Paul II,
Message for World Day of Peace,
1 January 2001)

Principle #4

To be human is to live in a culture of shared beliefs, values and meanings.

Culture sets humans apart from nature. Humans create culture. They create an order and a home around themselves in which it is good for them to live. But they do not do so alone. They create culture in communities. Every society has its own culture, defined by such things as people speaking the same language, doing things in a similar way, and placing the same value on actions and objects. Once established, culture also becomes a tradition, something we inherit from others. All humans live in a particular culture.

Theme 5

What are the sights and sounds of culture?

To fit in with a group, you have to look and sound and smell right. The friends that you hang out with have a distinctive culture. You know this when someone who "doesn't belong" wants in. The appearance of the outsider isn't right. Of course, there is a lot more to human relationships and ways of gathering than appearances. However, who can deny that certain physical qualities are important for fitting in and being identified with a group?

In this theme, you will have the chance to explore the sights and sounds of culture. You won't be going to art galleries or concert halls. You will, however, be taking a good look at the groups you belong to, listening to the music you hear every day, and asking how meanings and values are expressed within your culture. Understanding what symbols and rituals are, and how culture uses them, will also help you understand how religion uses symbols and rituals.

Focus your learning

- **Aware and Informed**
  What does culture look and sound like?

- **Practical and Active**
  How can I express myself effectively within culture?

- **Creative and Grateful**
  How can my understanding of signs, symbols and rituals increase my satisfaction of belonging to various cultural groups?

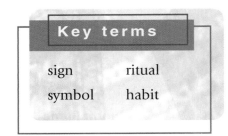

Key terms

sign	ritual
symbol	habit

The Oglala circle

The illustration above shows how the circle and tipi make the primary symbol on the flag of Oglala Sioux of the Pine Ridge Reservation.

The Oglala are members of the Lakota Native peoples. Their world view is different from the predominant world view in Canadian culture. Try to imagine living within their world view where the circle is a sacred symbol.

The Oglala believe the circle to be sacred because the Great Spirit caused everything in nature to be round except stone. Stone is the implement of destruction. The sun and the sky, the earth and the moon are round like a shield, though the sky is deep like a bowl. Everything that breathes is round like the stem of a plant. Since the Great Spirit has caused everything to be round, [humankind] should look upon the circle as sacred, for it is the symbol of all things in nature except stone. It is also the symbol of the circle that makes the edge of the world and therefore of the four winds that travel there. Consequently it is also the symbol of the year. The day, the night and the moon go in a circle above the sky. Therefore the circle is a symbol of these divisions of time and hence the symbol of all time.

For these reasons the Oglala make their *tipis* circular, their camp-circle circular, and sit in a circle at all ceremonies. The circle is also the symbol of the *tipi* and of shelter. If one makes a circle for an ornament and it is not divided in any way, it should be understood as the symbol of the world and of time.

(from P. Radin. *Primitive Man as a Philosopher.* New York: Dover, 1957, p. 227)

The circular nature of the ceremonial drum adds to its importance in Native American cultures.

What do you think?

What does the Oglala world look like?

Why is the stone a symbol of evil?

How does the circle give sense to their lives?

In your own life, are there symbols, like the circle, that have special significance for you?

Symbols are our best friends

Life can get pretty complicated. Sometimes our feelings and desires are so strong that we hardly know what to do with them. Consider the following examples:

Latisha is so attracted to Miguel that she is completely preoccupied with thinking about him. She can't get him out of her thoughts. She is up and down and all over the place with her feelings about him. She is excited to be near him but at the same time is afraid and unsure.

Adam is awestruck by the beauty of northern lights while on a wilderness camping trip. He wants to communicate what he saw and felt in his writing.

Ahmed wakes from a terrifying dream. In his dream the earth swallows him up and holds him captive and defence-less before a violent creature. This nightmare keeps recurring. He wants to be able to unload his fears with someone he can trust.

Marchelle gets anxious every time she is asked to write an essay. She can't sleep. She loses her appetite and breaks into hives.

Lynn has gotten into the habit of shoplifting small items. Last weekend she went on a shoplifting binge and now lives in fear and guilt. To cope with these feelings, she seeks comfort in painkillers.

As human beings, we seem to be a bundle of desires and fears, anxieties and joys. These desires, fears and emotions touch us so deeply that words alone are often not enough to describe them. That's why we need symbols. The word *symbol* means "thrown together." What are thrown together are our desires, feelings, emotions – things that are intangible – together with something that is tangible. For example, Latisha may express what she feels about Miguel with a flower. Adam might write a poem to express what he felt in the presence of the northern lights. When a tangible thing like the flower or a poetic image is thrown together with these powerful emotions and feelings, the flower or the poem symbolizes our feelings. It allows us to get in touch with deep experiences and feelings, such as those felt by Latisha, Adam, Lynn, Marchelle and Ahmed.

Symbols on their own do very little. They need to be connected with a context for them to make sense. Latisha's flower is only a flower, until she offers it to Miguel in a gesture of affection. Then it becomes a symbol. When used within rituals, symbols take on great power. We will explore how symbols are used in rituals later in this theme.

The cottage

For as long as I can remember, our family has gone up to the lake on the long weekend in May to open up the family cottage. We'd pile into the car early on Saturday morning, stop at the Tim Horton's for donuts, and drive for three hours, seeing who could spot the most moose. About half a dozen moose later, we'd arrive at the marina where Grandpa kept his boat.

Approaching the cottage dock in the freshly varnished cedar strip motorboat, Grandpa would always comment on how high the water was that spring. Meanwhile, my sister and I leaned over the side of the boat to look for our "pet" bass in the shadows of the dock. Then we all would make like pack mules and haul about a ton of stuff up the hill to the cottage, which stood boarded up against the winter snow and ice. Following Grandpa's orders, everybody had a job to do, and it had to be done just so. The shutters came off the windows in a certain order, and were piled up under the cottage in their special spot. The key to the cottage hung under the stairs. The key to the outhouse hung by the kitchen window. The key to the sauna hung next to the light switch in the tool shed.

Once everything was opened up, Mom would load the fridge, Dad would get the water running, while Grandpa got out the Maple Leaf and ran it up the cedar flagpole. We kids would have the job of collecting branches that had fallen over the winter, and starting a small fire in the fire pit near the water's edge. By noon the rushing around would stop. Mom would bring down the hot dogs and buns while Dad cut green sticks for skewering the hot dogs to roast over the open flames. And then Grandpa would start with his fish stories, with the fish in the stories getting bigger and more numerous every year.

And that's how it has been for as long as I can remember, except that Grandpa died a couple of years ago. But now it's Dad who comments on how high the water is in the spring. The shutters come down in the same order and are piled exactly as they have always been. The key to the sauna still hangs next to the light switch in the tool shed because that's where it belongs. The flag flies atop the cedar flagpole. And over hot dogs on the lakeshore, we remember Grandpa and his fish stories.

The long weekend at the cottage has become something of an institution. For me, it rates right up there with Christmas. It's what we do as a family. I wouldn't miss it for the world.

- The cottage for the person who is telling this story has become more than just a seasonal shelter on the lakeshore. In what sense has the cottage become a symbol? What does it symbolize?
- What rituals can you identify in the story? Why are they important to the storyteller?
- If this cottage were sold, would it continue to be a symbol to the new owner? Would it continue to be a symbol to the original family whose story we read? Why? How?
- How is "the cottage" a symbol in many parts of Canada?

Culture as a "memory box" of symbols

Jeff has had a crush on Audra ever since Grade 6. They had gone to a school dance together once or twice, and they often went to the same parties. But somehow the two of them had never gotten together until well into Grade 10. Jeff finally got the nerve to ask Audra out. After a few dates he even pulled out a beat-up old hockey skate box filled with photos, notes, and mementos that he had been collecting over the years. In the midst of all these treasures was a bundle of memories that he had collected related to Audra: photos of the two of them at the school dance and at parties, a note that Audra had written him in Grade 7, a gift that Audra had given him in Grade 8, and so on. This "memory box" was filled with little things that meant a whole lot.

Cultures are like Jeff's "memory box" – full of symbols. The symbols may differ from culture to culture, but each culture has such a memory box. The meanings, values and beliefs of a culture are stored in symbols. People draw on these symbols to help them find meaning in a world too complicated to understand. Some symbols are personal, like Jeff's collection; some are meaningful to family groups, like "the cottage." Others are shared by a large group of people (for example, by all Canadians, by Indonesian immigrants to Canada, by African Canadians, by Mohawks, by Christians, and so on).

When a symbol has deep meaning for the members of a particular group, we call it a cultural symbol. Such symbols are usually associated with significant ideas and beliefs held by the group. Sometimes, Canadians identify themselves as Canadians by wearing a Maple Leaf. Wearing it is a symbol of pride in being a citizen of Canada and a statement that one shares a common system of beliefs and values with other Canadians. In the Canadian Constitution, these beliefs and values are identified in the Charter of Rights and Freedoms. The Charter has become a symbol of Canadian rights and privileges.

In today's world, however, culture is rarely contained within the boundaries of one country. Because of television, the Internet, world trade and intercontinental travel, culture has gone global. This new global culture needs symbols to express commonly held beliefs and values. For that reason, we have global symbols, such as the Red Cross and Red Crescent.

Some symbols are religious. When groups seek to be in touch with the holy (whether expressed as Jesus Christ, the Holy Trinity, mana or Brahma), they will do so only with symbols. There is no direct contact or encounter with the holy. That's why religion makes use of symbols – sacred symbols, such as bread and wine, water, earth, plants, oil, rocks, sweet grass, incense and music – to symbolize what is higher and deeper than anything we know. The next theme will say more about this.

Everyday rituals

People create rituals out of everyday events. The things we do every day, we tend to do in the same way. The way we get up from bed, brush our teeth, take a shower, etc., quickly becomes a pattern, or *habit*. We ritualize everyday happenings: what we do at school, at meals, with our friends, when we come home from school. This is true for humans, and in many ways, it is also true of animals.

In the animal world this ritual behaviour comes from biological and social needs. Animals express their need for food, security, touch and care in gestures and actions that the other animals understand as a sort of code. Of themselves, many of these ritual gestures and movements do not appear to us to be relevant, but to the animals they are. These ritual gestures are often accompanied by sounds. Even the playful behaviour of a young cat or dog is a kind of ritual. Quite often, play is a means of learning how to live in their environment, or how to hunt and look for prey. With animals as with humans, rituals are first of all ways of dealing with certain everyday needs. A successful ritual is one that helps us meet these needs.

Human culture is made up of an almost infinite variety of rituals through which we seek to realize our goals. Some of these rituals just make life easier. Imagine if you had to think each morning – as if you had never done these actions before – how to get out of bed, how to brush your teeth, what to have for breakfast. Through repetition these rituals become automatic. And so our whole day is filled with rituals.

- What are some of your everyday rituals?
- How effective are your rituals in getting everyday things done?

We thank you

A year ago on Valentine's Day my parents gave me the shock of my life. It started when Mom told me and my brothers to get dressed in our good clothes because they were going to have some very special guests for dinner. When dinnertime came, the guests had not yet arrived, but we were asked to come to the table and sit down. The table was set with our best china, silver, and crystal. Strangely, there were only three places set, one for each of us. Mom and Dad stood by the table and said grace. Next to our plates we each found an envelope with our name written on it in fancy handwriting. Inside we found a letter from Mom and Dad in which they recalled all the times we had served them in a special way that year. Then they served us an amazing meal, and even did the dishes without asking our help! That Valentine's was really special. We really weren't expecting it, but they did it again this year. You can bet that I'll be looking forward to this next Valentine's Day!

- What is your reaction to this story?
- What was this ritual all about? Why do these parents serve their children on Valentine's Day?
- What does the ritual affirm? What do you think is the effect of the ritual upon the parents, upon the children?
- Do all rituals have this kind of effect? Why or why not?

Rituals are powerful!

On many occasions in life, such important changes take place that we need to mark them:

- being born
- being initiated into a community
- coming of age at puberty
- becoming an adult
- getting married
- becoming a mother or a father
- being sick and receiving healing
- experiencing moral failure and guilt and being reconciled
- aging and dying

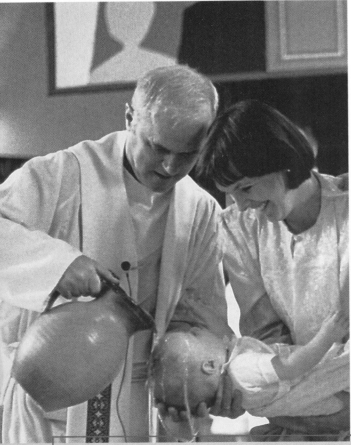

Each of us passes through most of these events at some point in our lives. Human culture has found ways of surrounding these significant moments with rituals and symbols. Later in the program, we will explore some of these rites in detail. At this point, we will look at a few traits of these powerful rituals:

- **A ritual passes on a tradition:** People through the centuries have given meaning to events such as births and marriages, sickness and death. Therefore, most important rituals have a long history. A ritual helps to pass on this history and the rite carries a memory of its own history.

- **A ritual needs our bodies:** All rituals have a bodily component. The memory carried in rituals is rooted in the body. And so rituals involve our bodies: they are washed, touched, embraced, anointed, released, etc. For example, baptism is a washing of the body, to purify us, to die to our former life, to put on Christ. It is not only a spiritual event; it is also bodily.

- **A ritual is accompanied by words:** The words of a ritual help us to give meaning to the event. They express and make real and effective what the symbolic ritual intended. Symbol and ritual need our human ability to speak to make the action complete. The embrace of a couple is not complete if it is not accompanied by a word that promises to be faithful. Often the words are sung. Rituals are closely allied with music and song.

- **A ritual forms a community:** The important rituals of life around birth, initiation, marriage, sickness and death are not solely intended for the individual. They are essential for building human community. Human birth is not a private affair; it is an event of the human community. The rituals around birth are ways of welcoming a child into the community.

The *Catechism of the Catholic Church* and symbols

"In human life, signs and symbols occupy an important place," the *Catechism* states. Why? Because humans are "at once body and spirit." For this reason they "express and perceive spiritual realities through physical signs and symbols." As we are social beings, we need signs and symbols to communicate with others through language, gestures and actions. The same is true for our relationship with God (see #1146). In addition, "a sacramental celebration is woven from signs and symbols" (#1145).

The Church's use of symbols and rituals

The Church has the mission to offer a special type of life and a special type of memory. It brings to memory the event of Jesus Christ and invites us to become part of this. As with all symbols and rites, the Church's sacraments have a bodily and a spiritual component. Each of the sacraments has something to do with our body: touching, washing, anointing, embracing, and so on. But it also has words attached to it, words that give these symbols meaning and make these symbols effective. In each sacrament, the words recall memories of what God has done in the past. We call upon the Holy Spirit to come and do for us now what was done for our ancestors.

The Church's symbolic actions

Life's events	Symbol	Ritual	Name of rite
birth	touch	signing with cross	rite of welcome
death and life experience	water	saying of creed immersion in water in the name of Trinity anointing with Holy Spirit	baptism in death and resurrection of Jesus
passage to maturity initiation into the community	oil touch through laying on of hands	being made part of the eucharistic community sealed with the Holy Spirit	confirmation
growth in maturity	bread and wine	praising and thanking God receiving communion	Eucharist
failure to grow spiritually / sin	touch	proclamation of forgiveness	reconciliation
getting married	ring embrace	exchange of promises sexual expression	marriage
service of leadership	oil laying on of hands (touch)	calling on the Holy Spirit to give priestly office	ordination to ministry
sickness	oil laying on of hands (touch)	anointing the sick person	sacrament of the sick
death	burial	invocation of baptism and the death of Jesus	funeral rites

Principle #5

To be human is to live in a culture with specific symbols and rituals that help us understand ourselves, God and the world.

Cultures express their deepest beliefs, values and meanings by using symbols and rituals. Since we are both spirit and body, we use material objects to signify spiritual realities. We express our greatest desires, convictions and ideas using symbols of all kinds. We make these symbols effective through rituals. Human life is surrounded by symbols and rituals. The human spirit seems endlessly creative.

What does religion have to do with culture?

A bit of advice passed on now and then goes "Never discuss religion or politics in 'polite company.'" How come? Is this good advice or bad advice?

One thing is certain, nearly everyone has an opinion on religion and politics, and usually a strongly held opinion at that. Whenever religion is brought into public debate, people line up on different sides of the issue. Consider, for example, an election campaign for public office. If a candidate voices a point of view that has religious overtones, we know that sparks will fly as people take sides. In Canada, whenever the bishops speak out on public policy issues, such as social justice in the economy, the story will be front-page news, and the editorial pages will be filled with opinions.

The point is, people are not indifferent about religion. Most people in our society may rarely go to church, but they still hold strong views about religion and its place in society. This theme is about the place of religion in culture. Why is religion important in our culture, even to people who say they have no religion?

Focus your learning

- **Aware and Informed**
  What role does religion play in culture?

- **Practical and Active**
  How can I discover more about the impact of religion on the life of my community?

- **Creative and Grateful**
  How do I appreciate the value of religion in my life?

Key terms

religion	liturgy
religious symbols	transcendence
religious rituals	

From earliest times...

Anthropologists believe that the earliest humans came from the African continent. Those who study traditional African religions note that Africans as a people are deeply religious. Religion permeates every aspect of their lives. Anthropologist Arthur Leonard writes, "[Africans] are in the strict sense of the word a truly and deeply religious people, of whom it can be said, that they eat religiously, drink religiously, bathe religiously and dress religiously. In fact, all that is sustaining or weakening in African life, has to be anchored in religion, whether it be the individual's relationship to the family, the clan and tribe, or morality, law, worship, politics, social status, economics, etiquette, wars and peace."* The whole of African life is the source of their religion.

If this is true of the descendants of the earliest human societies, religion must be rooted deeply in the very core of who we are as human beings.

(*from Emefie Ikenga-Metuh. *Comparative Studies of African Traditional Religions*. Onitsha, Nigeria: IMICO Publishers, 1987, p. 12)

religion:

Religion is a system of symbols and rituals. We form powerful beliefs, values, meanings and practices around these symbols and rituals about who we are in relationship to God.

religious rituals:

Symbols reveal the bond between us and the sacred. Sacred rituals enact this bond. We have the capacity to enter into the realm of the sacred, but only when the sacred approaches us through symbols and rituals. *Religious rituals* have the power to open up new ways of living and communicating with a power and energy that is higher or deeper than our own.

What do you think?

Take a look at popular movies and games. How many of them have spiritual themes or religious overtones? Why do you think this is so?

If you review advertising, how often do you find religious or spiritual themes? Why do these themes appeal to advertisers?

What are some of the most recognizable symbols in our culture? How many of them have a religious or spiritual basis?

Are we humans, by nature, religious? Why or why not?

"Together we can make a difference"

– Father Moses Michael Coady and the Antigonish Movement

Religious beliefs have often motivated people to act for change in their communities. This is a brief account of an important social movement in Canada's history that had its roots in Catholic social teaching.

Life for the average teenager in Eastern Nova Scotia in the early part of the 1900s held little promise of economic prosperity. The economy had been based largely on the one-family farm and fishing in close-knit, self-sufficient communities. A changing world economy and technological advances, such as large mechanized fishing boats, pushed rural Nova Scotians deeper into debt, poverty and dependency. The young people saw little future in staying home. They began to leave for other parts of Canada and the United States looking for jobs and opportunities. The local communities offered few opportunities for young people to use their talents, even if they decided to stay. Father Moses Coady, an outspoken priest of the Diocese of Antigonish, said in 1945:

> The bright child who gives signs of intelligence in school is immediately picked for a different career from that into which he was born. People will mortgage their farm, and workers will contribute their savings to the last cent to see that a favoured boy or girl gets a so-called chance in life… In our present educational procedure – which is essentially a skimming process – we are robbing our rural and industrial population of the natural leaders.

Father Moses Coady, inspired by the gospel and the Church's social teaching, was convinced that there was a way to deal with these emerging cultural and social changes for the betterment and well-being of these people.

liturgy:

In the Catholic tradition, *liturgy* is the Church's official act of worship. In liturgy, God interacts with us in the various situations of our lives. All liturgical rites use Christian symbols and rites to "retell" or "remember" the person of Jesus, particularly his death and resurrection.

He knew that the dominant culture favoured competitive individualism, in which there were a few "winners" and many "losers." This made the majority of the people passive, crippling their self-confidence. He saw the need for people to start identifying the problems in their own communities, to come up with alternatives, and to work together towards solutions. Father Coady worked at the grassroots level for and with the rural people. He organized community meetings, challenging the people to break out of their "culture of silence." From these large, "town hall" meetings, people organized "study clubs" – small gatherings that were often held in parishes. In these study clubs, the people would learn how to see their economic situation from a number of points of view so that they could understand what was taking place. They would learn how, by working together, they could make changes to improve life for the entire community. Besides these study clubs, St. Francis Xavier, a Catholic college in the area, offered courses to train leaders for this movement. The "Antigonish Movement," as it came to be known, was essentially about educating and empowering people.

> He organized community meetings, challenging the people to break out of their "culture of silence."

At a regional conference in 1938, one fisherman spoke about how he was no longer an "individual fighter" but now fought collectively. Cooperation with others resulted in more than economic benefits: "It teaches us to trust one another" and to "transact business… in peace and harmony with one another." Father Moses Coady was against centralized power, absentee owners and outside forces that kept the people of his community in economic bondage. He did not preach revolution, but rather a communal approach to solving local problems.

The Antigonish Movement transformed the culture and communities of the time. It drew on the scriptural vision of human beings sharing equal dignity in the image of God, and working together for the common good. The movement did not succeed in making long-term changes to the dominant economic structures. But it did succeed in promoting the cooperative movement at the grassroots, and it did bring about significant change for individuals and communities. Together they learned to understand and respond to social and economic tensions at the local level. By putting the social teachings of the Catholic Church into action, Father Moses Coady, and the many people who joined him in the cause, lifted up those who were poor, gave ordinary people a chance at an education, helped workers to organize, and provided the young people with renewed hope and opportunities to make a life in their own communities.

- What role did religion play in the Antigonish Movement?

- Was religion's role in this movement "religious," that is, focused on matters of faith and of its expression? What do you think?

- The Antigonish Movement, even though it brought about significant social benefits for many people, was unable to make long-term changes to the economic structures that were a major cause of the people's misfortune. Mother Teresa was once asked to comment on the seeming lack of success in her ministry to the dying poor of Calcutta. She responded that God did not call her to be successful, but rather to follow the teachings of the gospel. What do you think of Mother Teresa's comment, and of Father Coady's efforts to bring about social change?

Every society is religious

Many cultural anthropologists believe that religion is, by its very nature, human. By religion they mean our tendency as humans to call on something or someone that is higher or deeper than ourselves. They hold that all humans experience what they call transcendence. In other words, humans are naturally religious. Religion makes us human. The cultural anthropologist Peter Koslowski gives two areas where this search for transcendence shows: (1) Humans, he says, look for a way of getting a total picture of reality. They do so by asking where the world and humans come from, what the meaning is of all that has happened in history, and where the world and humans are going. People need this big picture. Religion seeks to make the big picture concrete. Religion will not rid the world of all struggle; there will always be a struggle over the world's resources. But religion calls us to be involved in overcoming the struggles and in working towards reconciliation and peace. (2) People desire growth, health, wholeness and freedom. Religion calls this the desire for salvation. We find ourselves caught in traps of our own making or in situations that are unjust or just plain evil. Religion generates the desire to be set free from these inhuman situations and gives us the faith or trust that this is possible. In other words, religion helps us to find a way of coming to grips with suffering and our feelings of isolation. Religion gives us a way of dealing with our experiences and desires by placing them in the larger framework of our bond with God.

transcendence:

Religious experience has to do with our relationship with a God whom we cannot see, hear, taste, smell, touch. That is, God is *beyond*, or transcends, our usual physical experience. God certainly knows that we humans are physical beings and that we relate in a physical way. That is why God reveals God's-self to us in a physical way by entering human history as a man, Jesus. God makes God's-self known to us through creation, but we must learn to "see" through creation to God, who is the source of all.

- How do you understand the statement: "Religion is, by its very nature, human"? How true do you find this statement?

- What are the two areas of life where the desire for religion shows? Do you experience these areas in your own life from time to time?

Religious views and practices in Canada

These statistical tables are the findings of a public-opinion poll of 1,500 Canadians, conducted in April 2000. The poll, done by Angus Reid for The Globe and Mail and CTV, gives us a snapshot in time of some of the religious views and practices of Canadians.

Do you believe in God?

	1500 RESPONDENTS	AGE			GENDER	
	Total	18 to 34	35 to 54	55+	Male	Female
Yes	84%	79%	85%	89%	82%	86%
No	14%	19%	13%	9%	16%	12%
Don't know	2%	2%	1%	2%	2%	2%

My religious faith is very important to my day-to-day life.

	1500 RESPONDENTS	AGE			GENDER	
	Total	18 to 34	35 to 54	55+	Male	Female
Strongly agree	39%	30%	39%	52%	33%	45%
Moderately agree	28%	29%	30%	25%	30%	27%
Moderately disagree	16%	20%	17%	11%	17%	15%
Strongly disagree	15%	21%	13%	9%	18%	11%
Not applicable/Not religious	1%	1%	1%	1%	1%	1%
Don't know	1%	–	0	1%	0	1%

Other than special occasions such as weddings, funerals or baptisms, how often did you attend religious services in the past 12 months?

	1500 RESPONDENTS	AGE			GENDER	
	Total	18 to 34	35 to 54	55+	Male	Female
Once a week or more	20%	15%	17%	31%	18%	22%
At least once a month	13%	14%	12%	13%	13%	13%
A few times a year	19%	18%	21%	18%	18%	21%
At least once a year	11%	13%	12%	6%	12%	10%
Not at all	36%	40%	37%	31%	39%	34%
Don't know	0	–	0	1%	0	1%

Do you agree with the statement that you don't need to go to church to be a good Christian?

	1500 RESPONDENTS	AGE			GENDER	
	Total	18 to 34	35 to 54	55+	Male	Female
Strongly agree	58%	61%	61%	51%	58%	58%
Moderately agree	23%	21%	22%	27%	24%	22%
Moderately disagree	7%	7%	7%	8%	7%	8%
Strongly disagree	10%	10%	9%	11%	9%	10%
Not applicable/Not religious	1%	2%	1%	1%	1%	1%
Don't know	1%	0	0	2%	1%	1%

My private beliefs about Christianity are more important than what is taught by any Church.

1500 RESPONDENTS	Total	AGE			GENDER	
		18 to 34	35 to 54	55+	Male	Female
Strongly agree	45%	41%	46%	47%	43%	46%
Moderately agree	26%	28%	26%	22%	27%	25%
Moderately disagree	13%	14%	14%	13%	25%	12%
Strongly disagree	12%	13%	11%	13%	11%	13%
Not applicable/Not religious	3%	3%	2%	3%	3%	3%
Don't know	1%	1	2	2%	1%	2%

The privatization of religion in Canada

Something has been happening to the way Canadian youth – and Canadians in general – live religion. Statistics show that while most youth see themselves as religious and believe in God, an increasing number no longer participate in the Church. Canadian youth find the institutional form of religion less and less relevant to their lives. They say that they don't need the Church to be a Christian or to be a good person. They don't sense that the institutional Church affects their daily behaviour. They appear not to need religion in its institutional form to help them integrate their daily experiences with the bigger picture of life, with God, with an ultimate meaning in life. The Church does not fit with their personal way of giving meaning to life.

Statistics bear out what cultural anthropologists have been saying for almost a century: Western culture has become secular.

secular:

worldly, not religious or sacred; living in the world.

secularize: to make worldly, separate from religious connection or influence.

(Gage Canadian Dictionary)

Major institutions and practices – such as hospitals, schools, social assistance, marriage, and so on – that used to be "religious," have moved more and more into the secular arena. This has shifted the search for religious norms and values away from the Church toward a more individual and private sphere. Religion in Canada, as elsewhere, is increasingly private. Other organizations are meeting human needs that used to be met by the Church. To participate in the life of the Church by regularly attending Sunday Mass and celebrating its major feasts has also become more and more a personal decision. I decide whether I participate. Quite a dramatic shift from the world of our grandparents! This privatization of religion is a movement that is taking Christ out of our culture.

...that true religion is fed by joy? A religion of long faces, fear, or obligation cannot be true. After all, religion is fundamentally a promise of freedom and salvation. What greater source of joy can there be?

- Why do you think only about 16% of Canadian-born young people between the ages of 12 and 24 participate in the Church's worship on a weekly basis?

- Are researchers correct in their assessment that people are religious, but mostly in a private way? Why or why not?

- If you were a priest in a Catholic parish, what would you do if a couple who never publicly participate in the life of the Church asked to be married or to have their child baptized in the parish church?

- If Father Moses Coady were alive today, what do you think that he would say about this trend toward privatization?

- When Pope John Paul II called the young people of the world together to celebrate their Catholic faith in World Youth Day gatherings, why did the young people respond by the millions? What do you think this says about the place of the Church in our society?

The effects of privatization on institutions

What happens when 77% of Canadians say they belong to a Church but only 20% participate in its life regularly? What happens when 70% say, "My private beliefs about Christianity are more important than what is taught by any Church"? A problem? Yes. But also a huge inconsistency. Surveys show that Catholics belong to the Church in a variety of ways. Some belong heart and soul to the Church and its way of living the mystery of God. They participate each Sunday; they are attentive to the feasts that celebrate the mystery of God; they participate fully in the social outreach because of their own convictions independently of what others do. They do so because they personally believe that faith is important for them and for the world in which they live. Others belong but do not participate in any real manner. They declare themselves Catholic and hold on to many of the Church's beliefs. But they feel no need to support the Church by taking part in its Sunday worship and its activities. Not with so many other things to do. But they want the Church to be there when their child is baptized, or when they get married, or when someone dies. They maintain a private spirituality and tailor what the Church holds in faith to their own needs. Still others want the Church to be there and would find it a real loss if the Church were to disappear. But they have no need or desire to be part of sustaining the Church. That is for others, not for them.

All this shows that at least 57% of the Catholic population has loosened its ties with the Church. Why did this happen? In Canada and elsewhere in Western culture, there has been a drastic decline in the participation of people in institutions generally. This declining participation has also affected the Catholic Church. Society pays a price for the growing lack of participation in institutions. The price is a feeling of isolation and a loss of a sense of belonging. Although institutions like the Church need not be as powerful as they were in our grandparents' days, institutions are part of the health of a society. Without support, institutions weaken and even die.

religious symbols:

Humans are linked with the sacred. The symbols we use in religion reveal this link. *Religious symbols* include things like the stars, the earth, cedar branches, smoke, oil and water. We use these things to represent immensity, power, growth, birth, cleansing, communion, and so on. These symbols manifest the sacred when they are accompanied by rituals and words.

Two million young Catholics came to Rome from all over the world to celebrate their faith during World Youth Day in August of 2000. The Pope said to them:

"Dear friends, at the dawn of the Third Millennium I see in you the 'morning watchmen' (see Isaiah 21.11-12).... Today you have come together to declare that in the new century you will not let yourselves be made into tools of violence and destruction; you will defend peace, paying the price in your person if need be. You will not resign yourselves to a world where other human beings die of hunger, remain illiterate and have no work. You will defend life at every moment of its development; you will strive with all your strength to make this earth ever more livable for all people.

"Dear young people of the century now beginning, in saying 'yes' to Christ, you say 'yes' to all your noblest ideals. I pray that he will reign in your hearts and in all of humanity in the new century and the new millennium. Have no fear of entrusting yourselves to him! He will guide you, he will grant you the strength to follow him every day and in every situation."

(excerpt from the homily of the closing Mass for World Youth Day, held in Rome, August 20, 2000.)

Young people bring life and new ideas to their local parishes. The gospel takes on new expression with each generation.

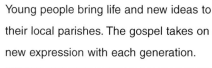

Reflections of a student on organized religion

Some people say that they can't find God in organized religion. They don't go to church because they say it's just filled with hypocrites. Some don't go because their experience of Church has been boring. These same people will often say that they prefer to find God by sitting alone on the seashore, or by taking a walk in the woods. Such a religious experience, they would claim, is more authentic, honest and pure than sitting in a church, taking part in the same rituals over and over, with people you don't know.

Well, sometimes I am in total agreement with these people. There have been times when, in the warmth of the sunshine, or the smell of fallen leaves, I have felt deep inside the desire to say "thank you" to God for being alive. And there have been many Sundays when I couldn't wait to get out of the church because the priest just wouldn't stop talking. But there was one time that makes me think that there's a point to organized religion.

Once I went to Church and the priest said something about it being "mission" Sunday. After his talk, he called up different groups of people – the readers, the musicians, the people who help give out communion, and a bunch of others. They all got some kind of blessing and were sent back to their places. Then he called up a group that he called the AIDS Hospice support group. He explained that there were a number of people in our community with the disease living in a house donated by one of the parishioners, and that this support group had volunteered their time to help the full-time nurses care for the sick residents. The people who came up included a couple of older people, some teenagers from my school, some middle-aged people, a gay couple, a nun. When this group gathered at the altar, the priest explained what they did: They helped the people that were dying of this disease get up from their beds; they helped bathe them, feed them, keep them company. The thought of spending time with these unfortunate dying people versus sitting on the seashore, enjoying the feeling of being alive, crossed my mind. Then it clicked. These volunteers, who seemed to have nothing in common with each other except their work with these AIDS patients, were able to do this because they were part of this Church.

Then another group came up – those who help out at the soup kitchen. Same thing: the people who came up had nothing in common but the fact they came to this church, and worked with the poor. It occurred to me that "organized religion" may be boring much of the time, but it did bring people together to live out what they said they believed in. As part of the "missioning" thing, the priest read a passage from the Bible that went something like, "see how they love one another."

At the end of Mass, I got blessed, too, and all I did was show up!

Darius Krall

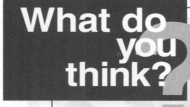

What do you think?

What do you think of organized religion?

What did Darius find "authentic" about his church experience?

What do you think the Church should do to be relevant to young people?

The importance of youth for society and the Church

The Church, while regarding young people as "hope," also sees them as "a great challenge for the future of the Church".... Alienation from the Church... lurks in many as a fundamental attitude.... On the other hand, many [young people] are driven by a strong impetus to find meaning, solidarity, social commitment and even religious experience.

The explicit proposal of Christ to the young man in the Gospel (see Matthew 19.16-22)... is a direct proposal to all young people.... In the Gospel young people in fact speak directly to Christ, who reveals to them their "singular richness" and calls them to an enterprise of personal and community growth, of decisive value for the fate of society and of the Church. Therefore young people... [must be] considered... active subjects and protagonists of evangelization and artisans of social renewal.

(*General Directory for Catechesis*, #182-183)

Principle #6

To be human is to live in a culture where religion plays an essential role in how we look at and live in the world.

Religion plays an essential role in human cultures. Religion touches on the trust within us that somehow reality makes sense, that there is a deeper underlying meaning of life. This is a trust in God. If our life together as human beings is not just an endless array of fragments – bits and bites – of unconnected events and objects, if life as a whole has meaning, it is because of religion. Our origins and our destinies, our lives in this world, make sense in light of a Creator God. That is why people form communities around religion.

Unit 2 review

In this unit, you examined the dynamic nature of culture as a context for meaning.

Aware and Informed

How would you define "culture"?

Culture is the set of meanings, beliefs, values and rules for living shared by groups and societies as the source of their identity. Culture sets humans apart from nature. Humans create culture. They create an order and a home around themselves in which it is good for them to live. But they do not do so alone. They create culture in communities. Every society has its own culture, defined by such things as people speaking the same language, doing things in a similar way, and placing the same value on actions and objects. Once established, culture also becomes a tradition, something we inherit from others. All humans live in a particular culture.

What does culture look and sound like?

Cultures express their deepest beliefs, values and meanings by using symbols and rituals. Since we are both spirit and body, we use material objects to signify spiritual realities. We express our greatest desires, convictions and ideas using symbols of all kinds. We make them effective through rituals. Human life is surrounded by symbols and rituals.

What role does religion play in culture?

Religion plays an essential role in human cultures. Religion touches on the trust within us that somehow reality makes sense, and that there is a deeper underlying meaning of life. This is a trust in God. If our life together as human beings is not just an endless array of fragments – bits and bites – of unconnected events and objects, if life as a whole has meaning, it is because of religion. Our origins and our destinies, our lives in this world, make sense in light of a Creator God. That is why people form communities around religion.

Practical and Active

How can I become more aware of how culture affects me?

Culture affects us in three basic areas of our lives: 1) our basic human actions, such as how we eat, sleep, work and pray; 2) our sense of belonging to a particular group of people; 3) our set of meanings, beliefs, values and practices within society. Culture is everywhere – it is like a pair of glasses that helps us to see and live in the world in a particular way. To be aware of our culture, we must look at it carefully and critically, identifying its elements, and then asking why it is so.

How can I express myself effectively within culture?

We can express ourselves effectively by recognizing the symbols and rituals of our culture, and learning to use these symbols appropriately and creatively. As social beings, we need to communicate with others, using the signs and symbols found in our language, gestures and actions. As Catholics, we use the symbols and rituals of our sacramental tradition.

How can I discover more about the impact of religion on the life of my community?

We look for a way of getting a total picture of reality by asking where the world and humans come from, what the meaning is of all that has happened in history, and where the world and humans are going. Religion seeks to make this big picture concrete. We also desire growth, health, wholeness and freedom. Sometimes we find ourselves caught in situations that are unjust or just plain evil. Religion generates the desire to be set free from these inhuman situations and gives us the faith or trust that this is possible. Religion helps us to find a way of coming to grips with suffering and our feelings of isolation. Religion gives us a way of dealing with our experiences and desires by placing them in the larger framework of our bond with God.

Creative and Grateful

You can answer these questions for yourself. The answer is found in your relationship with God.

How does culture enrich my life?

How can my understanding of signs, symbols and rituals increase my satisfaction of belonging to various cultural groups?

How do I appreciate the value of religion in my life?

Unit 3

The God question

Aim: to understand that Jesus' proclamation of the "kingdom of God" transforms lives and cultures

Theme 7

How did God shape the Hebrew culture?

When was the last time you asked yourself how your faith influences your culture? Most of us probably don't think much about the connections between our faith and our culture. The connections between what we believe and how we live aren't always clear. Often we make choices in life based on what "feels" right. Our choices in fashion, lifestyle, politics, diet, or morals are often made without a whole lot of conscious debate. We just go with what seems to fit who we are or who we would like to be.

This theme will give you the opportunity to explore what difference faith makes to culture by the way we live our lives. You will discover how faith in God shaped the culture of a nation. Through the stories of Moses, you will see how the Hebrew people's relationship with God formed them and their way of life. If God shaped the Hebrew culture, how does God continue to shape our culture today?

Focus your learning

Aware and Informed
How does our faith in God have a part in forming our culture?

Practical and Active
How can we be true to our faith convictions within our culture?

Creative and Grateful
How does faith in God enrich our culture?

Key terms

covenant

the Law or Torah

prophets

Chosen People

revelation

A story of stories

Our story of God has a long history. It began some four thousand years ago with the Hebrew people. It all started with a command and a promise. An old man, Abraham, and his old wife, Sarah, were commanded to leave their homeland, and were promised children and a land. And they believed this promise. They trusted this God enough to go from their birthplace and follow the promise to an unknown land. They found the land, but their trust in the promise of a child was severely tested. In their old age, when humanly speaking it would be laughable to still expect a child, Sarah delivered a son. Because there was famine in the land to which they had come, their offspring went to Egypt, where they ended up as slaves to the Egyptians. It was there that the greatest of their spiritual leaders was born: Moses, the founder of a people.

God made a new promise to Moses: the Hebrew slaves would be set free. Moses heard this promise from a voice in a burning bush. The voice said it was the God of Abraham. Because of what this voice was asking Moses to do, it gave itself another name – a name so holy that we dare not pronounce it. This revelation of the Holy Name was to form the Hebrew slaves in Egypt into a people, a nation. They became the Chosen People.

Chosen People

When God called the Hebrews out of Egypt through Moses, God chose them, the Bible says, "out of all the peoples on earth to be his people, his treasured possession" (Deuteronomy 7.6). Being the *Chosen People* was not so much a privilege as a mission. They were a "summoned" people. The people were to be a "light to the nations." They were to live the revelation of God to their ancestors for all the world to see and hear.

Moses

The birth of Moses was unlike that of the other great leaders and prophets of Israel. All of the great people, the ancestors of Israel, were born by God's grace. Their mothers were very old – they were infertile – and God looked upon them and had mercy on them. Moses was born without any such fanfare. But he was born in difficult times. At the time of Moses' birth, the Hebrew slaves were not permitted to keep their sons. The midwives were told to kill all male children because the Egyptians found that the Hebrews were becoming too dangerous. There were just too many of them. When the mother of Moses saw that her newborn child was a boy, she was afraid. She looked at the child and – the original Hebrew text says literally – "she saw that he was good (*tov*)," just as God, in the beginning when the world was still in its cradle, "saw that it was good."

She hid her child at first in her hut, but after three months she placed him in a basket on the Nile River. And just as long ago Noah had cast his boat upon the waters of the flood and was saved, a princess of Egypt saved the infant Moses, brought him up in Pharaoh's house, and gave him a name. He was to be called Moses – in Egyptian it meant "Son of," but in Hebrew it meant "drawn out." What a beautiful name! Drawn out of the water – saved or "the saved one." He who was saved as an infant was prepared all his life to save others. And God saw that it was good.

Michelangelo's sculpture of Moses depicts the greatness of the Jewish leader by making him physically larger than life.

Moses and the burning bush

Read the story of Moses and the burning bush in the Book of Exodus 3.1-14.

- What caught your attention in this story?
- How did you feel about what caught your attention?
- How does the story express the holiness of God?
- How is God named in the account?
- Why did God seek out Moses?
- What do these reasons say about God? What kind of a God is this?
- What is the power of the Name of God? When this Holy Name is called upon, what will it do for the people?
- Why is there such great reverence around the use of the Name of God in Hebrew culture?
- What is the meaning of the name YHWH?
- How does knowing a person's name allow a relationship to grow? How does knowing God's Name help our relationship with God to grow?

prophets:

Prophets were holy persons in Israel who were spokespersons for God. Because they were close to God through their prayer, they could communicate God's word through oracles, visions, judgments and symbolic actions. There were many kinds of prophets. But essentially, they were messengers of God amid the Chosen People.

This mosaic in northern Italy was created in the fifth century. It shows Moses removing his sandals because he is standing on holy ground. He turns around to see the hand of the LORD above him, as he approaches the burning bush.

The Holy Name of God

One of the most sacred accounts of the First Testament is the revelation of the Name of God to Moses at Midian. Some people call this account – Exodus 3.1-14 – the "revelation of revelations." The Name is so sacred that the Hebrew Bible gives us only its four consonants (YHWH). And in Jewish services the Holy Name is never pronounced because of the danger of misusing it. It is replaced with "Adonai" (the LORD) or with "Blessed is He!" or simply with "the Name." In our own Christian tradition, it is important to continue to respect this reverence for the Holy Name of God.

Where did the Name come from and what does the Name mean? The Name is forever linked with a place, a person and an event. The place is Mount Sinai, a desert mountain in the Sinai Peninsula; the person is Moses; and the event is a revelation of God that led to the liberation of the enslaved Hebrew people of Egypt. Moses received the Holy Name of God and was commanded to go with the power of the Name to the Egyptian Pharaoh. There he was to demand the freedom of the Hebrew slaves. He was to bring the Hebrew people to Mount Sinai so that there the whole people, like Moses, might experience the power of the Holy Name.

By the power of the Name, Moses led the slave Hebrews out of Egypt and brought them to Mount Sinai. There they experienced the desire of the LORD (YHWH) to adopt the Hebrew people. The experience of God at Sinai bonded these slaves into a nation. Translated, the Name means: "I am who am," or more literally, "I will be who I would be." The Name is not a noun. It is more like a verb or a promise: "I will be with you," "I am really there for you," or "I will show you who I am by what I do among you." We know the Name through stories of people who met God: "It was the LORD who did this; it was the LORD who said this." Forever after the story of this people was a story of the LORD *with* this people.

> ## revelation:
> God communicates God's-self to humankind in stages: through creation itself, through covenants (for example, God's covenant with Moses) and through the prophets. God's self-revelation is complete in Jesus. This *revelation* is passed on to all generations through the sacred Scriptures and apostolic tradition.

"I have observed the misery of my people... I have heard their cry... I know their sufferings, and I have come down to deliver them..." (Exodus 3.7-8).

- Why did God seek out Moses?
- What do these reasons say about God? What kind of a God is this?
- What is the power of the Name of God? When this Holy Name is called upon, what will it do for the people?

> ## Did you know...
> ...that the Name YHWH appears 6,823 times in the Hebrew Bible?

The song of Moses

Moses and the liberated Hebrew people sang this song to celebrate God's saving action. God continues to liberate people from all sorts of oppression. How can this become our song of praise and celebration?

I will sing to YHWH (the LORD), for he has triumphed gloriously;
  horse and rider he has thrown into the sea.
YHWH (the LORD) is my strength and my might,
  and he has become my salvation;
this is my God, and I will please him,
  my father's God, and I will exalt him.
YHWH (the LORD) is a warrior;
  YHWH (the LORD) is his name.

Who is like you, YHWH (O LORD), among the gods?
  Who is like you, majestic in holiness,
  awesome in splendour, doing wonders?
In your steadfast love you led the people whom you redeemed;
  you guided them by your strength to your holy abode.
YHWH (the LORD) will reign forever and ever.

(Exodus 15.1-3, 11, 13, 18)

Where do you go to find God?

These young people are becoming "B'nai Mitzvah" – Children of the Commandment. At a worship service, the Torah is passed symbolically from one generation to another; here, the grandfather passes it to his grandchildren. Personal responsibility for Jewish teachings is thus affirmed. A Bar Mitzvah (for boys) or Bat Mitzvah (for girls) is usually celebrated when the young person is about 13 years old.

At this moment during the worship service, the young B'nai Mitzvah stand before the open ark, which houses the Torah. Recalling the moment when the Israelites accepted the covenant at Mount Sinai, the rabbi bestows on these young people the priestly benediction: "May the Lord bless thee and keep thee..."

Did you know...

...that kings in Israel were surrounded by prophets? They helped the king know the will of God. Kings sought their advice because the will of God was central to good government.

"And they saw the God of Israel"

A mountain is an excellent place to meet God. There are peak experiences that can only be described using high, majestic images. And so when Moses came to Sinai, he went up the mountain, and you can almost imagine him saying to God: "Here I am, LORD, with my people – your people. We hardly know how to thank you." Imagine the LORD calling to him, "Moses, say to the Israelites: I, the LORD, have borne you on eagles' wings and brought you to myself. Listen to me and keep my covenant, and from all the peoples of the earth, you shall be my treasured possession. You will become a kingdom of priests, a holy people." Moses climbed down the mountain and told the people what God had said, and then climbed the mountain again to tell God what the people decided: "Everything that the LORD has spoken we will do." The LORD sent Moses down again – the LORD's go-between. He was to tell the people: "I am going to come to you in a dense cloud because I want to speak with you. I will make a covenant with you." (See Exodus 19.3-9.)

No one has ever seen the LORD. How could human eyes see the Holy One, the Creator of the heavens and the earth? The LORD is so completely other, so altogether different. When the LORD descended on Mount Sinai, the mountain trembled; thunder pealed and lightning flashed; smoke enveloped the mountain; the top of the mountain was full of fire. A human being can respectfully stand only at a distance from the mountain of God's presence. But the LORD does not want to be at a distance, so the LORD asked Moses to come to the top of the mountain. Moses took with him 70 elders of the people. And there, on the top of the mountain, the LORD made a covenant with Israel. When they were there they saw the LORD. But what did they see? They did not see the LORD's face or the LORD's form, but only what was under the LORD's feet, "a pavement of sapphire stone."

Did you know...

...why Moses selected 70 elders, and not 60 or 80? The number 70 represented the nations known by Israel at the time. In other words, through the symbolic number 70, Moses took with him all the nations on earth. No one is excluded from this covenant with the LORD.

- Where do we meet God?
- What do we see when we meet God?
- The story of Moses meeting God is full of symbols. If we were to tell our story of meeting God, how would we tell it?

When a man and a women exchange wedding vows, they enter into a covenant. They promise to be faithful, and to accept the conditions of a marriage commitment. What other covenants do we find in our culture?

What does a covenant look like?

Israel accepted to be the LORD's people. They had experienced their exodus from Egypt as a gift from God. They accepted the LORD's offer to be God's treasured possession. What did the covenant mean? What difference did it make to their lives as a people? Here are some changes that the covenant brought about in their lives.

(1) The Israelites became a people of the covenant

At the very foundation of this new people lay the LORD's act of liberation from slavery in Egypt. The LORD became the heart of this new people. They were the LORD's people. The LORD would be the centre of their life together. The covenant was the LORD's initiative. From this point on in their lives as a people, the LORD would dwell in their midst. All decisions, all life, required guidance from and consultation with the LORD. The LORD became their life.

In every Synagogue, the Torah scroll is kept in a special place. Its importance is expressed by the skill and high quality of the materials used to make it.

(2) The Israelites received a code of the covenant

For the Israelites, their whole life was based on the covenant with the LORD. The covenant was not an agreement among the people, but an agreement between the LORD and the people. The agreement was to be lived out by keeping a code. The Israelites called this code the Law or Torah. But the Torah was not law as we understand law in Canada; rather it was an instruction or a teaching of the LORD. It was an instruction for a freed people. If they kept this Torah, they would be a free people. At the core of this teaching are the Ten Words (the Ten Commandments).

(3) The Israelites had prophets as part of their leadership

In Exodus chapters 19 to 24, it is clear that Moses was the leader of the people. He was neither a politician nor a powerful military leader; he was a prophet and a lawgiver. Aaron and 70 elders assisted him. The people's covenant with the LORD was the most important aspect of their life as a nation. And so the Israelites needed leaders who could mediate between the LORD and the people. These go-betweens, or spokespersons for God, are known as prophets.

(4) The Israelites celebrated the actions and events of the LORD

The central celebration of the Chosen People was the Passover. It was celebrated on the Sabbath after the spring full moon. It commemorated God's liberation of the people from bondage in Egypt. The celebration was centred on a meal – the people ate lamb and unleavened bread and different herbs to remember the night when the LORD freed them. The main holidays of the Israelites were days on which they remembered what the LORD had done for them.

the Law or Torah:

The Torah is the heart of the First, or Old Testament. "Torah" is usually translated as "law." Here, "law" does not mean "legal rules," as we usually understand it, but "instruction." The *Torah* is God's instruction about the covenant: how to live in the mutually agreed-upon relationship with God. The Ten Words (Ten Commandments) are at the heart of the Torah. They are the code of the covenant with God.

What is a covenant?

A covenant is like a treaty or an alliance

In a world governed not by international laws but by military power, many peoples in the ancient world relied on the protection of more powerful rulers. They entered into covenants with these powerful rulers. The less powerful ruler would serve the more powerful one. Powerful nations spread their influence by making covenants. The Israelites adopted this political and cultural model of covenant to express the relationship between the LORD and the people. The LORD had been moved by the suffering of the Hebrews in Egypt and with a powerful arm had liberated them. The LORD loved them because they were weak and powerless. And so the LORD invited Israel to become the LORD's people and the LORD would be Israel's God.

A covenant has conditions

Most covenants have conditions attached. If the ruler provides protection and peace, the protected people promise something in return. In the covenant at Sinai, the response of the people is to be found in the code of the covenant. The code consists of the Ten Words or the Ten Commandments. The Ten Words are an instruction from the LORD on how to respond to the LORD. They are not arbitrary rules. They teach this people how to be a free people. This code or instruction is called the Torah or the Law (Exodus 20.1-17).

A covenant is sealed with a ceremony

A covenant is usually sealed with a ceremony in which the covenant is recited. As we read in Exodus 24.7: "Then he [Moses] took the book of the covenant, and read it in the hearing of the people; and they said, 'All that the LORD has spoken we will do, and we will be obedient.'" The covenant and its conditions are read and agreed upon in a ritual ceremony.

A covenant is celebrated with both parties present

Finally, there is a covenant celebration. In the Sinai covenant, it is sealed in a ceremonial meal. In Exodus 24.9-11 we read: "Then Moses and Aaron, Na'dab, and Abi'hu, and seventy of the elders of Israel went up, and they saw the God of Israel. Under [God's] feet there was something like a pavement of sapphire stone, like the very heaven for clearness.... and they ate and drank." It was a covenant meal. Did you know that the Eucharist is a similar covenant meal?

In this mosaic (from the same fifth century church as the one on page 60) Moses stands on the holy mountain and receives the Law from the LORD. Notice that the Law is depicted as a scroll and that Moses is shown with his hand covered so that it does not touch the holy scroll.

Did you know...

...that the ending *el* of Hebrew words or names such as Isra*el*, or Dani*el* means "God"? That is why "Israel" means "struggle with God."

The Ten Commandments

1. I am the LORD your God: you shall not have strange gods before me.

2. You shall not take the name of the LORD your God in vain.

3. Remember to keep holy the Lord's Day.

4. Honour your father and your mother.

5. You shall not kill.

6. You shall not commit adultery.

7. You shall not steal.

8. You shall not bear false witness against your neighbour.

9. You shall not covet your neighbour's wife.

10. You shall not covet your neighbour's goods.

(Exodus 20.2-17)

covenant:

Originally, covenants were agreements between a ruler and the people. They gave details about the rights and obligations of both parties. The word *covenant* is used in the sacred Scriptures to express the relationship between God and the Chosen People. A covenant is like an adoption agreement in which God agrees to love, feed, care for and protect the Chosen People. It is best expressed in the scriptural phrase: "I will be their God, and they shall be my people" (Jeremiah 31.33).

The Ten Words consist of two parts: the first three words concern the place of the LORD in Hebrew life and culture. The rest of the words concern the public and private lives of the people – like a code of conduct of God's people. All the Ten Words are about the relationship with the LORD. As Jesus said, the whole Torah (the Law) was summed up in the love of God and the love of neighbour. For him they were inseparable.

Pope John Paul II said during a visit to the Synagogue of Rome: "The Jewish religion is not 'extrinsic' to us, but in a certain way is 'intrinsic' to our own religion. With Judaism therefore we have a relationship which we do not have with any other religion. You are our dearly beloved brothers and, in a certain way, it could be said that you are our elder brothers."

Psalm 100.1-5

Make a joyful noise to the LORD, all the earth,
Worship the LORD with gladness;
come into his presence with singing.

Know that the LORD is God.
It is he that made us, and we are his;
we are his people, and the sheep of his pasture.

Enter his gates with thanksgiving,
and his courts with praise.
Give thanks to him, bless his name.

For the LORD is good;
his steadfast love endures forever,
and his faithfulness to all generations.

Principle #7

To be a Catholic in culture is to recognize that we form our relationship with God within culture.

For Catholics, our all-embracing covenant with God includes our culture. We have learned this from our Jewish ancestors in the faith. They taught us how God's self-revelation to the Hebrews was as a God of people, a God who would lead them and become part of their culture. To Moses, God revealed the Holy Name YHWH, which means "I am who am" or "I am with you." YHWH, usually spoken as "the LORD," accompanies any culture that truly seeks the well-being of all its people.

Theme 8

How does Jesus reveal God to us?

Listen to yourself the next time you describe an amazing experience to someone. What kinds of words and images do you use to convey something that is "just unbelievable"? Chances are, you will use a combination of facial expressions, tone of voice, gestures and words to try to communicate your experience. You will count on your listener to try to understand what it is that you are describing. Whether or not you succeed in communicating your experience will depend on what you do and say, the message itself, and what your listener does with all of that.

Jesus "communicates" God to us. In the last theme, you read how Moses encountered God in the burning bush and on the mountain. Do you remember the words and images used to describe this encounter? Jesus reveals God to us in an even more intimate way. We come to know God through Jesus – both through what he said and did, and through who he is.

In this theme, you will explore how Jesus taught about God and the kingdom of God through parables and through his very own life. As we grow in intimacy with God through Jesus, we also become more aware of how we are called to live with one another.

Focus your learning

- **Aware and Informed**
  How does Jesus reveal God?

- **Practical and Active**
  How can we speak of God, who is part of our experience, and yet so far beyond it?

- **Creative and Grateful**
  How does Jesus invite us to relate to God?

Key terms

kingdom of God	new covenant
parable	Incarnation
metaphor	

Speaking about God

Jesus reveals God to us completely and intimately. Jesus said, "whoever sees me sees him who sent me" (John 12.45). Through his teaching, his life, and his very self, Jesus shows us God. But how can we even begin to grasp the greatness of God? Jesus used the very simple and basic things in life to bring us to God, but he used these simple things in a special way. When he taught his followers about the kingdom of God, these simple things took on new and unexpected meanings. Jesus used metaphors to help us understand his message.

Metaphors are little jewels of language, used by poets and writers to give us a new way of understanding reality. God stimulates our imagination. Therefore, our best language about God is poetic. When we

Michelangelo illustrated the power of God during the act of creation in this painting on the ceiling of the Sistine Chapel in the Vatican.

speak about God we reach for the best the language can give us. And one of the highest forms of the poetic is the metaphor. With metaphors we create images that bring the reality of God within the reach of language. Metaphors create resemblances between the God who we cannot see or hear, and those things that we can see and hear that surround us. Biblical poetry speaks about God as a shepherd ("The LORD is my shepherd" Psalm 23) and points out the resemblance between God and a rock (Psalm 18) or an eagle (Exodus 19.4). The Bible portrays God walking in the garden, creating like a potter, appearing in a burning bush that does not burn up. "For now we see [God] in a mirror, dimly" (1 Corinthians 13.12), through fragments of images, through shards of the imagination. By using metaphors, we can see and understand more clearly.

kingdom of God:

The *kingdom of God* is a symbol used by Jesus to speak about God and God's actions among us. Jesus said the kingdom is among us. It is already at work in our midst, but the present moment is too limited to reveal all of it. The promise of the kingdom is that there is a whole lot more to come.

metaphor:

A *metaphor* is a figure of speech used in poetic language. In a metaphor the writer illustrates something about the nature of one thing by relating it to another thing. Metaphors help us to see things from a fresh perspective.

Did you know...

...that in the Jewish faith it is not permitted to have any images of God? Or that the early Christians struggled over whether paintings and statues of Christ should be permitted? God cannot be fully represented in any image. In the Eastern Church, icons are used as symbols to help the faithful focus on the mystery of God.

Our actions too are metaphors

Jesus once said to the crowds, "Be perfect, therefore, as your heavenly Father is perfect" (Matthew 5.48). Be perfect as God is perfect? That's impossible! But just as our language about God is metaphorical, so too are our actions. Our actions can only *resemble* God's perfection. That means that although we need to take Jesus' words seriously, our perfection is to be found in the perfection of God. Even when our actions are very good, they only resemble God's perfection. The desire to be perfect lies in the depth of the human heart, placed there by God. As St. Augustine, an early bishop of the Church (AD 354-430) said, "Our hearts remain restless, until they rest in Thee." The restlessness of our hearts is the constant tension between wanting to be perfect, and knowing that we can be only imperfectly perfect.

St. Augustine is usually shown dressed as a bishop and holding his "restless" heart.

Did you know...

...why Catholics use statues, crucifixes and medals? For the same reason that parents carry photos of their children in their wallets and purses – these objects remind them of those whom they love. We do not pray to statues. These images simply help us to focus our attention on God.

Incarnation:

Incarnation means that God became human and dwelt personally – in the flesh – among us in Jesus of Nazareth.

Jesus begins his work

When Jesus was about 30 years old, he "came from Nazareth of Galilee and was baptized by John in the Jordan" (Mark 1.9). This baptism by John marked the beginning of Jesus' ministry. It was a momentous occasion. All the gospels mention it because the event was accompanied by a revelation of God. As Mark tells it, "And just as he was coming up out of the water, he saw the heavens torn apart and the Spirit descending like a dove on him. And a voice came from heaven, 'You are my Son, the Beloved; with you I am well pleased'" (Mark 1.10-11). And then, according to Mark, the Spirit "drove" him immediately into the wilderness. There Satan, the tempter and deceiver, was with him in the wilderness, constantly tempting him to go on a different path than the one he had experienced in his baptism. At the end of the 40 days in the desert, Jesus was strengthened by a messenger of God. He had remained true to what he had experienced in his baptism. He told the tempter, "Worship the LORD your God, and serve only him," repeating the First Commandment. The gospel writers say that "after John was arrested, Jesus came to Galilee, proclaiming the good news of God, and saying, 'The time is fulfilled, and the kingdom of God has come near; repent, and believe in the good news'" (Mark 1.14-15).

- What happened to Jesus at his baptism?

- Who was the Spirit? What did the Spirit do?

- What does the voice from heaven say? What does this message from heaven mean?

- What does Mark say about the proclamation of Jesus? What is it about?

Historical data about Jesus

1. Jesus was a Jew, born of the Virgin Mary in Bethlehem sometime between 6 and 4 BC. He grew up in Nazareth, a town in Galilee.

2. He was called Jesus, which means "YHWH saves." His last name was not Christ. He was probably known as Jesus, son of Mary and Joseph, or Jesus the carpenter's son. Christ, which means "anointed one" or "Messiah," was a title given to him by his disciples after his death and resurrection.

3. Jesus' parents were deeply religious. Each year they went to the temple in Jerusalem (about a two-week journey) to celebrate Passover. One story tells of Jesus going with them at the age of 12. We know little about his life before he was 30. He lived in Nazareth and probably followed Joseph's trade. Justin the Martyr, who lived in the second century, said that Jesus was a maker of yokes and ploughs.

4. He was baptized by John the Baptist in the Jordan River in the 15th year of Emperor Tiberias, around AD 27.

5. Jesus began his ministry after King Herod arrested John the Baptist. Luke says that he was then about 30 years old.

6. Jesus called men and women to follow him and go to the places where he himself could not go. From among these disciples he called the Twelve. Just as Israel consisted of twelve tribes, the new Israel, which began with Jesus, was to be led by the twelve apostles. They were to be the vanguard. From the Twelve, Jesus chose Simon Peter to be the "rock" upon which he would build the Church.

7. Jesus proclaimed that the reign or kingdom of God was at hand. He did what he said he would do when, at the beginning of his ministry, he quoted the prophet Isaiah:

When early Christians decorated their places of worship, they often illustrated Jesus as the Good Shepherd (like this mosaic from northern Italy) because he used this title to refer to himself (John 10).

The Spirit of the Lord is upon me,
because he has anointed me to bring good news to the poor.
He has sent me to proclaim release to the captives
and recovery of sight to the blind,
to let the oppressed go free,
to proclaim the year of the Lord's favour.
(Luke 4.18-19)

8. Jesus taught about the kingdom of God by telling parables, healing the sick, providing for people's needs and forgiving sins. His public ministry lasted between one and a half and three years.

9. In AD 30, the Romans, in collusion with Jewish leaders, condemned Jesus to death. He died on the eve of Passover. Shortly after his death, the disciples reported that they had "seen the Lord Jesus." They proclaimed that he had risen from the dead, and was now the Lord who is with us until the end of time.

10. At Pentecost, the disciples were transformed by an experience of the Holy Spirit. They began to preach the gospel of Jesus to the ends of the earth. This ministry has continued for two thousand years. The popes have been the successors of St. Peter, the bishops are successors to the apostles, and all of the baptized are followers of Jesus.

What is a parable?

Few writers can tell a parable like American author Kurt Vonnegut. Here is an example of one of his parables from *Cat's Cradle*.

> *God has just created Adam. Adam blinks and looks around with fascination. After a while Adam turns to God and asks politely: "What's the purpose of all this?" God asks, "Everything must have a purpose?" "Certainly," says Adam. "Then I leave it to you to think of one for all this," said God. And God went away.*

- What does the story tell you? Did it go according to your expectations? Did it surprise you?
- Did this story happen historically? Is it purely fictional? Is there truth in fiction?
- If this story is a parable, what would you say is its purpose?

A parable is a story

Parables are short stories, often about ordinary events of day-to-day life. They are about people losing a coin, being hired to work, finding treasures, sowing seed, and squandering their inheritance. They tell about being a good person, always doing what you are supposed to do, cheating the boss, working with money, heaping up possessions, and holding banquets. Jesus' parables were based on daily life among his own people.

A parable is a comparison

A parable compares something we don't know (for example, the kingdom of God or God's way of acting) with something we do know (events from everyday life). Jesus makes some surprising comparisons. He compares the kingdom of God to a mustard seed, yeast, a pearl, a treasure, a father who has two sons, and so on. Some of his comparisons are quite daring.

A parable contains a crisis

All good stories have a beginning, a crisis and a resolution. So do parables. The crisis of the parable is the most interesting part. Sometimes the crisis is very gentle, like the seed sown by the farmer that grows without his knowing and becomes a stalk and develops a head of grain (Mark 4.26-29). Other stories take a strange turn. Our expectations of what is normal are challenged, overturned, or fulfilled in an unusual way. In the parable from *Cat's Cradle* quoted above, we might expect God to have a purpose for everything. The parable says that God scoffs at this idea, and suddenly we are left with a world where we have to make our own sense of things. This can be quite unsettling. What we thought we knew is being challenged. Parables challenge us to think differently about God and ourselves. In this sense, parables work like metaphors.

A parable has an ending

Some endings are happy – the shepherd finds his sheep; the father is reunited with his son. And others are tragic – the farmer who is heaping up his wealth dies before he can enjoy all the goods stored in his barns.

A parable is a story about God's kingdom, that is to say, God's way of acting among us

A parable gives us a brief glimpse into the mystery of the kingdom of God. The presence of the kingdom of God in the story gives the story its gentle and at times strange twists. In other words, the story is about God and the unexpected ways that God takes care of things. The story does not describe God's kingdom; it only makes a comparison. That is why parables are symbolic: they draw us into the mystery of God and how God relates to us. They raise questions. We don't know how God takes care of things; God is a mystery to us. But Jesus gives us some glimpses of God. His parables will help us when we look for ways of acting as Christians in our culture.

parable:

A *parable* is a story that compares something we don't know with something that we do know. A parable usually has a surprise twist that helps us see things in a new way. Jesus used parables to give us a glimpse of the mystery of the kingdom of God.

Jesus reveals his name for God

Remember the revelation of God's Name to Moses in the burning bush? It was an important turning point for the Hebrews. They became God's Chosen People. Their lives were marked by a covenant with God. And the LORD instructed them in this covenant through the gift of the Ten Commandments. All the symbols and rituals of Hebrew culture go back in one way or another to this event.

Jesus, too, revealed a new name for God – he called God Abba. The gospels do not tell of one specific moment – like Moses at the burning bush – when the name was given to Jesus. The gospels present it as a name for the type of relationship Jesus had with the LORD. One day the disciples asked Jesus to teach them to pray. In his prayer, Jesus revealed the name he gave to God: Abba. For Jesus it was a way of addressing the LORD in prayer. At the beginning of a prayer, Abba meant something like "Good Father" or "Dear Father." Here is the prayer he taught them:

> Father (Abba), hallowed be your name.
> Your kingdom come.
> Give us each day our daily bread.
> And forgive us our sins,
> for we ourselves forgive everyone indebted to us.
> And do not bring us to the time of trial. (Luke 11.2-4)

As followers of Jesus, we use the same name for God. We receive the same intimate relation with the LORD when we take on the life of Jesus in Baptism. Jesus prays, "Your kingdom come." Jesus asks Abba that our lives and our culture reflect what the LORD desires for them. Jesus too creates a new people and gives us a new code of the covenant.

new covenant:

With Jesus we talk about a *new covenant*. Through Jesus, God's original covenant with Israel became even more intimate, more personal. In the new covenant relationship, God personally enters into human culture in the person of Jesus of Nazareth. Jesus reveals this covenant relationship with God in his own person. "Jesus is the new covenant" through whom we become co-heirs of the kingdom.

Our Father,

who art in heaven,

hallowed be thy name;

thy kingdom come;

thy will be done on earth

as it is in heaven.

Give us this day our daily bread

and forgive us our trespasses

as we forgive those

who trespass against us;

and lead us not into temptation,

but deliver us from evil.

Amen.

Jesus according to John

We know little about the writer of the fourth Gospel, the one we call "the beloved disciple." We know that "The Gospel according to John" was written between AD 90 and 110, but we don't know who wrote it. It was most likely someone from a community led by a person called the beloved disciple, who appears in the Gospel but was not one of the twelve apostles. This Gospel differs from the Gospels according to Matthew, Mark and Luke. It tells a different kind of story about Jesus and uses different language to describe the events of Jesus' life. It is most obviously different in the way the Gospel starts. The prologue tells us that Jesus was with God as God's Word from the beginning. There is no story of Jesus' birth or early life. It starts instead with a beginning before time. As the Gospel says, whatever Jesus said and did during his life, he said and did as the Word of God. And so we may say that while Jesus is fully human, he is also a revelation of God. All that Jesus does and says in John's Gospel is symbolic of God. The story "The veil hiding God's face has been removed" is one of these symbolic stories.

The iconostasis (icon screen) separates the nave from the altar at this Ukrainian Catholic church. Its purpose is much like the "face veil" that hid the face of God (see below).

Revelation

At the resurrection, the veil that covered Jesus' head in the tomb is put aside. The writer of John's Gospel uses the veil as a symbol to show us that in Jesus we come to see God face to face.

The veil hiding God's face has been removed

When Peter and John enter the tomb of Jesus, the Gospel says they "saw the linen wrappings lying there, and the cloth that had been on Jesus' head, not lying with the linen wrappings but rolled up in a place by itself" (John 20.6-7). An interesting detail, but why report it? Why such attention given to the veil covering the face of the dead Jesus in the tomb? The Gospel writer saw more than a face veil, a sort of handkerchief used to cover the face of the dead. He recognized in the "face veil" an allusion to another face veil in the story of Moses. In Exodus 34.33-35 we are told that Moses used to cover his face with a veil after he had spoken with the LORD. Moses' face had become brilliant from the radiance of the LORD's presence, so whenever Moses returned from speaking with the LORD, he would cover his face with a veil. In other words, the face veil has something to do with seeing the LORD. The question is whether a veil is still required to see God. By putting the veil aside, "rolled up in a place by itself," Jesus demonstrates that he no longer needs a veil to see God's glory directly. He can see the LORD face to face. The disciples wanted to know where Jesus was after his death on the cross. And the beloved disciple saw in the discarded face veil a sign that Jesus was in the glory of God. The beloved disciple saw and believed. He realized that Jesus was with Abba/God. He believed that Jesus was indeed the Word of God, the revelation of God as Abba. To the question of Mary Magdalene, "Where is the Lord?" the story says, "He is with God." Jesus is in the bosom of God: he is the heart of God.

The Word became flesh

In the beginning was the Word,
    and the Word was with God,
    and the Word was God.
He was in the beginning with God.
All things came into being through him,
    and without him not one thing came into being.
What has come into being in him was life,
    and the life was the light of all people.
The light shines in the darkness,
    and the darkness did not overcome it.

The true light, which enlightens everyone, was coming
    into the world.
He was in the world, and the world came into being
    through him;
    yet the world did not know him.
He came to what was his own, and his own people did not
    accept him.

But to all who received him, who believed in his name,
    he gave power to become children of God,
    who were born, not of blood or of the will of the flesh
    or of the will of man, but of God.

And the Word became flesh and lived among us,
    and we have seen his glory, the glory as of a father's
    only son, full of grace and truth.
From his fullness we have all received, grace upon grace.
The law indeed was given through Moses; grace and truth
    came through Jesus Christ.
No one has ever seen God. It is God the only Son, who is
    close to the Father's heart,
    who has made him known.

(John 1.1-5, 9-14, 16-18)

Principle #8

To be a Catholic in culture is to commit oneself to the kingdom of God proclaimed by and personified in Jesus.

Through his proclamation of God's reign, Jesus revealed how God was present and active in human lives and culture. In his parables and actions, Jesus showed how God interacts with us in our everyday lives. God, he said, overturns or converts our normal expectations. Jesus personifies this image and activity of God. Jesus called God by a new name: Abba/Father. As we grow in intimacy with God through Jesus, we also become more aware of how we are called to live within our culture.

Theme 9

Christ and culture in conversation

Can we even begin to imagine that Jesus would want to watch Hockey Night in Canada or MuchMusic, go to school with us, or work with us at a fast food restaurant? Can we imagine Jesus as part of our street culture? What about Jesus being at an all-night rave? Or do we think that Jesus is present only in the church down the street? On the other hand, can we imagine that Jesus is absent from the street when there is violence or substance abuse? Do you believe that you can encounter Jesus anywhere within our culture?

In this theme, you will hear and read several stories from the Bible. You will hear how Jesus promised to be with his followers, even after his death and resurrection. Just as he surprised his disciples day after day with his teachings and actions, why should we not expect to be surprised by Jesus in our daily lives? Jesus wants to be close to us wherever we are. That is why he is with us through the Holy Spirit, and in a special way through his community of followers: the Church.

Focus your learning

- **Aware and Informed**
  How can I know that Jesus is present in our culture?

- **Practical and Active**
  How can my faith make a difference in how I live my life?

- **Creative and Grateful**
  How is God gracious and generous towards me?

Key terms

Church

kingdom of God as gift

grace

Why would Jesus want to be here?

What do you think?

Do you think that Jesus cares about the things you do every day?

The followers of Jesus were often left scratching their heads in wonderment at his teaching and behaviour. What kind of surprises do you think Jesus might have for us? Think about the many stories that involve Jesus' encounters with people who are poor or otherwise disadvantaged.

Jesus promised to be with us always. What do you think he meant by "always"?

Mary Magdalene, the first witness of the resurrection

The Bible tells many stories about Mary Magdalene. Perhaps the most important one happens after the disciples discovered that Jesus' dead body was missing from the tomb (John 20.11-18). Mary stood at Jesus' tomb weeping, for she had loved Jesus with all her heart. While the other disciples returned to their homes after looking into the empty tomb, Mary remained. She continued looking for the Lord. She wanted to find him.

Because her love compelled her to stay behind, Mary became the first to see Jesus. When she looked in the tomb, she saw two angels sitting where Jesus had been lying, and said to them, "They have taken away my Lord, and I do not know where they have laid him." Since her Lord was not there, she then turned away from the tomb to find him elsewhere in the garden. In her turning away from the tomb, she actually saw Jesus, but did not recognize him until he called her by name: "Mary!" The voice of the Lord calling her "turned" something inside her, just as she had physically turned her body around a moment earlier. The lover called the beloved and the beloved recognized the voice. She said in Hebrew, "Rabbouni!" ["Teacher!"] And like all the others throughout the centuries, women and men, who heard the voice of Jesus calling them by name, Mary was told to go and announce that Jesus lives. Love turned her around and enabled her to see, so she announced to the world, "I have seen the Lord!"

In Christian art, Mary Magdalene is often shown at the foot of Jesus' cross as described in the Gospel of John (see John 19.25).

Jesus appears to Mary Magdalene

A reading adapted from John 20.11-18

Narrator: It was very early on the first day of the week. Mary Magdalene, Peter and John had discovered that Jesus' tomb was empty, and the linens that had been wrapped around his body were lying there. Having seen the empty tomb, Peter and John returned to their homes, but Mary remained outside the tomb weeping. As she wept, she bent over to look into the tomb. She saw two angels in white, sitting where the body of Jesus had been lying, one at the head and the other at the feet.

Angel: Woman, why are you weeping?

Mary: They have taken away my Lord, and I do not know where they have laid him.

Narrator: When she had said this, she turned around and saw Jesus standing there, but she did not recognize him.

Jesus: Woman, why are you weeping? Whom are you looking for?

Narrator: Supposing him to be the gardener, she said to him,

Mary: Sir, if you have carried him away, tell me where you have laid him, and I will take him away.

Jesus: Mary!

Narrator: She turned and said to him in Hebrew,

Mary: Rabbouni!

Narrator: (which means teacher). Jesus said to her,

Jesus: Do not hold on to me, because I have not yet ascended to the Father. But go to my brothers and say to them, "I am ascending to my Father and your Father, to my God and your God."

Narrator: Mary Magdalene went and announced to the disciples,

Mary: I have seen the Lord!

Narrator: and she told them that he had said these things to her.

How Christ acts in our culture

What, if anything, do Catholics have to contribute to culture? How do they relate to culture? There has never been just one way of relating to culture. The way that Christians have reacted to and lived in culture depends a lot on how they think Jesus saw his culture. Theologian H. Richard Niebuhr identified five ways in which Christians through the centuries have related to culture:

1. Some Christians say that Jesus is *against* culture. They feel that Jesus wanted nothing to do with the world because it was too evil and sinful. He came not to save the world but to save us from the world. According to this view, since Jesus is against the world, people should separate themselves as much as possible from culture.

2. On the other extreme, some Christians think that Jesus is perfectly *at ease* in culture. Jesus was a faithful Jew who like other Jews tried to bring the Jewish way of life to its fulfillment. They say that Jesus had no real bones to pick with the Jewish culture of his time. Therefore, he wants us to embrace culture, not change it. According to this view there is no particular conflict between Christians and culture.

3. Others feel that because Jesus is the incarnate God, he was both *in* and *above* culture. He lived as a human but was also someone who could never be limited by a culture and so was above it. According to this view, people sometimes go along with cultural values, and at other times have nothing to say since Jesus is above such concerns.

4. Still others say that Jesus and culture will always be at *loggerheads*. It is as if Jesus lived in two worlds and these worlds were constantly at war with one another. They say that what we live here is only temporary. At some point the world will be renewed in Christ. According to this view, people live in a constant tension, caught between the values of culture and the values of faith.

5. Finally, Jesus is also seen as one who *transforms* culture. He came into the world to bring about a new and better order. This group believes that the things of this world can be symbols, or sacraments of Christ. ***This view seems to be the most consistent with Catholic thinking***, but there is evidence of all these views in the history of Christianity.

Church:

The *Church* is the community that was founded when God sent the Holy Spirit to Jesus' disciples at Pentecost. It is in this community that we can meet the risen Christ.

We are the hands and feet of Christ's presence

If Christ is absent because he returned to the Father, how can he still be present in our culture? Jesus promised to be with us always through the power and work of the Holy Spirit. We do not see Christ in the same way as his disciples did. Instead, we see his presence and activity through the way that the Holy Spirit works in us. The Holy Spirit makes Christ present in us and through us. So how can we talk about Christ in culture? Here are five ways that Christ is present.

1. Jesus acts through people

Jesus Christ enters into our culture through his communion with people. That is the main teaching of the Incarnation. The Word put on human skin and flesh, just like ours. Jesus does not act in our culture through some sort of magic. The transformation of culture into what God wants is the vocation of all human beings. The Holy Spirit is the one who seals us with Christ and makes it possible for people to become like Christ.

2. Jesus acts through people who freely choose to be in communion with him

Christians believe that God chose them, just as once God made Israel the Chosen People. A person's conversion to Jesus Christ is first of all an initiative of God's Spirit. To convert or turn to Jesus is to realize that Jesus is the way to fullness of life. This is not to say that non-Christians cannot act with goodness. God's Spirit blows where it will. But since in Jesus the goodness of God became incarnate, he is the way towards fullness of life.

3. Jesus acts through the Word of Scripture

The beliefs, values and meanings of Christians are not human inventions. They are revealed by God and are found in the Scriptures, which are the basis of the Church's teachings. To find their way in culture, Christians look to the Scriptures. Christians believe that Jesus is present in the Scriptures, especially so when they are proclaimed on Sundays among the assembled faithful.

kingdom of God as gift:

God's relationship with creation is characterized by generosity. At its heart, the relationship is not about laws and rules, but is a pure gift of generous goodness. We experience this in the abundance of creation and the gift or self-gift of Jesus of Nazareth.

- How is Christ present in Canadian culture?
- What influence do these different acts of Christ through Christians have upon our culture?
- How do you understand the partnership of God and people in culture? Why is priority given to God's initiative? What about our own initiative?

4. Jesus acts in the liturgy

The Spirit of Jesus Christ is active when the Christian community assembles to give praise and thanks in the Eucharist, particularly on Sunday. When the Church celebrates the initiation of new members, when it celebrates forgiveness, and when it celebrates the marriage of a man and a woman, the risen Christ is present and active among the assembly. When it ordains its ministers, when it anoints the sick, when it buries its dead, and when it celebrates the sacred moments (Advent-Christmas-Epiphany and Lent-Easter-Pentecost), Christ is present. These are the times when it remembers the death and the resurrection of Jesus. These are moments of growth for Christians, who need them so they don't forget.

5. Jesus acts in the witness of people

Jesus is also present when we do something for others: when we feed others, give them drink, visit them when they are sick or in prison, welcome the immigrant and the stranger, or clothe the naked. Jesus said that whenever we do these things for one another, we are doing them for him. In doing them we show something of the generosity of God and Jesus toward others. God is love and is near when we love one another. Love is our greatest gift, and helps Christ show through in people's lives. They put on Christ in their lives. How does this show? It shows in their joy, their freedom, their dedication to others, their warmth to others, their fidelity to friendships, their honesty, their trust and their hope. In their lives we can see traces of God that make them attractive as human beings. The greatest gift that a Christian can make to culture is to live a life of love.

As Catholics we believe that culture is a work of partnership. We create culture in partnership with God through Jesus Christ. God's Spirit takes the initiative. It is God's love that has flooded over the world, but this love needs people to help spread it. Together with God, people create a culture in which it is good for God and people to dwell. As St. Teresa of Avila said:

> *Christ has no body now but yours*
> *no hands but yours,*
> *no feet but yours.*
> *Yours are the eyes through which*
> *Christ's compassion must look out on the world.*
> *Yours are the feet with which*
> *He is to go about doing good.*
> *Yours are the hands with which*
> *He is to bless us now.*

The initiative of God's love, with Christ working through our actions, is called "grace."

Grace

Grace is the word Catholics use to describe God's generous love. It is God's gift of self to us. This love sought out the Hebrews in Egypt, made a covenant with them in the desert, brought them to the promised land, protected them as a hen protects her young, and in the end sent Jesus Christ. History is one giant gesture of God's abundance. It has changed humanity forever. This initiative was a free gift, given for no reason besides God's goodness. This self-gift of God touches us at our very core, helping us to respond to God's Spirit and gradually transforming us into the image of God. With this love, God's own life becomes active in our lives.

God's love is all gift; it is all grace. In the tradition of our Church we have given many names to this self-gift of God depending on the effect it has our lives as Christians. The *Catechism of the Catholic Church* speaks about sanctifying grace, actual grace and habitual grace (see #1999, 2000). Grace goes beyond our own experience; it does not depend on our feelings because it is ultimately about how God feels and acts towards us. But it is the source of our ability to love God and become like God. When Joan of Arc was asked whether she was in God's grace, she replied that she did not know: "If I am not, may it please God to put me in it; if I am, may it please God to keep me there."

grace:

Grace describes God's kind, merciful and absolutely generous love for us. Grace shows itself in God's gifts of creation but particularly in the person of Jesus Christ. It is shown in the offer of a free and joyful new way of life opened up for us by Jesus Christ. As Paul writes in the Letter to Titus, in Jesus "the grace of God has appeared, bringing salvation to all" (2.11).

To be a Catholic in culture is to manifest in creation and human society God's goodness and generosity. We do this by participating in the life of the Church.

Christ comes into culture through people who have been baptized into the life, death and resurrection of Jesus. These people, followers of Jesus, are known as the Church. They tell the world about God's superabundant graciousness and generosity. God wants people's lives to be filled with the graciousness of God and for them to be set free from all the obstacles to true life.

Unit 3 review

In this unit, you explored how Jesus' proclamation of the kingdom of God transforms lives and cultures.

Aware and Informed

How does our faith in God have a part in forming our culture?

For Catholics, our all-embracing covenant with God includes our culture. We have learned this from our Jewish ancestors in the faith. They taught us how God's self-revelation to the Hebrews was as a God of people, a God who would lead them and become part of their culture. We form our relationship with God within culture.

How does Jesus reveal God?

Through his proclamation of God's reign, Jesus revealed how God was present in people's lives. In his parables and actions, Jesus showed how God interacts with us in our everyday lives. Jesus called God by a new name: Abba/Father.

How can I know that Jesus is present in our culture?

Christ comes into culture through people who have been baptized into the life, death and resurrection of Jesus. These people, followers of Jesus, are known as the Church. Through the witness of their lives, they tell the world about the superabundant graciousness and generosity of God.

Practical and Active

How can we be true to our faith convictions within our culture?

God made a covenant with Moses and the people of Israel: "I will be your God, and you shall be my people." God gave them the Law, the Ten Commandments, to follow as conditions of this covenant. Jesus renewed this covenant, summarizing the Law in the two great commandments: "Love God. Love your neighbour." By keeping this law of love, we can remain true to our faith within culture.

How can we speak of God, who is part of our experience, and yet so far beyond it?

Metaphors are little jewels of language that allow us to use images and imagination to speak about and understand reality that is beyond our immediate experience. Jesus' parables were metaphors, telling us that God's kingdom "is like" something that we are familiar with, and yet very different; for example, like yeast in dough that makes the bread rise.

How can my faith make a difference in how I live my life?

We are the hands and feet of Christ's presence in the world. We create culture in partnership with God through Jesus Christ. God's Spirit takes the initiative. It is God's love that has flooded over the world, but this love needs people to express it. As St. Teresa of Avila wrote, "Christ has no body now but yours…."

Creative and Grateful

You can answer these questions for yourself. The answer is found in your relationship with God.

How does faith in God enrich our culture?

How does Jesus invite us to relate to God?

How is God gracious and generous towards us?

Section II
Christ in our culture

Section aim:

to explore our culture in light of the principles established in Section I

Unit 4   Relating to oneself: Who am I?

Aim: to understand that each individual becomes fully a person through relationships with God and others

Theme 10

Self-understanding in our culture

The person who looks back at you every morning from the bathroom mirror is complex, full of questions, full of ideas, hopes and dreams, and connected in so many ways to other people. That person is you, of course. But if you asked all of the people who know you well to write down who you are, you would get as many descriptions of your identity as the people you asked. And if you yourself were to write down who you are, your own description would be different again. Even your own description would change over time.

In this theme, you will explore how our culture's vision of the individual influences how you see yourself, and as a consequence, affects how you live. God also has a vision of who you are. Jesus spent his public ministry telling us not only about God, but also about who we are in the sight of God. We call the gospel the "good news" because it frees us from untruths, including untruths about ourselves. The good news of Jesus helps us to see ourselves as we really are – beloved by God.

Focus your learning

- **Aware and Informed**
  Who am I?

- **Practical and Active**
  Who shapes my identity, and what can I do about it?

- **Creative and Grateful**
  How does God see me?

Key terms

self-understanding   individualism

self-esteem

My identity

When someone asks who I am, my first response is to give my name. My name is only part of my identity, though, not the whole thing. To know my name is not enough to know me. It isn't enough either to know where I live, who my parents are, or what jobs I have. My identity lies somewhere else, in something more important. I get in touch with it more when I try to answer the question, "What am I like?" My identity is tied up with what is most important to me. It can be easier to answer that for others than for ourselves.

If you want to know someone's identity, you may want to know what sort of commitments this person has made. What does the person find good or valuable? So if your best friend says that she or he is a Catholic, that means not only that your friend has a Catholic background, but that her or his stand on questions on what is good, valuable, desirable or worthwhile comes from this commitment. A person who has an identity knows where she or he stands.

René Descartes and a new way of looking at the self

Four or five centuries ago, new ways of thinking about the world, about ourselves and about God emerged. These "ways of knowing" are still shaping the way we think about these things today. In other words, we did not invent how we think about ourselves; neither did our parents or even our grandparents. Our thinking is shaped in many ways by our Western culture, which has been evolving for many centuries. In 1642, the French philosopher René Descartes searched for a new way of knowing – one that would be based solely on his own authority. He wanted to find something that was absolutely clear and distinct upon which he could build this way of knowing. So he undertook a doubting experiment. He began to systematically question everything that people of his time held as certain truth: from God, the Scriptures, Jesus and the Church, to the world around him, and all the way to the principles of mathematics. At the end of the experiment the only thing that was certain to him was his doubt. In other words, all he knew was that he didn't know anything for certain. He was what we call a skeptic. But how is a skeptic to live in this world? Descartes' answer was that a skeptic must find certainty in his or her own thinking. One of his most famous phrases became "I think, therefore I am." This skeptical attitude before the world, others, God, sacred Scripture and everything religious has stayed with our culture to this day. Unfortunately, the "I" of Descartes is only a shell of the real self. It is isolated from everything else, even from the body. Still, Descartes' idea of this disembodied thinking self has influenced Western culture ever since.

Did you know...

...that although René Descartes wrote in French, he wrote his now famous "I think, therefore I am" in Latin: *Cogito, ergo sum.* When he is quoted today, he is often quoted in the original Latin.

Modern ways of looking at the self

We all look at ourselves differently. But we share a lot of common characteristics that set us apart from people who lived, let's say, five hundred years ago, or from those who live in non-Western cultures. On the next two pages you'll read about seven tendencies that people in Western cultures have when it comes to identifying who they are. These are general tendencies; probably no one holds all of them exactly the way they are stated. Together, though, these tendencies help us form a picture of orientations in our society. You may recognize yourself in several of them. Our culture has shaped us in these ways without us necessarily being aware of it.

individualism:

Individualism is another name for the isolation of the self in Western culture. Our culture puts greater emphasis on the individual than on the community. For this reason, there is often a conflict in our culture between the rights and value of the individual, and the common good of society. The common good assumes respect for the person, but it also requires well-being, justice, stability and security for the group. Personal and social good must develop alongside each other.

The seven tendencies of individualism

1. I am free

In modern terms, to be free means that I am not bound by anything or anyone. Freedom is my highest dignity. *I* must be able to decide. *I am* responsible for myself. Others must respect my autonomy. Nothing outside of me can place a claim on my freedom except when my freedom encroaches on the freedom of another. The only authority I accept is one that protects my freedom from the attempts of others to take it away.

2. I have rights

I possess rights, which have been enshrined in a number of declarations of human rights, including Canada's Charter of Rights. These rights protect my freedom and dignity.

3. I am equal

I have the same claim to freedom, dignity and rights as everyone else. Like everyone else, I am interested in myself and use my power to further my own interests. The English philosopher Hobbes said in 1651 that this equality is never secure. People, he said, are like wolves to one another. They will take whatever they can get away with. Therefore, nations need governments to protect people's rights and equality. For this reason, all citizens must have a voice in government or in decisions that affect them.

4. Only reason binds me

I accept things only when the reasons for accepting them are compelling. If no evidence can be given that takes away my doubt, I am inclined not to accept things. I do not accept things on the basis of authority unless the authority first gives reasons that are evident to me. My mind is like my soul – it is what most identifies me. Knowledge that comes through observation and experience – "empirical" knowledge – has been a very powerful influence in the development of modern science and technology.

5. I am isolated from everything

In relationship to the world and to others, I am an observer. To acquire empirical knowledge, I have to treat the world as an object. I am expected to be objective, not to act out of my involvement with things or people. I am like a painter who paints a landscape. The painter is not part of the landscape, but rather an observer of the landscape. The painter creates a perspective that shows how she or he sees the landscape. As an isolated individual, I see everything from my own perspective.

This drawing by Leonardo da Vinci shows the lines of perspective from where he observed the subject of his painting. His perspective determines how we see it too.

6. I am master of the earth

Because I am separate from the world, everything else becomes an object for me to observe. Even human beings become an object of study. My relationship to the earth changes. It is no longer God's good creation, and so I am no longer responsible for safeguarding its goodness. The earth is an object. I can use or exploit it as I see fit for my benefit and happiness. Everything must make way for me. In the same way, I am master over my own body.

7. I am godless

In a world where everything is centred on me, God has no place except at the limits of my life (only in times of sickness, death or natural disaster, for example). God is squeezed out of a culture that operates out of self-interest.

Western culture, which has promoted this view of the human self, is identified as a culture of individualism. We place too much value on individualism when we don't balance it with concern for the common good.

- What is your overall impression of these traits?
- Where do you see these traits in our culture?
- How have these traits contributed positively to society?
- How have these traits had a negative or dehumanizing effect on our culture?

self-understanding:

How do I understand myself? Who is the "self" in self-understanding? I usually identify myself by giving facts, such as name, address, occupation, telephone number, or e-mail address. Every time I answer the question "Who?" I say something about the self. "Who did this?" "Who said this?" "Who owns this?" "Who feels this?" Our culture tends to see the self as isolated from others, and some even think of the self as somehow separate from the body. But self-understanding cannot happen without the other. The other is essential for me to be a self. At the heart of who I am lie the things that I am committed to, things that are of crucial importance to me.

Who informs you, forms you

(By John McMahon, excerpted from Dreams, Dilemmas, Decisions, *National Office of Religious Education, 1994, pp. 16-17.)*

The title, "Who informs you, forms you," has more than one meaning. The most obvious meaning is that the person or organization providing you with information has a great influence on you and your beliefs. That is one reason why we believe that freedom of the press to report what is going on is so important. If one group of people were allowed to control the flow of information, that group could control what we believe by controlling what we know. When many groups share control over the flow of information, then a larger variety of views, impressions and opinions are available to us. This reminds us that we must carefully choose our information sources. A steady diet of false or poorly chosen information will give us a distorted and inaccurate view of the world.

The word "inform" has another meaning that applies to media. "Inform" can mean "to give form to" or "to fill with a certain quality." The media don't just give us information; they change the form of our thinking and perception. This is an awesome amount of power for any one person or group to have, especially when you consider the amount of time many people spend watching TV.

This might not be a problem if TV programs were produced by a great variety of people. But the TV programs most people watch are made by a relatively small group of people who have similar beliefs and economic status. Most programs are made by white, middle- or upper-class people, and are paid for by large corporations that advertise their products during the programs in order to make money. Media-makers work to promote their own interests. This is not necessarily evil; it is as true of religious broadcasting as it is of the Playboy channel. In order to evaluate the media, each of us needs to decide whether the spiritual, political and economic interests of the media-makers are the same, more or less, as our own.

And what about values? Values are not added to a TV program or newspaper article. Values are, in part, like lenses through which reality and experience must pass on their way to our minds. They are both the lenses that media-makers use in interpreting the reality that they present to us, and the lenses that come between us and the programs we watch. If our values are very different from those of the media-makers, we can have two possible reactions. We may reject the view of the world presented by the media. Or (and this is more likely), our values will gradually be moulded and changed to match those of the media. We will have been "informed" by the media in both senses of the word.

self-esteem:

Self-esteem is an awareness of one's own worth. Our culture presumes that I can give this esteem or love of self to myself. Esteem, however, can only be fulfilled by others. I can exist only by having others affirm me. This is human existence at its most fragile level. In a culture where the self has become isolated – and one hardly knows how to live in the gracious recognition of God – it is no wonder that self-esteem is so difficult.

Avoiding manipulation

How can we keep from being manipulated in this way? The most important thing is to recognize that the media may be trying to manipulate us. Whenever you watch a favourite TV program, ask yourself some questions: Who is the good guy in this show? Who is the bad guy? Why does the producer want me to believe this about the characters? Another set of useful questions might be the following one: Who made this program? Why? Are my interests and their interests the same? Does the picture of reality I am being shown here correspond with the world as I know it?

Another way to defend ourselves is to consciously seek out different sources and media than we usually do. Read magazines other than your usual favourites. Watch other news programs than the ones you usually watch. Listen to radio stations other than those that are most popular. This will help you to weaken the hold that any one of them has on your imagination.

The final and perhaps most important way to avoid being manipulated by the media is to be very clear about your own beliefs. We should always keep our values clearly before us and compare them to the programs we watch and the things we listen to. It is easy to be lulled by television. Creators of media messages do not want us to be critical of them. They make their programs as friendly as possible, so that we will not question what we are seeing. It is our duty as thinking, Christian people to question them constantly.

- What is the meaning of the title, "Who informs you, forms you"?

- How do you think the media shape the lives of people in your community in terms of their dreams, values, ideas of good and bad, understanding of various professions, etc.?

- In what ways do the media distort reality as you know it?
  - in presenting violence?
  - in presenting teenagers?
  - in presenting families?

- Research how different media cover the same event. Try to include as wide a variety of media as possible, including radio, TV, newspapers, Internet, magazines, French and English, and "alternative" media. How does the reporting differ? How do different media affect your perception of the event?

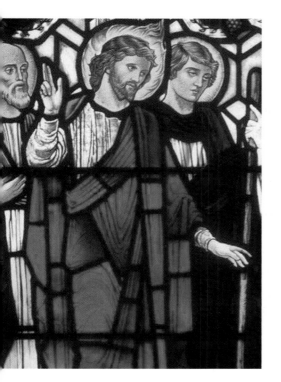

Who do you say that I am?

At one point in his life Jesus asked the disciples to tell him who they thought he was. They had been with him for some time. It was not a trick question. Jesus was asking them about his deepest identity. And Simon Peter got it just right. He said, "You are the Messiah, the Son of the Living God" (Matthew 16.16). Simon Peter clearly understood the central commitment of Jesus. It was God and God's work among us. But what do you think Jesus would say if *you* were to ask him, "Who do you say that *I* am?" It might be hard to answer exactly as Jesus would, but the points below would stand out. They make a dramatic contrast with the seven tendencies of individualism on pages 88 and 89.

1. Jesus wants me to call God Abba/Father
Jesus' greatest wish is that my relationship to God as Abba/Father would be like his own. Jesus prayed that God would make a home with me. For Jesus, I am most myself in my relationship with God. I am not isolated or cut off from others. I am in a covenant relationship with God. This is my deepest identity. →

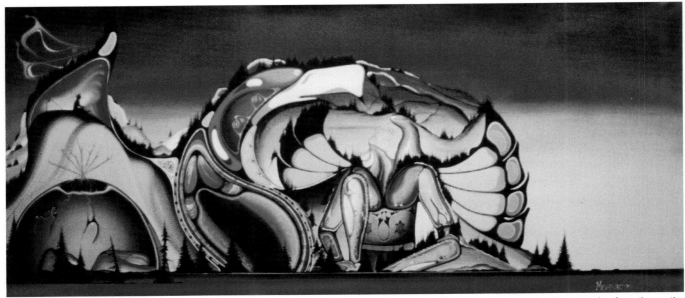

Native spiritual traditions express respect for the earth. This painting by Anishinabe artist James Simon shows several spirits emerging from the earth, as a person (upper left) seeks their help.

2. My relationship with Abba/Father is my freedom

Even though I am created, I am free. Christians can agree with modern philosophers that freedom is essential. But freedom is never a possession. Before I can be free, I must be set free. In other words, freedom is a gift that we cannot give to ourselves. In fact, so strong are the obstacles to freedom, that God sent Jesus to unbind us. The thing that binds us, and has power over our freedom, has many names. It is most frequently called sin. Being set free from these obstacles to our relationship with God is what Christians call salvation. I am made whole through the saving action of Jesus.

3. The earth is good and is a gift of God

I am not the master of the earth. The earth belongs to God. God declared the earth to be good for itself, not just for me. I must respect the earth as a gift, and my relationship with the earth should be one of thanksgiving, praise and stewardship rather than exploitation.

4. Other people are as important – perhaps even more important – than myself

The world does not turn around me. Jesus taught that whoever seeks their own life, loses it. My life cannot be centred solely on myself. Remember the story, "Flower, Mister?" The other is never really completely outside of me. He or she commands me, beckons me, questions me, begs from me, and cares for me. For Jesus, my relationship to him and my worship of God must also be a commitment to others.

5. Before Abba/Father, all are equal

When Peter is asked to make a distinction between the Jews and non-Jews, he says, "God shows no partiality" or, "God has no favourites" (see Acts 10.34). All are in the love of God. That is the basis of the goodness of all creatures, the basis of their equality. As the American Declaration of Independence proclaims, "All [people] are created equal." Equality is part of us as relational beings.

- What is the main difference between the image of self in Western culture and the image of self in the proclamation of Jesus?

- How does a person's relationship with Abba/Father make a difference to how they identify themselves?

- How is the "other" important for the self?

- What do you think Jesus would say to our culture about our preoccupation with the rights of the individual?

The Road Not Taken

Two roads diverged in a yellow wood,
And sorry I could not travel both
And be one traveler, long I stood
And looked down one as far as I could
To where it bent in the undergrowth;

Then took the other, as just as fair,
And having perhaps the better claim,
Because it was grassy and wanted wear;
Though as for that, the passing there
Had worn them really about the same,

And both that morning equally lay
In leaves no step had trodden black.
Oh, I kept the first for another day!
Yet knowing how way leads on to way,
I doubted if I should ever come back.

I shall be telling this with a sigh
Somewhere ages and ages hence:
Two roads diverged in a wood, and I –
I took the one less traveled by,
And that has made all the difference.

From THE POETRY OF ROBERT FROST
edited by Edward Connery Lathem,
© 1969 by Henry Holt and Company, LLC.
Reprinted by permission of Henry Holt & Co., LLC.

Theme 11

The desire for God is written in the human heart

What is your deepest longing – something even more important than having enough water to drink or enough air to breathe? Many of us just don't take the time to find out what our deepest longing really is. We don't think about getting enough to drink every day; we just drink – that is until the day comes when there is nothing to drink. Then our thirst brings our need into sharp focus and it becomes the only thing we think about.

Just like our bodies, our spiritual self also thirsts, but sometimes it's hard to recognize what will satisfy that thirst. Many people are so used to ignoring the signs of their spiritual thirst that they don't even realize it's there. We sometimes experience it as an emptiness deep down inside. How have you tried to fill that thirst?

Some people try to fill it by eating and drinking. Others try to fill it with pleasures. Some people try to fill the emptiness in their lives with work. Others with friends. Science tells us that nature abhors a vacuum – when there is an emptiness, something rushes in to fill it. This theme is about our spiritual thirst, and about how Jesus wants to fill us so completely that we ourselves become fountains of God's love for others.

Focus your learning

- **Aware and Informed**
  What do we hunger and thirst for?

- **Practical and Active**
  How do my relationships with others help me to grow?

- **Creative and Grateful**
  How does Jesus satisfy my hunger and thirst?

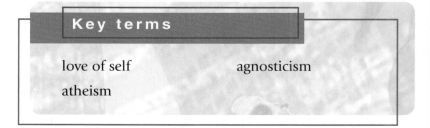

Key terms

love of self   agnosticism

atheism

Nietzsche's madman

Have you heard of the madman who lit a lantern in the bright morning hours, and ran to the marketplace, crying again and again, "I seek God! I seek God!" Many people who did not believe in God were standing around just then, so he caused much laughter. "Why, did he get lost?" said one. "Did he lose his way like a child?" said another. "Or is he hiding? Is he afraid of us? Has he gone on a voyage?" They just yelled and laughed. The madman jumped into their midst and pierced them with his glances.

"Where is God?" he cried. "I will tell you. *We have killed him –* you and I. We're all his murderers. But how did we do this? How were we able to drink up the sea? Who gave us the sponge to wipe away the entire horizon? What did we do when we unchained this earth from its sun? Where is it moving now? Where are we headed? Away from all suns? Are we not plunging continually? Backward, sideward, forward – in all directions? Is there any up or down left? Are we not straying as through an infinite nothing? Do we not feel the breath of empty space? Has it not become colder? Is not night and more night coming on all the while? Must not lanterns be lit in broad daylight? Do we not hear the noise of the gravediggers who are burying God? Do we not smell God's decomposition? Even gods decompose. God is dead. And we have killed him.

"How shall we, the murderers of all murderers, comfort ourselves? What was holiest and most powerful has bled to death under our knives. Who will wipe this blood off us? What water is there for us to clean ourselves? What festivals of atonement, what sacred games will we have to invent? Is not this deed too great for us? Must not we ourselves become gods simply to seem worthy of it?"

Here the madman fell silent and looked again at his listeners; and they, too, were silent and stared at him in astonishment. At last he threw his lantern on the ground, and it broke and went out. "I come too early," he said. "My time has not yet come. This tremendous event is still on its way, still wandering – it has not yet reached the ears of humanity. Lightning and thunder require time; the light of the stars requires time; deeds require time even after they are done, before they can be seen and heard. This deed is still more distant from them than the most distant stars – *and yet they have done it themselves.*"

Later that same day the madman forced his way into various churches and there sang "Eternal rest to God!" When he was led out and asked to explain himself, he is said to have replied each time, "What are these churches now if they are not the tombs and sepulchres of God?"

(based on Walter Kaufmann's translation of Neitzsche's *The Gay Science* [New York: Random House, 1974] #125)

Friedrich Wilhelm Nietzsche (1844-1900)

atheism:

People throughout the ages have said that there is no God. But only in the West has atheism, the denial of God's existence, become such a strong part of culture. In the 1991 census, 12.5% of Canadians declared that they had no religious affiliation.

agnosticism:

Agnostics say they don't know if God exists. They prefer to remain indifferent. The movements of atheism and agnosticism are parts of Western culture.

- What would it feel like, according to Nietzsche, if God were no longer experienced in our culture?
- What aspects of the story of the madman ring true or false about our culture? Where is God in our culture?
- How could this gradual disappearance of God in culture be linked to the individualism of our culture?

Our culture of self-fulfillment

Live in the lap of **Luxury** at Oak Tre Valley Es

The ultimate travel expe

Put on a happy face!

Now you can eat as much as you want.

Style and Sophistication

SKIN PROBLEMS? TRY OUR PRODUCTS AND SAY GOODBYE TO THE BAD SKIN BLUES

Diamond Jewellery

Get your very own **Fishin' Freddy Bear!** Limited Edition Buy yours now!

WANT TO LOOK BETTER THAN YOU THOUGHT YOU COULD?

WE HAVE WHAT YOU NEED TO GET YOU WHERE YOU WANT TO BE

Look like a model in just 7 days with the amazing **No-Diet Weight Loss Plan!** The quickest way to a happier YOU!!!

What do you think?

Is there room for God in our culture?

How do you think Jesus would react to our culture's messages of what it means to be fully human?

What is true/false about our culture's understanding of what it means to be fully human ?

I will set you free

The Old Testament prophet Jeremiah is not known for mincing words:

> Cursed are those who trust in mere mortals
>> and make mere flesh their strength,
>> whose hearts turn away from the LORD.
> They shall be like a shrub in the desert,
>> and shall not see when relief comes.
> They shall live in the parched places of the
> wilderness,
>> in an uninhabited land. (17.5-6)

He contrasts them to those who trust the LORD. Of them he says,

> They shall be like a tree planted by water....
> It shall not fear when heat comes...;
> ....
> in the year of drought it is not anxious,
>> and it does not cease to bear fruit. (17.7-8)

The Scriptures proclaim that God saves. Human life is based on trust in God. True freedom is a gift of God. Happiness is to be found in the LORD.

What do Jeremiah's words mean for our culture? Our culture promises happiness and fulfillment in quite a different way. The media proclaim that human fulfillment can be bought, and that we as consumers can choose how we are to be fulfilled. We recognize the value of food, shelter, health care, education, arts, sports and leisure to help people live from day to day and achieve their potential. Is Jeremiah saying that these things are not important? Or is he saying that there is something even more important?

The Prophet Jeremiah (part of Michelangelo's ceiling in the Sistine Chapel)

love of self:

The gospels assume that we love ourselves. They add, however, that this love of self must equal our love for others. "Love your neighbour as yourself," the second commandment says. In other words, loving your neighbour goes hand in hand with loving yourself.

The following stories from the gospels tell about God setting people free. As you read each one, think about what the prophet Jeremiah was saying about trusting in God.

The paralyzed man	John 5.1-18
The woman caught in adultery	John 8.1-11
The man born blind	John 9.1-12
The raising of Lazarus	John 11.1-44
The crippled woman	Luke 13.10-17

- How is the person in the story not free?
- How does Jesus set this person free?
- What might be a modern parallel to this story?

Jesus and the woman at the well – a dramatic reading (John 4.3-42)

Narrator: Jesus left Judea and started back to Galilee. But he had to go through Samaria. So he came to a Samaritan city called Sychar, near the plot of ground that Jacob had given to his son Joseph. Jacob's well was there, and Jesus, tired out by his journey, was sitting by the well. It was about noon. His disciples had gone to the city to buy food. A Samaritan woman came to draw water.

Jesus: Give me a drink.

Woman: How is it that you, a Jew, ask a drink of me, a woman of Samaria?

Jesus: If you knew the gift of God, and who it is that is saying to you, "Give me a drink," you would have asked him, and he would have given you living water.

Woman: Sir, you have no bucket, and the well is deep. Where do you get that living water? Are you greater than our ancestor Jacob, who gave us the well, and with his sons and his flocks drank from it?

Jesus: Everyone who drinks of this water will be thirsty again, but those who drink of the water that I will give them will never be thirsty. The water that I will give will become in them a spring of water gushing up to eternal life.

Woman: Sir, give me this water, so that I may never be thirsty or have to keep coming here to draw water.

Jesus: Go, call your husband, and come back.

Woman: I have no husband.

Jesus: You are right in saying, "I have no husband"; for you have had five husbands, and the one you have now is not your husband. What you have said is true!

Woman: Sir, I see that you are a prophet. Our ancestors worshipped on this mountain, but you say that the place where people must worship is in Jerusalem.

Jesus: Woman, believe me, the hour is coming when you will worship the Father neither on this mountain nor in Jerusalem. You worship what you do not know; we worship what we know, for salvation is from the Jews. But the hour is coming, and is now here, when the true worshippers will worship the Father in spirit and truth, for the Father seeks such as these to worship him. God is spirit, and those who worship him must worship in spirit and truth.

Woman: I know that Messiah is coming. When he comes, he will proclaim all things to us.

Jesus: I am he, the one who is speaking to you.

Narrator: Just then his disciples came. They were astonished that he was speaking with a woman, but no one said, "What do you

---

Did you know...

...that wells were important places in the history of the Israelites? Several prominent biblical figures met their future spouses at wells. The same thing happens here, but in a symbolic sense. Here the Samaritans, through the woman, espouse the way of Jesus.

	want?" or, "Why are you speaking with her?" Then the woman left her water jar and went back to the city.
Woman:	Come and see a man who told me everything I have ever done! He cannot be the Messiah, can he?
Narrator:	They left the city and were on their way to him.
Disciple:	Rabbi, eat something.
Jesus:	I have food to eat that you do not know about.
Disciple:	Surely no one has brought him something to eat?
Jesus:	My food is to do the will of him who sent me and to complete his work. Do you not say, "Four months more, then comes the harvest"? But I tell you, look around you, and see how the fields are ripe for harvesting. The reaper is already receiving wages and

is gathering fruit for eternal life, so that sower and reaper may rejoice together. For here the saying holds true, "One sows and another reaps." I sent you to reap that for which you did not labour. Others have laboured, and you have entered into their labour.

Narrator:	Many Samaritans from that city believed in him because of the woman's testimony, "He told me everything I have ever done." So when the Samaritans came to him, they asked him to stay with them; and he stayed there two days. And many more believed because of his word.
Samaritans:	It is no longer because of what you said that we believe, for we have heard for ourselves, and we know that this is truly the Saviour of the world.

Jesus meets a Samaritan woman at the well of Jacob

The woman whom Jesus met at the well must have had a deep thirst for life that she was unable to satisfy. After all, she had been married five times. She came to draw water, but that day she got much more than water. Jesus, too, was thirsty when he arrived at the well. In this story, the thirst of the woman and of Jesus is symbolic of a different kind of longing that comes from within. Satisfying this interior thirst contributes every bit as much to staying alive as does having enough water to drink.

There were many barriers to overcome in this meeting between Jesus and the Samaritan woman. Jews and Samaritans had the same ancestry, but over the generations they became enemies. To meet Jesus, the Samaritan woman had to overcome the hatred, fear and distrust that were rooted in her culture and upbringing. How could Jesus, a Jew, help a Samaritan?

Jesus tells the woman that he could give her water that would make her never thirst again. The woman says to him, "Are you greater than our ancestor Jacob who gave us this well? Give me this water." In reply, Jesus asks the woman to call her husband. The woman answers quite honestly, "I have no husband." In John's symbolic language, the woman is saying, "I have no God." Jesus says, "You are right. Your people have had five husbands – that is, all sorts of gods – and your present one is not your husband." (Jesus speaks like a true prophet here. The prophets of old often spoke about Israel's relationship with the LORD in terms of marriage relationships.) The woman then asks, "How are we to worship this God?" Jesus replies, "All of the ways that you seek for God are not true worship. There is only one true worship." "Where can I find this?" she asks. "Must I wait until the Messiah comes?" "No," says Jesus, "you do not have to wait. I am the one who can lead you to true worship."

Did you know...

... that Samaritans were Israelites who did not worship in the temple in Jerusalem? Some became followers of Jesus shortly after his death and the first resurrection appearances. The Samaritan story may well have been intended to help Samaritan Christians be recognized as being equal to Jewish Christians.

For the woman, Jesus' reply, "I am he," came as a revelation of the LORD. (Remember how Moses heard God's Name: "I am"?) Here Jesus tells her that he is "I am." With this revelation, the woman forgot everything else – she left her water jar behind and ran to tell the people in her town what she had discovered. She became a disciple – in fact, an apostle – announcing to the people that she had met Jesus the Messiah. →

She had found what she was searching for. Jesus had satisfied her inner thirst. She was free.

Notice how Jesus gradually deepened the meaning of their conversation. As Jesus revealed who he is, the woman also learned a great deal about *herself*. She learned about her own thirst for life and for love, about her own sinfulness, and about her own experience of worship. As she learned about herself, the barriers of race (between Jew and Samaritan), religious prejudice (about the right place to worship God), and political differences (over the laws about uncleanliness), all came tumbling down. As she learned the truth about herself, she learned who Jesus is – the Saviour of the world.

- What is the conflict between the Jews and the Samaritans?

- What is the woman seeking in all her questions to Jesus? What does she really want?

- What does the water in the story symbolize?

- How does the woman come to know that Jesus is the Messiah?

- Why do you think the disciples were astonished to see Jesus talking with the woman?

- What effect did the woman's words have on others in her community?

The saint of the "little way"

One pope called her "the greatest saint of modern times." Yet, we would never have known her had she not been ordered by one of her own sisters to write the story of her childhood. She later completed her story in two other autobiographical letters. In this autobiography there are no great deeds, no extraordinary experiences, no mystical visions, no soaring prayer life. From the outside, she was remarkably ordinary. She was born Thérèse Martin in 1873, the youngest of five sisters. The family were extremely devout Catholics. When she was only five her mother died. At that time, her father took the family to live in Lisieux in France. That is why she is now known as St. Thérèse of Lisieux. Her two eldest sisters entered a Carmelite convent there and when Thérèse was 15 she joined them. Later, another sister entered the same convent. Thérèse died nine years later of tuberculosis at the age of 24. Only 27 years later, in 1925, Pope Pius XI declared her a saint. Why? Because within 10 years after her death her autobiography *The Story of a Soul* had become an international best-seller. Her spirituality was contagious. Many tried to imitate her in her love shown to others in the little things of everyday life. Her spirituality became known as the "little way."

What is there to report on her life? She did not want to stand out and be noticed. She wrote to her father shortly before entering the convent, "I, too, [like Jesus,] wanted to be without comeliness and beauty, alone to tread the grapes, unknown to all creatures." Her life was ordinary and uneventful as lives in convents tend to be. But she gave the smallest things of life with all its daily irritants the attention of love. The love showed in her face that was forever smiling. As someone said, "Smilingly, Thérèse went through her years in the convent, graciously, guilelessly, sunnily smiling." It was not a smile of happiness but a smile of love. The smile covered her little sacrifices for other sisters in the convent and her own suffering. Smiling for the other was for her the only permissible way to suffer. When other nuns described her, even 40 years later, they always remembered her beautiful smile. She describes her

Mother Teresa on our thirst for God

The greatest disease in the West today is… being unwanted, unloved, and uncared for. We can cure physical diseases with medicine, but the only cure for loneliness, despair, and hopelessness is love. There are many in the world who are dying for a piece of bread but there are many more dying for a little love. The poverty in the West is a different kind of poverty – it is not only a poverty of loneliness but also of spirituality. There's a hunger for love, as there is a hunger for God.

When you know how much God is in love with you then you can only live your life radiating that love. I always say that love starts at home: family first, and then your own town or city. It is easy to love people who are far away but it is not always so easy to love those who live with us or right next to us. I do not agree with the big way of doing things – love needs to start with an individual. To get to love a person, you must contact that person, become close. Everyone needs love. All must know that they're wanted and that they are important to God.

Jesus said, "Love one another as I have loved you." He also said, "Whatever you did to the least of my brethren, you did it to me," so we love Him in the poor. He said, "I was hungry and you fed me… I was naked and you clothed me."

(Mother Teresa, A Simple Path, pp. 79-81. Random House Canada, 1995)

---

little way as a "way of spiritual childhood, the way of trust and total surrender." All her little actions, she says, are like rose petals strewn before Jesus with no concern about achievement. Leave your actions to God. Expect everything from God. Thérèse saw herself as a little child who knows only one thing: to love.

In minute detail she wrote about how she practised her little way with a fellow sister who irked her by making irritating noises during prayer; with the sister who often accidentally splashed her face with dirty water as she worked in the laundry; with the cranky old sister in a wheelchair whom she daily "piloted" to the dining room. All little things, insignificant really. But Thérèse trusted that God delighted with "little ones," with the little deeds of life, as long as they were done out of love. What she sought was the happiness of others.

Thérèse teaches us that to be holy, one does not need to do great deeds. One does not need to make a big splash in the world to be a full person. Ordinary life is holy when it goes beyond ourselves and does what Thérèse did: "I have no other means of proving my love for You other than that of strewing flowers, that is, … profiting by all the smallest things and doing them through love…. While I am strewing flowers, I shall sing, for could one cry while doing such a joyous action? I shall sing even when I must gather my flowers in the midst of thorns, and my song will be all the more melodious in proportion to the length and sharpness of the thorns."

"Let anyone who is thirsty come to me,
and let the one who believes in me drink.
As the scripture has said,
'Out of the believer's heart
shall flow rivers of living water.'"

(John 7.37-38)

The *Catechism of the Catholic Church* and the search for God

"The desire for God is written in the human heart." Why? Because people are created by God and for God; and God never ceases to draw us toward God. Only in God will we find the truth and happiness we never stop searching for. (#27)

Unit 4 review

In this unit, you explored how each individual becomes more fully a person through his or her relationships with God and others.

Aware and Informed

Who am I?

Jesus wants me to call God Abba/Father. I am in a covenant relationship with God. This is my deepest identity. We are created free. Sin binds our freedom, but God sent Jesus to free us from the bondage of sin. I become more fully a person through my relationships with God and others.

What do we hunger and thirst for?

The desire for God is written in the human heart. We have been created by God and for God. Only in God will we find the truth and happiness we never stop searching for.

Practical and Active

Who shapes my identity, and what can I do about it?

Our culture has a strong influence over how we perceive ourselves. Our culture is greatly influenced by the various information media. "Who informs us, forms us." Who do we listen to in our culture? Do we listen to the Word of God in the midst of the thousands of media messages that seek to shape our self-perception?

How do my relationships with others help me to grow?

Jesus taught his followers to love their neighbours as themselves. In other words, loving my neighbour goes hand in hand with loving myself. Jesus also said, "Love one another as I have loved you." And, "whatever you did to the least of my brethren, you did it to me." The more that we love others, and seek the good of others, the more we ourselves grow in love and goodness.

Creative and Grateful

You can answer these questions for yourself. The answer is found in your relationship with God.

How does God see me?

How does Jesus satisfy my hunger and thirst?

Unit 5

Relating to the other:
The voice of the other in me

Aim: to explore relationships with others from a Catholic perspective

Theme 12
Friendship

We all enjoy having friends. That's clearly a good thing. But it is still important for us to know what friendship is all about. From the day we are born, we enter into relationships: with our parents and caregivers, extended family, doctors and nurses, the parish priest, and all sorts of other people. We find ourselves dealing with people in many different ways. But some relationships are special: we choose our friends. We choose them from all others, and want to be with them. We put extra time and energy into our relationships with them.

How do friendships make us better people? How do we help our friends be better people? What do we do when our friends betray or abandon us? This theme is not about the psychology of friendship, but about looking at how we relate to other people, and how Jesus calls us to be even better friends to others than we can imagine ourselves.

Focus your learning

- **Aware and Informed**
  How important is friendship?

- **Practical and Active**
  How can I be a better friend?

- **Creative and Grateful**
  How have friendships helped me to grow?

Key terms

golden rule   Christian self-understanding

the other   reciprocity

What do you think?

How are relationships life-giving? How do they make life richer?

If certain relationships are not life-giving, what is destructive about them?

How do some relationships end up in betrayal?

What do we do with the pain that relationships can sometimes bring?

How do cultural factors influence relationships? When do they support relationships? When are they an obstacle?

What place does the gospel or the person of Jesus Christ have in relationships?

The face

A person's face is a wondrous reality! From the time we are babies until we grow old, we are affected by face-to-face relationships. It starts with the mother whose eyes seek out the eyes of her newborn to welcome the infant into the world. By her smile she draws a smile from the baby; by singing and speaking face to face with the baby she develops a lifelong bond. Each face is like no other – it has a genetic history and shows someone's ethnic heritage and family traits. No two are exactly the same. We are each unique in the entire world and in all of history.

Our faces are naked – they are the one place where we expose ourselves totally to another. That's why, when we meet another person face to face, our meeting is so intimate. When we are face to face, the mystery of the other person is before us, and ours before them. Imagine for a moment being face to face with your mother, friend, girlfriend/boyfriend, teacher, the class bully, a famous musician, a beggar. Each face is different, each one a different message, and each one a different call upon you. No face is neutral. That is why it may be hard to look someone in the eyes. We may feel that the other is too much for us. We may feel small, shy, guilty, tense, uncertain, full of fear, or shamed. We may also feel welcome, beautiful, interested, happy, confident or relaxed. Our face is the site of language and communication. Our face speaks with the eyes, the smile, the frown, or a thousand other ways. All our senses congregate in our faces – smell, touch, taste, sight and hearing. It is no wonder that the face can attract and unsettle us at the same time.

The French philosopher Emmanuel Levinas says that when we are face to face with another person, the other's face is like a visual version of God's commandment, "You shall not murder." The face is so exalted that we may not do anything that "murders" its sanctity and uniqueness. The face of another person, he says, is a trace left behind by all-holy God. In each face God speaks to us. It is no wonder that when we are face to face with one another our feelings and emotions can be intense. The face speaks to us and cannot be ignored. The face does not leave us neutral. If ever we thought that we were settled, that we needed no one else, that we had things under control and were happy with things, being face to face with another can make us reconsider. The face calls us to honesty. The other's face often seems like our master, revealing our innermost thoughts, selfishness, or even our desire to be rid of the other. The face calls us forth from ourselves to relate to the other.

- Describe an experience of being face to face with someone.
- What do faces tell you?
- How are faces traces of God? If each face is a trace of God then each face has something unique to say about God and each face is needed for us to know God. What do your classmates' faces say?
- Can a person become merely an object when you are face to face with them? Explain.

Reciprocity and trust

Society and communities cannot function without people helping one another. We clear snow from our neighbour's walkway; we turn down the music at a party so that our neighbours can sleep; we lend money; we give up our seat on the bus to an older person. These are just a few of the ways we do things for others. But are all these acts of kindness without any self-interest? Not always. We may not expect anything in return immediately, but in the back of our minds there is the expectation, knowledge or at least hope that somewhere down the road someone will reciprocate. So it is not totally without self-interest. I help you now, expecting that in some way you will help me in the future. Society actually depends on this reciprocity, though, as the glue that holds it together. The glue is the trust we give each other in society.

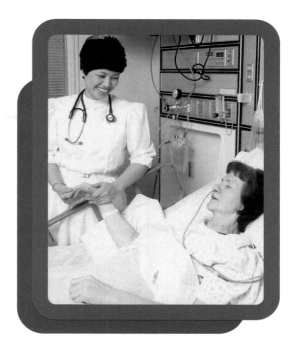

Social analysts point out that over the past 25 years this glue has been weakening. Our society is losing its trust in the honesty of people. One survey showed that in 1973, 36% of 18- to 24-year-olds thought most people were trustworthy. In 2001 that trust had dwindled to 20% (National Opinion Research Center, University of Chicago). It means that young people today are less trusting than young people in the 1970s. What has happened? Are people less trustworthy? Or have we lost trust and become more suspicious? For society to function we cannot always rely on a background check. Only when people trust their fellow citizens will they feel free to contribute to society, to give to charities and to participate in cooperative activities.

reciprocity:

Reciprocity is the expectation that if I do something for someone else, this person will at some point do something in return for me. This give and take is motivated both by unselfishness and by self-interest. Our culture depends on reciprocity, but it has been gradually decreasing because of a lack of trust.

the other:

The Scriptures call the other "your neighbour." The other is a very concrete person, so unique that we cannot lump this person together with others. The other has a name, a particular face and unique eyes. The other is ultimately a stranger to me because I can never know him or her fully. The other's face reveals itself to me as a plea, a command never to harm or to murder. The other is for me an image of God.

- Why do you think that the level of trust in our society and among high school students has declined?
- What activities do you avoid because you don't trust the other person(s)?
- On a scale from 1 to 10, what is your level of trust toward
  - your friends?
  - your parents?
  - sales people?
  - health care professionals?
  - school administration?

Did you know...

... that in ancient Israel, censuses were not permitted. Why? Because a census does not respect the uniqueness of each person. People cannot be added up. A census proposes that a human can be reduced to a number. King David, we are told in 2 Samuel, "was stricken to the heart because he had numbered the people" (24.10). That's how holy people are!

Betting your soul

Faust (a play written by the German writer Johann Wolfgang von Goethe) is a masterpiece of modern literature. The main character, Dr. Faust, captures perfectly the Western ideal of the self-made, independent, rational human being. In the play, Dr. Faust is tempted to enclose himself totally in this world and to let go of his spiritual side. Even though the play was written around two hundred years ago, Faust is like us in many ways.

Dr. Faust lives life through his senses, fully immersed in everything Western culture has to offer. He likes the new rights and freedoms of ordinary citizens and is drawn to the new powers that his culture is giving to the individual. It is a heady experience to be set free from the tyranny of others. He is fascinated by what the sciences are promising with their new inventions. He is a skeptic, doubting the beliefs and values held out by others, particularly the Church. Yet something still gnaws at him.

Despite his attraction to what the world offers, he realizes that he is a prisoner to this world of the senses. He feels trapped.

At first he tries to escape into the world of magic – not unlike today's flight into the world of virtual reality video games and science fiction. But he soon realizes that he cannot escape this world. Magic ends up being just another way of controlling, of being in charge. He then tries mysticism, thinking that the self would lose itself by being absorbed into God or nature. God would be all. The self would be gone, and thereby set free. But he can't go down this road either, because one day he hears church bells announcing Easter. The sound makes him warmly remember the proclamation of the gospel from his youth. He remembers with an ache in his heart the Bible's image of himself: "I, a mirror image of divinity!" Immediately after this admission, he says: "And never ever to you!" referring to the world of the senses. That is, "I have never ever been a mirror image of what culture has made me out to be!" Deep within himself Faust believes that he does not have to be a slave to what his culture says he is.

And yet, he cannot let go of the attraction that his culture's image of the self holds out to him. One day while out walking, Faust is followed by a black poodle. The poodle stands for the spirit of his culture. One might expect that he will reject the poodle, but he doesn't. In fact, he invites the poodle into his study. In other words, Faust lets the spirit of culture into his home, since he knows he cannot live without it. His need to live in culture on one hand and his desire to be free of culture on the other becomes the struggle of his life. How can one live in this culture, accept it, and at the same time not become its prisoner?

Enter Mephistopheles. In the play, Mephistopheles is the tempter, a magician, a representative of the dark forces of chaos and disorder. Mephistopheles tries to seduce Faust into giving himself totally to the spirit of the culture. He makes a wager with Faust, promising happiness in this world. He will be Faust's servant and give him whatever he wants. Mephistopheles – like the seducers on television today – promises that he will conjure up for Faust whatever will make him happy. In return, Faust has to promise that in the next life he will be a slave to

Mephistopheles. Mephistopheles wants Faust's soul. Faust accepts, but on one condition. Mephistopheles has to win his soul. And so, Faust and Mephistopheles enter into a wager. Faust says, "You win the wager and you may rule me from the day you can give me such enjoyment that I'll say, 'Stay with me – you are so beautiful!'"

Mephistopheles uses magic to show Faust all that human ingenuity and technology can offer and to bring Faust enjoyment. He does everything to make Faust experience beauty and fulfillment of the senses, trying to make Faust believe that this world is enough. He wants Faust to forget that he is an image of God and that his destiny is with God. He wants him to give up his eternal destiny for a temporal one. At no point, however, does Mephistopheles succeed. Every time Faust is about to give in, he remembers his Jewish and Christian ancestry.

Mephistopheles comes closest when Faust meets Margaret. Mephistopheles arranges that she fall in love with Faust. The tempter wants it to be a purely sensuous affair, one that will force Faust to say to her, "Stay with me – you are so beautiful!" But in their sensuous love, Faust sees a spark of the divine. Moreover, sensuous love is not enough to bind Margaret to Faust. She seeks a higher love than one that's confined to just the senses. And this higher love is beyond the power of Mephistopheles to conjure up. He cannot offer Faust anything that will make him forget who he really is. He is an image of divinity whose destiny is more than sensuous happiness.

Wrestling with temptation

In the story of Dr. Faust and Mephistopheles, the image of the tempter is one of a magician. In the story of Jesus' temptation in the desert (Matthew 4.1-11), on the other hand, Jesus is tempted by the devil. Just as Jesus had to wrestle with temptation, we too must deal with temptation in our daily lives. Even as we try to find fulfilling relationships with others, our self-interest tries to get the better of us.

Christian self-understanding:

When we think about Christ in our culture, we begin to see ourselves in a new way. This new self lives out of relationships with others. It is not afraid to listen. It is a self who lives out of a trust and faith in another. In these relationships I am no longer in control; I am no longer the source of my freedom or of making myself. This is the self of a believer who is not afraid to celebrate being in relationship with God.

- How is Doctor Faust like us?
- How is advertising like Mephistopheles? How does advertising seduce us?
- What memory of himself do the Easter bells evoke in Faust? Why is this memory so different from what he was experiencing?
- What would be something about which you might say: "Stay with me – you are so beautiful"?
- How did the love of Margaret break the pact between Faust and Mephistopheles? What did Faust experience in her love?
- How are we tempted to "wager our souls" in today's world?

Friendships in the kingdom of God

Jesus had some intense friendships in his life: with his mentor, John the Baptist; with Lazarus whom he raised from the tomb; with the beloved disciple in the fourth gospel who reclined next to him at the Last Supper; with Mary and Martha whom he visited often; with Mary Magdalene who came looking for Jesus after his death; and with many other people. He said that friendship was based on love and that one could have no greater love than this: to lay down one's life for one's friends (see John 15.13). And that is what he did. "You are my friends," he said to his disciples. With them he shared his heart.

Jesus with Martha

Whenever Jesus speaks or acts, ordinary actions and things we thought we knew take on new meaning. For Jesus, the kingdom of God transformed everything, including friendships. Friendship is never to be prized simply for the good feeling of closeness that it provides, or for the privilege of being with someone you like. For Jesus, everything, including friendship, is for others. Friendship is a gift that must be passed on. It is a vocation – a call to extend to others the benefit you have received. You can't keep it for yourself. The call is not always easy. It is a call to serve others in the way that Jesus served.

At one point in the gospels Jesus told his friends what he wanted them to do for others. He told them to go to all the towns and villages where he had not been able to go and do there what he did. "Tell people," he said, "that the kingdom of God is at hand." He told them to heal the sick and bring peace to the homes that extended hospitality to them. He called them to go on a journey without any provisions. They were not to wear sandals; they were not to bring a change of clothing, a staff, a bag for food, bread, or money. They were to go and rely totally on the hospitality of others. Read the following texts about the lifestyle to which Jesus invites his friends:

Luke 9.1-6	Jesus sends out the twelve disciples
Luke 10.1-11	Jesus sends out the seventy
Mark 8.34-38	What it takes to find one's life
Luke 18.18-30	What must I do?

Jesus sought a friendship that was totally for others. He did not give us practical details on how to be friends in a totally self-giving way. But in the gospels, we read about the ideals that he set for his disciples in their situation. There are many things that can get in the way of these ideals. For Jesus, one stumbling block to friendship was wealth. Other stumbling blocks included things like the desire for honour and recognition. Such things can keep us from being the sort of friend that Jesus is calling us to be. If friendship that is completely other-centred seems impossible, we must remember what Jesus told his disciples. One day when they complained that he was asking the impossible, he said, "What is impossible for mortals is possible for God" (Luke 18.27). Trust God.

> ### golden rule:
>
> The *golden rule* – "Do to others as you would have them do to you" (Luke 6.31), or "In everything do to others as you would have them do to you" (Matthew 7.12) – presents a good summary of Christian morality. When we apply it, we deal with others in the same way that we would like them to deal with us, not asking for anything in return.

This is my commandment,

    that you love one another as I have loved you.

No one has greater love than this,

    to lay down one's life for one's friends.

You are my friends if you do what I command you.

I do not call you servants any longer,

    because the servant does not know what the master is doing;

    but I have called you friends,

    because I have made known to you everything

    that I have heard from my Father.

(John 15.12-15)

Theme 13

Intimacy, sexuality and love

Few things in life both thrill and scare us more than intimacy with another person. We want to be close to another and to be loved, but at the same time we sometimes fear coming close. We may have felt the pain of betrayal and rejection before, and we cannot help but think, "Will I be hurt again?" On the other hand, we also cannot help but think how wonderful this relationship could be.

In this theme, you will explore the meaning of love, sexuality and intimacy from the perspective of our faith. The Bible, after all, has more than a thousand references to love. It tells hundreds of stories about love and intimacy, self-giving, and even betrayal and rejection.

Our perspective on love, when seen through the eyes of our culture, may have become jaded, but our relationship with Jesus can renew our faith in love.

Focus your learning

- **Aware and Informed**
  Why is intimacy important?

- **Practical and Active**
  How can I be a better lover?

- **Creative and Grateful**
  Where does love lead me?

Key terms

sexuality	body
intimacy	marriage

What is intimacy?

I met Danielle four weeks ago. We have done some neat things together. She loves snowboarding and we have gone to Panorama two weekends in a row. She is fun to be with. She has a beautiful smile and laughs easily. One evening we went walking in a snowstorm along a cross-country ski trail and talked – all about our families, growing up, school, what our plans are, and some of the things we have done. At school I told my good friend Zack about her. He looked at me and with a grin he asked, "So have you done it yet?"

There are a number of ways of being intimate. Zack was interested in only one. Had they had sexual intercourse? He thought that having sexual intercourse was the be-all and end-all of a relationship – the only point of being together, in fact. But love and intimacy come in many packages. In our culture, we use only one word for love. Other cultures, like that of the Greeks, have many words to express the complexity of the mystery of love.

intimacy:

Intimacy is the close bond that exists between human beings, whether as friends or as associates. The bond is intimate because it touches our innermost being, our spiritual and physical core. Because we are sexual by nature, intimacy is always sexual, but it does not necessarily involve having sexual relations. We cannot be divided spirit from body. Intimacy involves the whole person.

body:

The human body is more than its cells or its biological makeup. It is not just *a* body, but *my* body. It is not an object. It is me, and it shares the honour and dignity of being in the image of God. Catholics call the body the temple of the Holy Spirit. This is why our bodies are part of the covenant between a man and woman, which we call marriage.

- The reading says that there are different ways of expressing intimacy in human relationships. How is intimacy expressed in each kind of love?
- Why is the intimacy that is appropriate for one kind of love not necessarily appropriate for another kind of love? How do we know the difference?

Five kinds of love

Companionship

This is the love that one has for an associate, a classmate or a comrade in an adventure. This is a relationship based on companionship and a sharing of common interests or goals, but it does not involve emotional closeness. The Greeks called this love *hetaireia*.

Sexual love

Love in the sexual sense is a passionate love, pleasurable, spontaneous, and even instinctive. It is the love of mutual attraction between a man and a woman. *Eros* is the Greek word for romantic, or sexual love.

Family love

This is the love children have for their parents and parents for their children. It is a love that sprouts naturally. It is not earned, and is often quite emotional, with deep attachments. The Greeks used the word *storge* to name this family love.

Friendship

The Greeks called the warm and tender affection felt between two friends *philia*. This is the love that Jesus had for Lazarus. When Lazarus' sisters sent for Jesus when Lazarus was ill, they reminded Jesus of his friendship: "Lord, he whom you love (*phileo*) is ill" (John 11.3). A love between friends is mutual and supportive. One does not leave a friend in the lurch.

In this scene of creation from the Sistine Chapel, Michelangelo suggests God's gift of sexuality to humanity. As God extends his hand to touch Adam with the gift of life, he brings Eve (the figure wrapped in God's left arm) so that each will have the other's love and companionship.

Charity

Charity is a special kind of love. The Greeks called it *agape*. We wish others well even when they do not do anything in return. It is an unconditional love, a love that is willing to sacrifice. It does not matter what a person does to us; he or she may offend us or treat us badly. *Agape*-love reaches out to this person. *Agape*-love does not have to like the person, since it is not dependent on the emotions. *Agape*-love does something – a favour, a gesture, an offer of help – for a person, whether deserving or not. This is the highest form of love. It can even be given to enemies. Jesus referred to *agape*-love when he said, "Love one another as I have loved you" (see John 13.34).

Sexuality

The whole area of sexuality is one of the great mysteries of human life. In addition to being mysterious, sexuality is sometimes feared. Sexuality is the force and energy, experienced both spiritually and bodily, to be creative in response to life. Our sexuality orients us toward others – it underlies our desire for love, friendship, community and family. Sexuality allows for communion between persons. "Man and woman were made 'for each other' – God… created them to be a communion of persons… and complementary as masculine and feminine." (*Catechism of the Catholic Church*, #372)

Sexuality fills us with the astonishment of the Man face to face with the Woman in the Book of Genesis. "This at last is bone of my bones and flesh of my flesh," he said in awe (Genesis 2.23). The next verse adds, that is why "a man… clings to his wife, and they become one flesh." The Man was no longer alone – he had found a helpmate. No wonder God exclaimed: "This is good; indeed, it is very good."

No other drive is more effective in breaking us out of the constant concern for ourselves. At the level of sexuality, the other is not a burden; the other is a delight because there is nothing more desirable. As Ron Rolheiser writes, "For this reason, sexuality lies at the center of spiritual life. A healthy sexuality is the single most powerful vehicle there is to lead us to selflessness and joy" (*The Holy Longing*. Toronto: Doubleday, 1999, pp. 192-193). But the opposite is true as well. The fire of sexuality can also turn ugly. There is no more powerful disorder in us than an unhealthy sexuality. Unhealthy sexuality hardens us in our selfishness. Nothing will make us more unhappy.

What, then, is sexuality and what is its relationship to sexual intercourse? Let us make some distinctions. →

sexuality:

Sexuality is the force and energy to be creative in response to life. We experience this force both spiritually and bodily. Our sexuality orients us toward others – it underlies our desire for love, friendship, community and family. Human love and communion are not only spiritual. They are also physical, taking into account the fact that we are male and female. "Man and woman were made 'for each other' – God… created them to be a communion of persons… and complementary as masculine and feminine." (*Catechism of the Catholic Church*, #372)

marriage:

"God created man and woman *together* and willed each *for* the other…. In marriage God unites them in such a way that, by forming 'one flesh,' they can transmit human life: 'Be fruitful and multiply, and fill the earth.' By transmitting human life to their descendants, man and woman as spouses and parents cooperate in a unique way in the Creator's work."(*Catechism of the Catholic Church*, #371-372)

Our desire for the other

Sexuality is the spiritual and physical drive within us that fuels our desire to be with others and to create life for others. It is an authentic source of life in us. A healthy sexuality is the desire in us for love, friendship, family, community, creativity – all the things that urge us to go beyond the self to the other. We feel that it is not good to be alone. God said this about Adam, the first human being, and it is also true about us.

Sexual intercourse

Our sexuality finds its creative meaning and expression in sexual intercourse. Sexual intercourse is physical; it is the meeting of two persons in a physical sexual consummation. This physical act – the becoming of "one flesh" – is also intensely spiritual if it is a true and loving encounter of two people. In the sexual act the body becomes a symbol of one person's love for another. And when a married man and woman enter into the rituals of lovemaking, the body as symbol comes alive and creates a communion between two people. For this reason, sexual intercourse is sacred. The sexual act is a symbol of a much deeper desire for the other, which God has placed in us.

Intimacy – the language of sexuality

Sexuality uses the language of intimacy. Sexuality is a tender and sensuous language that communicates our deepest self to another. We celebrate and desire the other, not for his or her usefulness, or his or her ability to give pleasure. Intimacy involves gestures of tenderness and truthful communication of our intimate selves. To be healthy, sexuality does not require sexual intercourse. In fact, chastity is a necessary part of a healthy sexuality. It is quite possible to be healthy sexually without having sexual intercourse. On the other hand, it is also possible to have sexual intercourse with another without ever achieving real love or intimacy with that person.

Sexuality – it will make saints out of us yet!

If sexuality is God's gift to us, it will lead loving married couples and chaste single people into a deeper and deeper covenant with God. Healthy sexuality stimulates spiritual growth. Try to imagine the journey of life along the various stages of sexuality: from the first stirring of sexuality in search of intimacy, to meeting someone attractive, to wanting sexual intercourse within a committed relationship, to marriage, and to becoming the father or mother of a family. Through the years we grow. The horizons of life broaden. We become more generous and loving. All of us are called to journey to holiness. We live as sexual beings in relationship to one another on this journey. Some are called to marriage and family life. Others are called to lives of celibacy in the service of others. Whether we live our lives in a married or a single state, we do so as sexual beings called to holiness.

- Why can it be difficult to talk about sexuality, but particularly about sexual intimacy?
- Why does sexuality and its physical expression demand so much respect and sensitivity?
- Why are there so many rules around sexual relations?

The Song of Songs

Among the books of the Bible, one has always caused astonishment. We call it the Song of Songs. It is exactly that: the song of all songs – the ultimate love song. Why and how did this love song ever get into the Bible? It survived against all odds. The writer must have been a woman. Only at the end of the Song is she identified as "the Shulamite." Throughout the song we find love words describing her. She is *sosanah*, a lily. This woman in love is compared to a scented flower, a garden, a vine or vineyard, a mare, a dove, myrrh, honey, wine and milk. She is called dawn, sun and moon. She evokes the beauty of the earth and the universe. Her lover, too, is called by many images: he is a cluster of henna in blossom, an apple tree, a gazelle, a fawn, a king, and a treasure of fine gold. Their love for one another is celebrated in the orchard, with frequent references to the exuberance of nature – filled with plants, fruits, valleys in blossom, and products from the field and animals.

The writer does a daring thing in her song. She writes about the love between a man and a woman in the context of Hebrew culture. She questions a lot of the conventions of the time, such as, for instance, the convention of arranged marriages. Ordinarily, a woman was brought to the house of her in-laws and transferred from the authority of her father to the authority of her husband. Not here! The Shulamite suggests to her beloved that he come and live in the house of her mother, thereby turning the convention on its head (3.2). Another convention was that in arranged marriages, love came after the marriage, because only after the arrangements were made did the couple get an opportunity to be together. Not here! The woman and the man are not married and celebrate their love outside of the convention. She is not presented as a loose woman, nor does the poem advocate free love. She is a free woman and she wants nothing more than to be true to the one she loves. It is perhaps one of the only texts of the Bible where a woman is praised as a lover, rather than as a mother or a wife. A third Hebrew convention was for the two families to exchange gifts. Marriages, as in so many places even today, were also financial transactions between the families. Not here! Love cannot be bought: "If one offered for love all the wealth of his house, it would be utterly scorned" (8.7). This was certainly a daring move at the time!

The poem describes love as purely as it can. It is a love that exists for itself. It is without guilt, without fertility. It is a joyous celebration of living and of loving – a pure gift of one to the other. It glorifies the event of love. Such love is a symbol of the love and union that God enjoys with Israel – but also with us.

Read the Song of Songs from your bible.

- What is the attitude of the Song of Songs toward *eros*-love?
- How can the bodily love and sexual desire of the woman and the man toward one another be a symbol of God's love?
- Choose one verse of the song that you like and explain what it says about sexuality.
- Compare the Song of Songs with contemporary love songs.

Christian marriage: where *eros* and *agape* meet

We attach a high value to marriage. So much so, that when two Christians marry, they are a sign not only of the spiritual value of *eros*-love, they also become a symbol of *agape*-love. St. Paul teaches that marriage is a primary place of *agape*-love. He compares the love of husband and wife to Christ's love. This makes marriage a high calling indeed. In the Letter to the Ephesians (5.25-31) he writes, "Husbands, love your wives, just as Christ loved the church and gave himself up for her... 'For this reason a man will leave his father and mother and be joined to his wife, and the two will become one flesh.'" The giving up one for the other that happens in marriage is a true expression of *agape*-love. The love for the other sets no conditions; it is to be a love in good times and in bad, in sickness and in health, for richer and for poorer. It is like the commitment and covenant Christ made with his followers. Marriage is therefore a primary sign of that commitment and covenant that Christ made never to abandon his followers. He would remain with them until the end. A married couple promises nothing less.

- How is marriage a way of living *agape*-love?
- A Catholic marriage takes place in the Church and is blessed by the Church. In light of the reading, why is it appropriate that it take place in the Church?
- How is a Catholic marriage a coming together of *eros*-love and *agape*-love?

Peter, do you love me?

At times it is awkward that the English language has so few words to say love. It is easy to miss the point, which is what happens in the English translation of the story of Jesus appearing to the apostles, who had been out fishing all night on the Lake of Tiberias. After eating with them, Jesus asked Simon Peter, "Simon son of John, do you love me more than these?" We know Peter's answer, "Yes, Lord; you know that I love you." But what did Jesus really ask Peter? What Greek word for love did he use? Jesus asked Peter whether he had *agape*-love for him. But Peter answered, "Yes, Lord; you know that I have *philos*-love for you." Jesus, in other words, asked Peter if he loved him with a love that is unconditional, with a love that hopes for no reward. Peter, remembering his betrayal of Jesus just days before, knew that his love did not measure up to what Jesus asked of him. His love, he knew, had been painfully conditional – he loved Jesus as long as it did not cost him anything. By saying "I love you as a friend," Peter told Jesus that he was weak and immature. He was no longer the braggart of the night before Jesus died, when he boasted that he would follow Jesus even if none of the others would. Now he was humble and more truthful about himself.

But Jesus did not give up. He asked him a second time whether he loved him with *agape*-love. Peter, however, remained humble. He did not claim to be better or do more than what he could do. He again ➤

said to Jesus that he loved him as a friend. When Jesus asked him a third time, "Simon son of John, do you love me?" he acknowledged that he could not ask of Peter more than what he could give. The third time, Jesus asked Peter whether he loved him with *philos*-love, as a friend. Peter, the braggart, again humbly, but also sad, because of what this impetuous bravado had done to Jesus, said again, "You know that I love you." Only as a truthful and humble Peter could he take care of and feed others. But Jesus also said to him that a time would come when Peter's love would grow and mature and reach *agape*–love. One day he would give his life for the Master.

- What was Jesus asking of Peter? What could Peter give?
- Why could Peter not give more? Why couldn't he give *agape*-love to Jesus?
- How does one grow to become capable of *agape*-love?

Jesus and Peter

When they had finished breakfast, Jesus said to Simon Peter, "Simon son of John, do you love me more than these?" Peter said, "Yes, Lord; you know that I love you." Jesus said to him, "Feed my lambs."

A second time Jesus said, "Simon son of John, do you love me?" Peter answered, "Yes, Lord; you know that I love you." Jesus said to him, "Tend my sheep."

Jesus said to him the third time, "Simon son of John, do you love me?" Peter felt hurt because he said to him the third time, "Do you love me?" And he replied, "Lord, you know everything; you know that I love you." Jesus said to him, "Feed my sheep. Very truly, I tell you, when you were younger, you used to fasten your own belt and to go wherever you wished. But when you grow old, you will stretch out your hands, and someone else will fasten a belt around you and take you where you do not wish to go." (Jesus said this to indicate the kind of death by which he would glorify God.) After this he said to Peter, "Follow me."

(See John 21.15-19.)

The *Catechism of the Catholic Church* and sexuality

Sexuality affects all aspects of our being, body and soul. It especially concerns our affection for others, and our capacity to love and to procreate. In a more general way, it relates to our natural ability to form bonds of communion with others.

(See #2332.)

Theme 14

A life of generosity

When we see things around us that have been there for as long as we can remember, sometimes we stop noticing them. This can happen with people or with the everyday things in our world around us. It is easy to take things for granted when we get so used to them. Only when they are suddenly missing do we notice that they are gone. Only if they are "turned upside down" do we see that they are different.

Jesus, especially through his parables, turns our everyday world upside down. By surprising us, he helps us to notice what we have been missing – that God's kingdom is present. We just need to see with new eyes. In this theme, you will explore God's generosity, which is evident all around us, if only we take the time to look. You will imagine how we could transform our culture if we reflected God's generosity in our own choices and lifestyle.

Focus your learning

- **Aware and Informed**
  How can living according to the beatitudes transform our culture?

- **Practical and Active**
  How does Jesus want me to love others?

- **Creative and Grateful**
  Why do you think God loves us so much?

Key terms

grace   charity

The power of a generous life

An old black man lived in a small town. He had been an "Uncle Remus" figure to countless young people, teaching them to hunt and fish. He was greatly loved. He owned a small piece of land, and continued to live there alone after his wife died.

One day it was discovered that a valuable strain of copper ran right through his property. Local business leaders wanted to get him off his land and mine the property. The old man had no use for money; all he wanted was to stay in the only home he had ever known.

Finally, the businessmen threatened him with lynching. At the appointed time, these leaders showed up at his front porch. The town preacher was there with the black man. He stepped forward and said: "John knows that he is going to die. He has a last will and testament that he wants me to share with you. He gives his fishing rod to Pete, because he remembers the first bass Pete caught with it. He wants his rifle to go to James, because he remembers teaching him to shoot."

Item by item, the old man gave back in love to those who would kill him. The people left, one by one. The man's grand-son asked, "What kind of will was that, Grandpa?" "The will of God, son," the old man replied.

(from William Bausch, *A World of Stories for Preachers and Teachers* [Mystic, CT: Twenty-Third Publications, 1998])

charity:

Jesus invites us to love *(agape)* one another. He invites us to live a life of generosity. This life exists in God's generosity and grace, as lived out in our generosity and graciousness to one another! This is the order of grace, the new way of dealing with one another, that Jesus came to preach in the kingdom of God.

- What act(s) of generosity do you see performed in the story?
- Where does the motivation to be generous come from? (Compassion? *Agape*-love/charity?)
- How did Pete, James and the others receive John's act of generosity? How did they respond?
- How might our society benefit from an attitude of generosity, even in the face of hatred and self-interest?

Volunteering

Volunteers fill in the cracks of society, often giving a human face to our institutions. They are the welcoming face at a church or hospital. They visit shut-ins. They join the youth choir. They serve at soup kitchens. They give blood. They coach community sports teams. They act as big sisters or big brothers. They hold car washes for the United Way and work behind the scenes at community theatres and sports meets. They prepare the lunch after a funeral.

Every year, the CBC radio station in Ottawa holds a volunteer recruitment day. On that day it broadcasts from one of the local shopping centres and invites community social agencies to help people decide where they might best volunteer. By the end of the day, people have shown their capacity to love by pledging thousands of hours to these agencies, helping them bridge the cracks of life in society. There is a lot of generosity in our communities.

Who volunteers in our society? Volunteering data show that people who belong to a church or a civic organization, such as Kiwanis or the Lions Club, give much more of their time to good causes than those who do not belong to any group. In 1996, 73% of members of civic organizations and 55% of church members volunteered. Only 19% of those who did not belong to these groups volunteered. The same people who volunteer their time are also more generous when it comes to financially supporting good causes. Volunteers give two or three times as much of their income to charities as those who do not volunteer. Our commitment to others is a community affair. Volunteers show us *agape*-love in action.

Your parish offers many opportunities for participating in volunteer activities, everything from reading at Mass to helping out those in need.

- What would a community be like without volunteers?
- What would our school be like without volunteers?
- Why do you think that people who belong to a church or civic organization are more likely to give their time, energy and money?

Glad to help my peers

My most meaningful contribution as a volunteer has been peer tutoring in mathematics. When I was in Grade 10, I helped six students (both male and female) to improve their math skills and test results through recess, lunch and after-school sessions. This free service was organized through the school.

Tutoring my peers was a meaningful experience for me because it allowed students who really needed help to continue with better grades toward their graduation and future employment. I was more than happy to participate in such a worthwhile program.

Erika Chafe

God's wonderfully generous world

Do you remember the parables of Jesus? At first sight they are simply stories of people doing everyday things. But the stories are also metaphors. They take everyday events and put them alongside the kingdom of God. Obviously the everyday stuff of Jesus' time is different from the everyday stuff of the twenty-first century. The majority of people in Jesus' time were peasants. Farming and the land were their primary focus, and the world seemed much smaller. Even the family, the village and the city were different than they are today. There were still slaves and kings. However, many of the things that went on between people were not so different from what goes on today. Jesus told stories about sons who take off or become angry. He told about a world of cheaters, of absentee landowners, of widows who challenge a good-for-nothing judge, and of greedy people who would murder their master's son.

Jesus is able to draw all of these aspects of life into stories about the kingdom of God. The stories create tension because most of us have pretty set ideas about what we think God is supposed to do in our world. The parables tell us something different about God and our expectations. What kinds of things do they say?

1. With God the present moment is precious

The kingdom happens all around us. It does not come with a grand display or a big splash. It happens as imperceptibly, but just as surely, as the growth of a seed into a plant. Our present moment is bursting with all sorts of surprises, if only we had the eyes to see. Jesus tells us about God as one who acts in solidarity with people day in, day out.

2. With God, the first shall be last, and the last first

God is especially there when things become tragic or when someone gets ostracized, bullied, pushed aside, excluded, or pronounced unclean or different. The privileged and the powerful are toppled from their thrones, anyone walking along the street gets invited to the banquet, and the last one hired becomes the first paid. God is especially close to those who are poor, excluded, who suffer and who are sad. The kingdom excludes no one – not even those who die. But none of this happens with great fanfare. The kingdom is often hidden.

3. With God there are all sorts of hidden miracles

We want God to intervene with power when things go wrong. But God doesn't. The parables tell us that God is active in the most ordinary events of life. That's where the little miracles of life take place. But we don't always see them, because God acts in hidden ways. In the parable of the sower who sows and loses much of his seed among thorns, on rocky paths and in soil that is too shallow, the miracle is the unexpected great harvest. In the parable of the Good Samaritan, the miracle is the unexpected generosity of the Samaritan for the man who is beaten and thrown into the ditch. It happens for the woman when she finds her lost coin, and for the shepherd when he finds the lost sheep. Life is filled with miracles and with gentle generosity, but one must have eyes to see and ears to hear.

The code of the new covenant

We call Jesus the new covenant because the relationship with God that Jesus proclaimed is so different from the one that came through Moses. Just as God's covenant with Moses had a code in the Ten Words, so the new covenant in Jesus has a code too. This code is found in the Sermon on the Mount. Like Moses, Jesus went up a mountain and spoke to his disciples, but his language was radically different. The Ten Words are presented as commands: honour your father and your mother; you shall not steal; you shall not murder. In the beatitudes, on the other hand, Jesus declares certain people to be blessed. They are called the salt of the earth or the light of the world. Then Jesus makes some comparisons. Moses told people not to murder, but Jesus tells us not even to be angry with our brother or sister. We may not call them names, and must always reconcile. Moses permitted oaths, but Jesus instructs people not to swear at all. Let it be just "yes" and "no." Where Moses permitted people to get even with their neighbours, Jesus says to turn the other cheek. Moses said you may hate your enemy, but Jesus says to love your enemy and pray for those who persecute you. "Be perfect as your heavenly Father is perfect," he says.

With Jesus there is a shift from mere obligation to generosity. Love is the highest principle of the new covenant. It is not our love, but God's *agape*-love. This is not a covenant brought about by our efforts. It is God's initiative. God's infinite love dwells in our midst because of Jesus. So live out of that love. Receive it! Know that you are loved! What does that mean? It means to live without fear. It means to live generously. Jesus shows us how life can be lived at its most generous. What are the rules for moral living? Jesus tells us: Live out of the awareness that you are infinitely loved by God. He sends his Holy Spirit to dwell within us, giving us the power to share not only our time and talents, but our very selves. Don't ask what the minimum is that you must do to stay in this love! Strive for perfection! Be as generous as you can be.

grace:

Grace describes God's kind, merciful and absolutely generous love for us. Grace shows itself in God's gifts of creation. But grace is particularly manifest in the person of Jesus Christ. Through his redemptive living, complete self-surrender on the cross and rising from the dead, Jesus shows us just how complete God's love is. As Paul writes in the Letter to Titus, in Jesus "the grace of God has appeared, bringing salvation to all" (2.11). The gift of God's grace allows us to imitate Jesus' selfless love for others.

Prayer of St. Ignatius of Loyola

Lord Jesus, teach me to be
    generous;
teach me to serve you as you
    deserve,
to give and not to count the cost,
to fight and not to heed the
    wounds,
to toil and not to seek for rest,
to labour and not to seek reward,
except that of knowing that I do
    your will.

Theme 15

Me and institutions

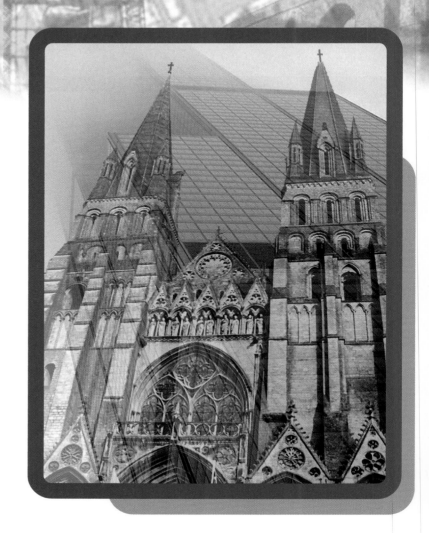

What's the first thing that comes to mind when you hear the word "institution"? Chances are, if you and your classmates were to create a list of ways to describe this word, you would come up with many different meanings, some positive, others negative.

The fact is, "institution" does have many meanings in our culture. Institutions are a necessary part of our social fabric, and, for the most part, improve our quality of life. On the other hand, just as people are capable of both good and evil, so too institutions are a reflection of this human characteristic. Institutions are no more perfect than people are.

In this theme, you will explore the world of institutions, and your relationship to them and within them. You will probably find that they are a bigger part of your life than you may at first think.

Focus your learning

- **Aware and Informed**
  What are institutions, and how are they important to me and society?

- **Practical and Active**
  How can we relate to institutions in ways that are life-giving?

- **Creative and Grateful**
  How do institutions enrich my life?

Key terms

institution

expressions of culture

multicultural societies

Surrounded!

We are surrounded by institutions. We live in families, go to school, and belong to a parish. We have jobs at local businesses. We drive on city streets and take public transportation (provided by the institution of government). We save our money in a bank account (owned by the institution of the bank). Everything we do in society involves one institution or another.

Institutions show us how we are expected to live in society. They direct us on how we can best get things done, how we can realize our talents and abilities, and how we can best serve the common good. We don't usually learn our rules, customs and behaviour from books or from some list of do's and don'ts. We *live* them as our beliefs, values and practices. Most of our ways of doing things are inherited and are part of the institutional framework of our culture.

Over the centuries our ancestors have set up and refined the institutions that shape our lives. Some, like the family, are natural institutions. Marriages and the family go back to our earliest history. But not all families are alike. The great diversity of family structures in Canada is very recent. Other institutions, such as the police force, justice system, health system and education, have been developed over time to meet particular needs.

Institutions are as good as the people who are part of them and who are willing to put their efforts into them. We are all responsible for making institutions life-giving, or for changing them if they become destructive. As Jesus said of a sacred institution of his time, "The Sabbath was made for humankind, and not humankind for the Sabbath" (Mark 2.27).

expressions of culture:

A culture's sets of meanings, beliefs, values and practices are formed around the basic human needs (the need for food, housing, health, religion, work, communication, etc.). Each culture expresses these needs differently. Also, each set of meanings, beliefs and values interacts with other sets to form a total set of beliefs, values and meanings.

What do you think?

Why are there institutions?

How do they come to be?

Why do they continue?

Why do some institutions come to an end or change radically?

Why do we need rules?

Why take part in institutions?

Studies over the last 40 years show that in North America the glue that keeps communities together is weakening. Social indicators point to stagnation and decline in community participation from the late 1960s into the new century in all sorts of areas of life: newspaper reading, running for public office, entering the seminary, attending public meetings, going to church, joining unions, giving blood, working on community projects, and even eating the evening meal with the whole family. This decline in participation is showing up everywhere.

People seem less committed to one another. They are less ready to pitch in and throw their energies at a community project. People's ways of participating in an organization or a community today do not necessarily mean meeting other people and working with them. More often than not it means simply sending money or writing a letter from home to support a cause. It does not mean going to a meeting where they would have to rub shoulders with people. People prefer to use the Internet or the telephone rather than to meet face to face.

Why is this happening? Robert Putnam, a social analyst from Harvard University, lists four reasons for this decline in community participation[1]:

1. Time and money Everyone is much too busy. People do not have the time to give to others or to help organizations or institutions and still maintain their day-to-day commitments. According to Putnam, time is only one small factor in the decrease in involvement. People are doing less and less together. They are spending more time doing things by themselves.

2. Urban sprawl More and more people live in suburbs, where there are fewer opportunities to join organizations, volunteer, or engage in community activities. The suburbs do not encourage socializing. The distance to downtown, to a meeting place, club, organization or activity, is just too great. The downtown is replaced with the shopping mall.

3. Television and the Internet We spend so much time watching television (young people average 24 hours per week) that we have little time left for more social activities. Much of our leisure time is spent alone. Putnam feels that much of our declining involvement in institutions and with others is because of our excessive consumption of television and the Internet for entertainment.

4. Generational change Generational change refers to the slow, steady and persistent shift from a generation who made it a point to participate in community, to the current generation who are less and less involved. In other words, the change has to do with our time. Younger people today are much less likely to be involved in the community than people their same age 30 years ago. The change is dramatic. In almost all areas of community involvement, young people between the ages of 18 and 29 are about 50% less likely to be active than their grandparents were. According to Putnam, this is the biggest reason for the overall decline in participation.

- Do you agree with Putnam's assessment? Why? Why not?
- Of all the institutions and organizations in which you are involved, how many are more or less a private involvement, and how many are social with a real interaction with others?
- How much time during the day are you involved socially with others? (Family, school, church, sports, visiting, etc.)

---

1 Robert Putnam. *Bowling Alone.* (New York: Simon & Schuster, 2000), p. 283.

A new generation of community shapers and institution builders?

A study by Reginald Bibby published in 2001 indicates that "a fairly high 65% of teens say that they expect to be involved in their communities in the future." This finding is consistent with current research in the United States by William Strauss and Neil Howe, who find that teens are "gravitating toward group activities… in such areas as team learning and community service." These researchers believe that today's teenagers are going to be "community shapers" and "institution builders."

- Who's right? Is Putnam's analysis correct, or do you think Bibby's observations are closer to the truth?

Institutions are like covenants

An institution is an organization in society that takes care of particular needs. Part of the nature of institutions, like the family or the school, is that each one has a whole set of rules. Sometimes we want to shake off those rules, thinking that without them we will be more free. But freedom actually needs some kind of structure around it to keep it from becoming anarchy. Freedom needs institutions. Institutions provide rules and a stable framework that help us to live in society. They allow us to exercise our freedom without infringing on the freedom of others. At their best, institutions are meant to work for the common good.

In light of this link between institutions and freedom, let us take the traits of covenants and apply them to institutions. (You may want to refer to Theme 7 again to refresh your understanding of "covenant.")

Institutions help us to become a free people

For the Israelites, the covenant made them into a free people. They were to be a liberated people through an act of the Lord. Christians believe that who we are, and our life together in communities, is a gift of God. Our interaction with one another through institutions is one of the ways in which we work together with God to become free. Institutions provide a structure to help us live out our covenant with God.

Institutions need rules and a commitment

For the Israelites, the covenant had certain conditions attached to it. The code of their covenant was the Ten Words (Ten Commandments) of the Lord. Through these commandments, the Lord showed them how to live as free people without violating one another's freedom. Similarly, today's institutions have conditions attached to them. They are not always clearly written on tablets of stone, but the rules are there. They don't carry the same weight as the Ten Words of the Lord. Sometimes, in fact, the rules are not just, and fail to lead to true freedom. At times we may even have to fight certain rules because they are destructive. But our response should be to work at changing the rules, rather than destroying the institution. Human institutions are as good as the people who are part of them, so it is up to us to work to improve them. Institutions need our participation, not our indifference or our refusal to be part of them.

Institutions are powerful and require prophetic leaders

In the covenant with the Israelites, the leader, Moses, was a prophet. He was a man of great vision because he had seen the Lord. Our institutions need great visionaries as well: people who have a prayerful, obedient relationship with God and who can translate that relationship into a practical way of life. These people may be our politicians, parents, caregivers, teachers, principals or priests. But they can just as easily be someone who is not obviously in a leadership role. It is important to always keep your mind open to look for true wisdom in people.

Institutions need participation and celebration

One way the Israelites remembered their covenant was to celebrate the moment of their liberation by the Lord. In the same way, we need to celebrate our institutions – our family, our parish, our school – for the gifts that they bring to our lives. It is true that we may be sad or angry at times when these institutions fail to give us freedom. Our very anger and sadness is a testimony of our desire for freedom. Rather than giving up on institutions when they fail us, we need to remind ourselves of the gift that they have been to us, and celebrate that. Without our participation and celebration, these institutions lose their life force.

institutions:

In every culture, systems of meanings, beliefs and values grow up around basic things like food, housing, health, education and the economy. Over time, they become stabilized and take on a lasting form in social structures. We call these stable social forms *institutions*. Some examples of institutions include things like family, the state, agriculture, health care, religion, economy, sports and communication. Each one has its own rules that provide structure to our lives and allow our freedom to be realized.

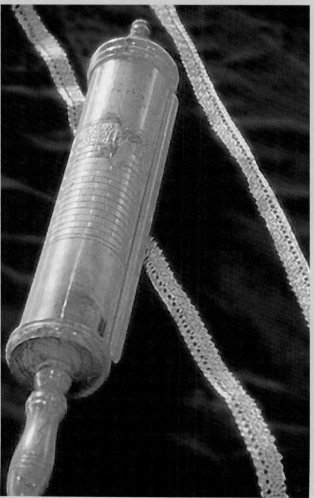

When the LORD is near...

When the LORD came to Moses, a whole new people came into being. Israel became the LORD's own people. The covenant with God created all sorts of new institutions and transformed others. It set a different standard with high expectations. When the Israelites entered the Promised Land, they used the Torah, the LORD's instruction, to structure their culture and life.

Jesus did not radically change the institutions of his own people. He was immersed in Jewish culture and participated in its institutions. He clearly valued the institutions, but at the same time, he made it his work to bring them back to what he saw as their original purpose.

The question Jesus asks of institutions is quite simple, but also quite radical: "When the LORD is near and you really trust in this nearness, what would you do in your homes, what would you do in the temple, in commerce, in politics?" We may be inclined to say out of fear, "I'd be on my best behaviour. What will happen to me if I don't shape up?" That's not what Jesus appears to have had in mind. To act out of fear or out of any other self-serving motives is not worthy of us. He might well say to us, "Listen, don't fear God. Trust God. With God near you, you will be able to do the right thing. So, don't fear. I'll set you free." Our fears today are much more the fears that come from what others may say or think. We want desperately to be accepted by others and we are willing to do almost anything to be popular. Jesus would say, "Only one thing is important. Trust in God and all the rest will be given you besides."

- What would you do differently at home, at school, at Church, or at work if you realized the LORD were near?
- Would you change the way you participate in these institutions? Why? Or why not?
- What would be your motivation for making changes?

The Torah still provides the foundation of Jewish culture and life. Because of its importance, copies of the Torah scrolls are stored in protective cases like the one pictured on the left. Often the Torah is further protected by a prayer shawl (*Talit*), which is wrapped around it when it is moved.

Jesus and the institutions of his culture

If Jesus was a living witness of God, does it show in his relationship to the institutions of his time? Jesus lived the life of a Jew in the first century. He came from a family. He lived in a village for 30 years where he was a carpenter after his father. He went to the synagogue and worshipped in the temple in Jerusalem. He interacted with all groups within Jewish society – those in charge and those at the fringes. He lived in an agrarian society. He preached and healed the sick in and around the town of Capernaum on the shore of the Sea of Galilee. But everywhere he went, he brought a particular perspective. He had experienced something else – the "kingdom of God" – that allowed him to see things with different eyes. It was so different that he began to gather a new community around himself – a community of disciples who became the vanguard of the Church.

So what did Jesus do, for instance, with the temple, one of the most important Jewish institutions? The temple in Jerusalem was also important to Jesus. As Luke tells us, Jesus and his parents went there each year for the Passover. During his public ministry, Jesus and his disciples went to Jerusalem, even though it would have meant one or two weeks of walking. For Jesus, the temple was the place where God dwelt among the people.

The only time in Jesus' life when he was visibly angry and even violent was when he cleansed the temple by chasing the buyers and sellers out with a whip. He

When he was twelve, Jesus stayed in Jerusalem after his parents had left. He stayed behind so he could go to the temple where he listened to the teachers and asked them questions (see Luke 2.14-50).

protested against the commercialization of the relationship with God. He overthrew the tables of the money changers, saying that they had made the temple a "den of thieves" (Mark 11.17). We might interpret from his actions that Jesus was opposed to the animal sacrifices in the temple. Or did he react so strongly because he felt that the temple had lost its original purpose of being a house of prayer, a place to meet the LORD? When Jesus was questioned about this, he went so far as to say, "Destroy this temple and in three days I will build another." In other words, Jesus realized that the temple had to be a place for *all* the nations to meet God. And *this* temple, made of stone, mortar and wood, and located in one specific place, could not fulfill this mission. Instead, Jesus said, "I will raise up a temple – a new place to meet God, and this place will be my own body."

That's a pretty radical transformation of the institution of religion – to destroy the existing symbol and transfer its power to a new symbol: Jesus. The place to meet God is now a human being. After Jesus' death and resurrection, his followers worshipped God in Christ through the Holy Spirit. Their beliefs, worship and lifestyle spread through many other nations. God was present in all those who were baptized in Christ Jesus. In other themes we will explore how the nearness of God transforms other institutions.

multicultural societies:

Canadian society is multicultural. We have not one set of beliefs and values, but many. We refer to this diversity as our "cultural mosaic." A number of Canadian institutions, such as the family, are complex and changing, because they incorporate many different beliefs and values.

Like a refiner's fire

The prophet Malachi, who lived in the first half of the fifth century BC, had high hopes for Israel. He dreamed of the day when the temple would be restored, the day when the LORD would once again dwell in the midst of the people. But he knew the presence of the LORD would also act as a force to bring the people to new health. He saw his people as a people whose spirits were drained. Listen to his prophetic oracle:

> See, I am sending my messenger to prepare the way before me, and the LORD whom you seek will suddenly come to his temple. The messenger of the covenant in whom you delight – indeed, he is coming, says the LORD of hosts. But who can endure the day of his coming, and who can stand when he appears?
>
> For he is like a refiner's fire and like fullers' soap; he will sit as a refiner and purifier of silver, and he will purify the descendants of Levi and refine them like gold and silver, until they present offerings to the LORD in righteousness. (3.1-3)

Gratitude

Our Christian participation in institutions is at its core one of gratitude. We are called to be grateful for the chance to enhance and, at times, challenge the groups through which we live our lives. It is because we are loved first by God, through Jesus, that our gratefulness is even possible. Often, it is through institutions that God's kingdom of justice and peace unfolds.

Unit 5 review

In this unit, you explored your relationship with others from a Catholic perspective.

Aware and Informed

How important is friendship?
Jesus taught that friendship is based on love and that one could have no greater love than this: to lay down one's life for one's friends. And that is what he did. "You are my friends," he tells us.

Why is intimacy important?
Intimacy is the close bond that exists between human beings. This bond is intimate because it touches our innermost being, our spiritual and physical core. Because we are sexual by nature, intimacy is always sexual, but it does not necessarily involve having sexual relations. Intimacy is the bond of love, friendship, community and family.

How can living according to the beatitudes transform our culture?
With Jesus' teaching on the beatitudes, there is a shift from mere obligation toward God and one another, to generosity. Love is the highest principle of the new covenant in Jesus. Jesus calls us to live out of the awareness that we are infinitely loved by God. He sends his Holy Spirit to dwell within us, giving us the power to share not only our time and talents, but our very selves. Jesus calls us to live generously.

What are institutions, and how are they important to me and society?
Institutions are organizations within society that take care of particular needs. Institutions have rules and structures that reflect the values and beliefs of society. They show us how to live in society so that we can exercise our freedom without infringing on the freedom of others. They promote the common good.

Practical and Active

How can I be a better friend?
The golden rule is a simple and effective guide: "Do to others as you would have them do to you."

How can I be a better lover?
God created us for one another. In life we have different sorts of relationships, and different sorts of love, each with its appropriate expression of intimacy:
- companionship
- friendship
- family love
- sexual love
- charity

To be better lovers, we must learn how to be appropriately intimate in each type of situation, and to respect the sacred nature of our sexuality.

How does Jesus want me to love others?
Jesus invites us to love one another in a spirit of generosity. This *agape*-love is life lived in charity toward one another. It is God's gift of grace that allows us to live in this manner.

How can we relate to institutions in ways that are life-giving?
Our Christian participation in institutions is at its core one of gratitude. We are called to be grateful for the chance to enhance and, at times, challenge the groups through which we live our lives. It is because we are loved by God that our gratitude is possible. Often, it is through institutions that God's kingdom of justice and peace unfolds.

Creative and Grateful

You can answer these questions for yourself. The answer is found in your relationship with God.

How have friendships helped me to grow?

Where does love lead me?

Why do you think God loves us so much?

How do institutions enrich my life?

Unit 6

Relating to civil society: Living together in solidarity

Aim: to explore our relationship to civil society from a Catholic perspective

Let's celebrate time

When is the last time you heard someone say, "I have to kill some time" or "I'm just passing time"? How do you understand these statements? Do you have time to kill?

On the other hand, when did you last hear someone say, "Sorry, I just don't have time" or "Maybe another time"? Do you think that people who use these expressions are complete opposites in terms of their pace of life? You may even have heard the same person use both expressions.

Focus your learning

- **Aware and Informed**
  What is time for?

- **Practical and Active**
  How can the Catholic perspective on time help me to live a fuller life?

- **Creative and Grateful**
  How do we "keep the Lord's Day holy"?

How much time do you have? What do you use your time for? Is time your friend or your enemy? In this theme, you will have a chance to reflect on your experience of time, and on the understanding of time in our culture. You will discover that the Catholic understanding of time is something to celebrate, especially in our rushed lifestyle.

Key terms

time	Sunday
Christian time	Sabbath

On time

Because time pervades everything, it is difficult to grasp. One of the things that makes it difficult to understand time is that it has two different meanings. There is the time we call cosmic time, and what we might call "lived time." Cosmic time is the stuff of calendars, years, months and days, measured by the earth's rotation and interaction with the sun and the moon. When we speak of nanoseconds or geological eras, we are talking about cosmic time. Cosmic time is measurable by clocks and watches. But lived time is something quite different. If you were to ask, "What time is it?" someone could answer, "It's 2:15," (which is an example of cosmic time), or, "It's time to have a party," (which is an example of lived time). We experience and live with time differently than we measure it. Lived time is a time for doing things. So what is it time for anyway? That depends on you, on your family, the school, culture, society, the state, and in a very special way, on God.

Time

Time is a measurement of movement or events. For example, the days, months and years measure the motion of the earth around the sun; our activities from birth to death measure our lives. Time is often approached by what it is time *for* – time to plant, to eat, etc. If anything reveals what time means to us, what it is *for*, it is our commitments and our promises. They will determine what sort of story we tell when we give an account of our lives.

Christian time:

Christian time celebrates the focal point of human time: the story of God with us. It celebrates the memory of particular events that continue to shape our covenant relationship with God. The central events of Christianity remember Jesus' death and resurrection and his incarnation. Easter and Christmas are the high points of the Christian calendar. Every Sunday is like a "little Easter," when we remember and celebrate the life, death and resurrection of our Lord. Christians know that Jesus is the beginning and the end of time. He is the Lord of history.

What do you think?

What is your experience of time?

How is it that we can experience time as moving both slowly and quickly?

When time seems to move slowly, does that mean it takes longer in cosmic time? Or is the speed at which we experience time something in us, like when we experience time as moving slowly when we are bored?

Time in our culture

What we do is a reflection of what we value. The way we spend our time says a lot about what we think is important. But do we think as carefully about how we "spend" our time as how we spend our money, for example? Culture influences our decisions about how we use our time. The experience of time within our culture has changed over the last few generations in at least four important ways:

1. We experience the loss of leisure
2. We experience confusion about the importance of our elders, tradition and history
3. We have no clear expectations for the future
4. We lose sight of the larger picture

1. We experience the loss of leisure

When your parents were teenagers, they read in the papers about how by the end of the twentieth century their biggest concern would be how to spend all their leisure time. People thought that advances in technology would provide them with more consumer goods even as they worked less. However, instead of dealing with increased leisure time, people today are finding that technology is speeding up the pace of life. Technology even seems to be dictating the pace of life. It is forever promising us something newer, faster, better, or more exciting. Time seems rushed. We have come to expect instant communication, immediate solutions, constant entertainment, immediate attention, life at the push of a button, whether it is from a machine or from another person. Technology is about doing more, and so, we are busier than ever.

2. We experience confusion about the importance of our elders, tradition and history

Because changes in technology happen at such a rapid pace, we spend much of our time worrying about keeping up with the changes. We feel that if we don't get the latest in gadgetry or fashion we will be left behind. But how do we decide that a certain change is good? In the days when changes did not come as quickly, people turned to those who had experience with life: parents and grandparents. People would turn to their religious traditions and to those who were considered wise elders in the community. In today's world, it seems that our parents and grandparents can no longer guide us in how to respond to these changes. It is often the children who show their parents how to operate the computer or entertainment equipment! Youth often consider their parents to be out of step and out of date. The same is felt about traditions. Many people feel that our Catholic faith tradition, which goes back two thousand years, does not speak to our time. The same applies to the study of history. History and tradition are often not considered important because people feel that the past is so different from the present that it can have little to say to our age.

But we cannot do without the past. There is a saying, "Whoever forgets history is bound to repeat it." Often we repeat the mistakes of the past because we refuse to deal with them. We are born into a culture that has institutions, customs and traditions that we inherit without being aware of their history. We are people with a past, though. Our past is a treasury of human wisdom, but also of our human folly. If our culture is pushing us to ignore our past, it is at our own peril.

3. We have no clear expectations for the future

People who forget the past – both its wisdom and folly – will have a hard time knowing what to expect for the future. If we forget the past, we don't have much to guide us in shaping the future. The future will happen without a vision. It will happen, but it will be driven by whatever is the fad in the present. For a while there was a strong belief (which many people still hold) that technology and the advances of human knowledge would make the future so much better. All sickness would be cured; there would be no more hunger; everyone would be free; and human rights and justice would govern the relations between people. Reason and technology would accomplish all of this in the future. But the future became the present, and this hope in human progress has been dealt a serious blow. The same reason and technology that brought us improvements in medicine, travel, communications, agriculture, etc., also produced the nuclear bomb, biological weapons, ecological disasters, and climate change. The best of human plans do not always achieve what they set out to do. They often have so many unintended results that we might question the ability of human reason alone to create the perfect human society.

Christians do not rely on technology or human rational planning alone. They believe that the past not only shows them how to live with grace and hope, but also reveals the great obstacles of the power of sin, the hardness of the human heart, and excessive pride in their own accomplishments. For them the future is a promise based on a trust in God. We are not the creators of the world or of its future. We are co-creators. The future is Christ's.

4. We lose sight of the larger picture

What is the present? Have you ever tried to hold on to it? The present is about doing. The present is an opportunity in which I can do something or a situation in which I experience something. The present is where I show who I am and what I can do. I can do something about the situations in which I live. I can begin something new, take initiatives, and exercise certain capacities or talents. But where do I direct my ability to change things? What do I do with my capabilities? It has often been said, that, if we don't know where we are coming from, we won't know where we are going. If we are not aware of our Catholic background, we can hardly know what sort of direction we should commit ourselves to as Catholics. The present becomes very confusing if we have no experience from the past to guide us.

Today's Western culture is having great difficulty finding a direction, partly because it loses sight of the larger picture. Life has become so complex, that we find it difficult to see how everything is interrelated. The only direction it seems to accept is, "If something is doable, it must be worth doing." That attitude means that there is nothing to stop researchers from making the most dangerous bombs and chemical poisons, bioengineering new organisms, testing dangerous drugs on animals, or cloning animals and human beings. Because it is possible and possibly profitable, someone will do it. If it destroys the earth for future generations, so be it. If it means that we will exploit workers in less developed countries, we are justified by so-called market forces. The present can move towards healthy and ethical commitments. But it can also move towards destruction that endangers all God's creation. The present is what's most important.

"The time is fulfilled"

The first time Jesus speaks in the Gospel of Mark he says, "The time is fulfilled, and the kingdom of God has come near" (Mark 1.15). In one of his first words in the Gospel of John, he speaks of "my hour" (John 2.4). Time plays an important role in the life of Jesus. So what was time *for*, as far as Jesus was concerned? Time was for God. If there was one commitment in his life, it was the kingdom of God and Abba/Father. For him the kingdom of God and the covenant relationship with Abba/Father was time in its fullness. Time could not be more complete or full. As he said to his disciples, "Strive first for the kingdom of God" (Matthew 6.33). All the rest will be given you besides.

With Jesus, this fullness of time came into the world. Pope John Paul II said, "In Jesus Christ... time becomes a dimension of God." In the Book of Revelation Jesus is presented as the beginning and the end of time. For Christians, time turns around Jesus and his life, as the most important event in history. For this reason, Christians experience time as full of tension. The kingdom of God may have become present in Jesus, but the present cannot carry it completely. A prayer by Archbishop Oscar Romero says this beautifully:

Archbishop Oscar Romero stood with the poor of his land against the violence and repression that they suffered. While he was celebrating the Eucharist in the cathedral in San Salvador on March 24, 1980, he was shot down at the altar, a martyr for his faith and his struggle for justice.

It helps, now and then, to step back
    and take the long view.
The kingdom is not only beyond our efforts,
    it is beyond our vision.
We accomplish in our lifetime only a tiny fraction of
    the magnificent enterprise that is God's work.
Nothing we do is complete,
    which is another way of saying
    that the kingdom always lies beyond us.
No statement says all that could be said.
No prayer fully expresses our faith.
No confession brings perfection.
No pastoral visit brings wholeness.
No program accomplishes the church's mission.
No set goals and objectives include everything.
This is what we are about:
We plant seeds that one day will grow.
We water seeds already planted, knowing that they
    hold future promise.

We lay foundations that will need further development.
We provide yeast that produces effects beyond our
    capabilities.
We cannot do everything
    and there is a sense of liberation in realizing that.
This enables us to do something,
    and do it well.
It may be incomplete, but it is a beginning,
    a step along the way,
    an opportunity for God's grace to enter
    and do the rest.
We may never see the end results,
    but that is the difference between the master builder
    and the worker.
We are workers, not master builders,
    ministers, not messiahs.
We are prophets of a future not our own. Amen.
            ("Prophets of a future not our own,"
            in *Return to Sedaqah: Prayers*)

Celebrating the mystery of Christ throughout the year

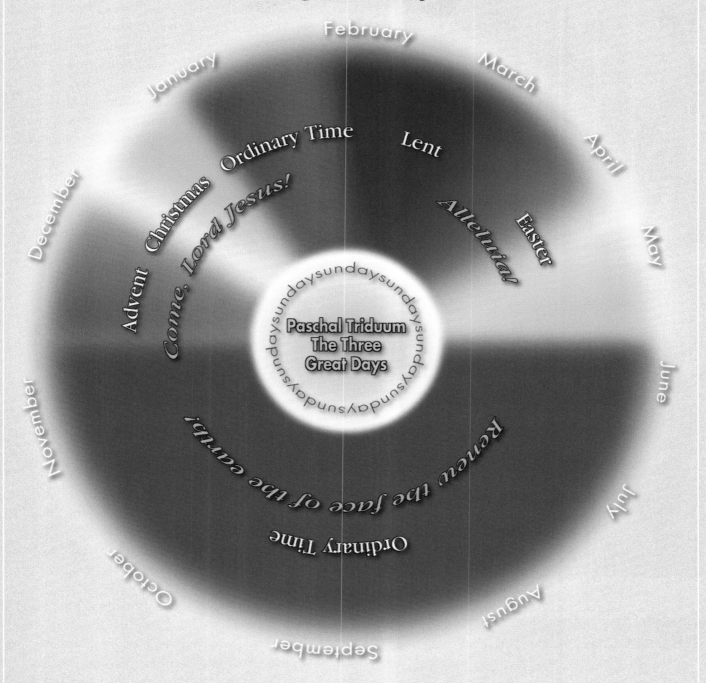

February

January

March

Ordinary Time

Lent

December

Christmas

April

Advent

Come, Lord Jesus!

Alleluia!

Easter

May

**Paschal Triduum
The Three
Great Days**

sunday sunday sunday sunday sunday sunday sunday sunday sunday

November

June

Renew the face of the earth!

July

October

Ordinary Time

August

September

*What Sunday is to the week,
the Paschal Triduum is to the year.*

Sunday

The oldest feast for Christians is the Sunday. Since Jesus was raised from the dead "on the first day of the week," that is, the day after the Jewish Sabbath, from earliest times Christians have gathered on Sundays. Sunday is our weekly Easter, the day that Christians remember Christ's resurrection from the dead. Easter is the event where believers "see the Lord." Just as the revelation of God to Moses became a focal point and transformed Jewish time and history, Easter transforms time for Christians. Christian time bears the imprint of the resurrection. God sees the world through the victory of Jesus and we are invited to do the same. If we are to live this time and if Easter is to colour our life, we must celebrate it in the rituals of the life, death and resurrection of Jesus. We do this primarily when we gather on Sundays for Eucharist. The Sunday Eucharist is a memorial of Jesus' death, resurrection and his promise to come again. We also do it on the special feasts that remember the resurrection and the incarnation. We do it by recalling each Sunday one of the words or events of Jesus in the gospel reading. We do it so that we may gradually put on Christ and be shaped into his image. The more our time becomes this remembrance of Jesus, the more our time becomes the fullness of time. Christ is the guide, the Lord, the shepherd, in all this.

Sunday:

Sunday is the day of the Lord, the day that Jesus rose from the dead. For Christians, the resurrection is the central revelation of God, the revelation of Jesus as the Lord and Christ. Catholics gather on Sundays to celebrate the memorial of Jesus in the Mass.

Sabbath

The Sabbath is the seventh day, on which God rested after the creation of the heavens and the earth. The Sabbath is a day of rest not only for people, but also for animals and even the earth. Rest, not work, is the priority. It signifies that the earth and all it contains are a gift from God. It did not come into being by our work. For the Jews, the Sabbath is a day of rest. Christians made Sunday their Sabbath because creation was completed on that day in the resurrection of Jesus. "Sabbath time is time off the wheel, time when we take our hand from the plow and allow the essential goodness of creation to nourish our souls."*

(*Wayne Muller, *Sabbath: Restoring the Sacred Rhythm of Rest* [Bantam, 1999])

W hen the Easter candle is signed before it is lit and brought into the Church for the Easter Vigil, the presider says:

Christ yesterday and today,
the beginning and the end,
Alpha and Omega;
all time belongs to him,
and all the ages;
to him be glory and power
through every age and for ever. Amen.

(from the Sacramentary, p. 247)

Theme 17

The voice of justice

When was the last time you felt your gut tighten at something that was just not fair? Why are we outraged when we see an injustice being committed? We have all felt vulnerable or unfairly treated at some point in life. We value justice because we know how fragile it can be. Anybody can be a victim of injustice. That is why we invest so heavily in our police forces and security systems. That is why we seek protection in numbers and strength.

But when is justice done? Is justice simply the protection of our self-interest and security? Or is there more? Jesus taught about doing justice in one sentence: "Do unto others what you would have them do unto you."

Focus your learning

- **Aware and Informed**
  When is justice done?

- **Practical and Active**
  How can the golden rule lead to a more just society?

- **Creative and Grateful**
  Who advocates for justice in our lives?

In this theme, you will explore how this simple teaching of Jesus works in situations of justice and injustice. Canada is known around the world for being a just society. How does Jesus challenge us to improve on that?

Key terms

justice

distributive justice

judicial justice

common good

rights

golden rule

social encyclicals

Hear what the LORD says:
    Rise, plead your case before the mountains,
    and let the hills hear your voice.
Hear, you mountains, the controversy of the LORD,
    and you enduring foundations of the earth;
for the LORD has a controversy with his people,
    and he will contend with Israel.

"O my people, what have I done to you?
    In what have I wearied you? Answer me!
For I brought you up from the land of Egypt,
    and redeemed you from the house of slavery;
and I sent before you Moses, Aaron, and Miriam."

"With what shall I come before the LORD,
    and bow myself before God on high?
Shall I come before him with burnt offerings,
    with calves a year old?
Will the LORD be pleased with thousands of rams,
    with ten thousands of rivers of oil?"

He has told you, O mortal, what is good;
    and what does the LORD require of you
but to do justice, and to love kindness,
    and to walk humbly with your God?

(Micah 6.1-4, 6-7a, 8)

What is justice?

The image of justice, a blindfolded woman holding scales in her hand, is a powerful statement. Justice refuses to defer to rank. Before justice all are equal. The rich should have no advantage over the poor; the powerful should not be treated differently from the ordinary citizen; men should not be privileged over women, the born over the unborn, or the handicapped over the healthy. Before God all people are equal. This principle of the fundamental equality of all is upheld even by those who do not believe in God. It has become enshrined in the constitutions of democratic countries. But what does that equality consist of? The generally accepted definition of justice is to render to the other what the other is due. What do we owe the other? How far does the equality go? Am I allowed to own a bigger house than you? Is it all right to be paid more for one job than another? Must I treat my little sister the same as my parents? How do we distribute goods in society? How do we maintain equality in the face of an unequal distribution of goods? How do we avoid the maxim of the pigs in George Orwell's *Animal Farm*: "Some are more equal than others"? That's where the scales of justice come in. The scales of Lady Justice show that justice is a balancing act. When is the distribution of things (property, salaries, dignity, power) inequitable enough that it jeopardizes the fundamental dignity of the human person? Justice requires a lot of weighing and a lot of discussion to arrive at even a semblance of equality in the distribution of goods.

- What is justice?
- When is justice done?

The Universal Declaration of Human Rights and the Canadian Charter of Rights and Freedoms

Bruce Springsteen performs at the Amnesty International concert given in Paris on Thursday, December 10, 1998, to celebrate the fiftieth anniversary of the signing of the Universal Declaration of Human Rights.

On December 10, 1948, the General Assembly of the United Nations adopted and proclaimed the Universal Declaration of Human Rights. The Declaration contains 30 articles that define basic human rights. These articles are not binding by law, but they are considered by most member nations to be the basis for global justice. Some highlights are

- the right to life, liberty and security of person
- the right to an education
- the right to participate fully in cultural life
- freedom from torture, or from cruel and inhuman treatment or punishment
- freedom of thought, conscience and religion
- the right to a standard of living adequate for health and well-being

The Canadian Charter of Rights and Freedoms, enacted on April 17, 1982, was developed based on the principles contained in the Universal Declaration of Human Rights. Similar to the Declaration, it spells out the basic rights of citizens. It guarantees these rights and freedoms subject only to laws that a free and democratic society would accept as reasonable. The Charter is a part of the Constitution of Canada. It applies to all Canadian citizens and to the institutions of government that create and enforce our laws.

(Both of these documents can be downloaded from the Internet.)

justice:

Justice is based on the distribution of goods (not just material goods) in society and the equality of all its citizens. *Justice* is the virtue that gives each person his or her due in the distribution of goods.

rights:

Rights are those things in society to which we are entitled. Some are legal rights (for example, laws that entitle us to a lawyer if we are arrested). Other entitlements are based on human dignity itself, such as people being entitled to food, shelter, work and security of person.

distributive justice:

When we use the word justice, we usually mean distributive justice. *Distributive justice* is the equitable and fair distribution of the goods of society.

The cultural setting for justice

Some years ago a number of board games appeared that were based not on competition but on cooperation. These cooperative games were meant to counteract games that are based solely on competition. The competitive games, however, clearly win out in popularity. They pit one player against another, and there is something exciting about trying to outwit the other. In general the winner takes all. Some people see in this competitiveness a model for life in society. Recent "reality" TV programs have taken the idea one step further, putting people in a situation where they have to scheme against and betray one another in order to win the prize. The motto is "take as much as you can," and the winner is the one who has taken the most. If we extend this to society, it would mean that the strongest, the smartest, the most gifted in sports or music, or the most beautiful would have the right to take for themselves a much greater share of the available goods. This is reflected in our culture – in sports, politics, business, and even education.

judicial justice:

Many societies use courts and a legal system to decide between the conflicts arising from abuses against justice. The goods under consideration here are much more than economic goods. They also include the right to the integrity of one's body, one's honour and dignity, life, security from invasion of privacy, etc. Because our justice system pits two interests against one another, it requires lengthy argumentation, usually involving lawyers and judges.

Is there anything that limits the amount of goods, money or property that a person can acquire in our society? Outside of taxes and criminal law, there is very little. Our society feels that it shouldn't impose limits. It relies instead on something called the market. This way of thinking sees society as a marketplace in which people compete for the goods that are available. And in the marketplace, the competition, or lack of it, determines what one receives for the goods and who receives the goods. Any limits are set not by people, but by "what the market will bear." This is the model of capitalism, the model that prevails in most Western countries. This way of dealing with one another in society works well if you are powerful, smart, gifted or beautiful. But the market does not work as well for those who have little power, education or practical sense. Those without "purchasing power" are left on the sidelines.

Our Church teaches that a society based solely on competition and on the market is unacceptable. A market economy without restrictions leaves out too many people. A society that leaves out the poor is not a just society. St. Ambrose, a bishop in the fourth century, said it well when he spoke of ➔

The influence of economic systems

What should society do to ensure that goods are distributed more equally? Since governments play an important role in this, much will depend on how governments understand the importance of competition and cooperation. Three political-economic systems have prevailed in recent times:

- In *capitalism*, which operates out of a free market, few restraints are put in the way of individuals or corporations to produce and accumulate wealth.

- In *communism*, a central bureaucracy regulates the production and distribution of goods.

- In *democratic socialism*, the state exercises some control over the market. Those who are less capable of taking care of themselves receive support from the state to take care of their basic needs.

Since the fall of the major communist governments in eastern Europe and the former Soviet Union, the communist approach to producing and distributing goods has lost much of its influence. The influence of democratic socialism is under pressure from powerful multinational corporations. The push for global free trade undermines the power of individual governments to implement social programs within their own borders. Capitalism, with its emphasis on a market-driven global economy, has become the major influence on how goods are distributed in our world.

the rights of the poor. To the rich he said, "You are not making a gift of your possessions to the poor person. You are handing over to him what is his. For what has been given in common for the use of all, you have arrogated to yourself. The world is given to all, and not only to the rich." Our faith demands of us to put the basic needs of all people first, before thinking about luxuries for some.

Canadian society is characterized by both the competitive market model, and genuine concern for the welfare of its citizens. For example, universal health care (ideally) ensures that everyone who needs health care will receive it. Our "social safety net" includes welfare programs for those who cannot work. Employment insurance programs help those who have lost their jobs make ends meet until they find other work. As well, thousands of volunteers work in communities to improve the quality of life of others, especially the disadvantaged, through programs such as Big Brothers and Big Sisters. Food banks and soup kitchens provide food for the hungry. Even so, the "holes" in this safety net can be large, and many people slip through. Poverty continues to be a serious issue in our society. One in five children in this country live below the poverty line. We must do more.

Letters on social justice by Catholic leaders

In 1891 Pope Leo XIII began a new practice for the Catholic Church. He issued a letter on the dignity of human work and on the rights of workers. He spoke of their right to organize into unions, to receive a just wage and to own private property. It created quite a stir. It was the first time that the Catholic Church had looked at modern societies and culture and then taken a position on issues of social justice. Big business told the Church leaders to mind their own business and not to interfere with the affairs of factory owners, business leaders and bankers. They argued that the Church should take care of "souls," that is, the spiritual welfare of people. Business and industry would keep the world going and deal with the "real" issues. The Catholic Church held that it is not possible to separate the spiritual from the material. From that point on, a whole series of letters and documents have been written to try to put into practice the golden rule of Jesus: "Do to others as you would have them do to you" (Luke 6.31).

The following is a partial list of these writings of the Catholic Church:

1891 Pope Leo XIII

The condition of work   This encyclical asked the state to pass laws to protect workers. Everyone has a right to work. Workers have rights: to form unions, to receive a just wage and to own private property.

1931 Pope Pius XI

Reconstruction of the social order
On the fortieth anniversary of Pope Leo's letter, Pius XI affirmed what Leo had written on work. He also condemned excessive capitalism and communism. He proposed the principle of subsidiarity, which states that what individuals or small groups can do must not be taken over by the state. He asked for international cooperation.

1961 Pope John XXIII

Christianity and social progress
Pope John, who late in his life called together the Second Vatican Council, wrote a letter on Christianity and social progress. His letter criticized the rich nations for not doing more for the poorer nations. He insisted that the world's nations were becoming dependent on each other, and he wanted workers to participate in this new world. He encouraged collective bargaining for workers.

1963 Pope John XXIII

Peace on earth   In this letter, addressed to Catholics and all people of good will, Pope John talked about human rights and human dignity. He asked nations to seek the common good and to stop the arms race.

The golden rule

What advice did Jesus give about justice and the distribution of goods? He said little about issues of justice directly, but a lot indirectly. Clearly, for Jesus a major obstacle to full human life is wealth. The gospel is full of warnings to the rich: "Woe to you who are rich, for you have received your consolation" (Luke 6.24) or "How hard it is for those who have wealth to enter the kingdom of God! Indeed, it is easier for a camel to go through the eye of a needle than for someone who is rich to enter the kingdom of God" (Luke 18.24-25). To the rich young man who wanted to be perfect Jesus said, "Sell all that you own and distribute the money to the poor" (Luke 18.22). For Jesus, *agape*-love was the fullest level of life. But before he summoned the young man to give up all his wealth as a measure of his love and generosity, Jesus asked him to keep the commandments. Be just! It is as if

he told us to give others what is their due, and to live according to the instructions of the commandments. Jesus did not impose love. We can love only if we have been loved first. So how would Jesus guide us in our everyday dealings with one another? Jesus says, "Do to others as you would have them do to you" (Luke 6.31). This is how Jesus urges us to do justice. Don't consider only yourself; keep in mind the other, even in your use of money and property. This is known as the golden rule.

1967 Pope Paul VI

The development of peoples Pope Paul wrote especially about the need of rich nations to help develop poorer nations and insisted that world peace depended on this. He proposed fair trade practices and a tax on rich nations to help poor nations.

1971 Pope Paul VI

A call to action This letter was written on the eightieth anniversary of Pope Leo's letter. In it, Pope Paul talked about the development of big cities, about racial and sexual discrimination, and about Catholics getting involved in political action.

1981 Pope John Paul II

On human work Pope John Paul showed how work is a spiritual activity. He affirmed the rights of the disabled. He sought stronger family life and reaffirmed the right of workers to join unions.

1987 Pope John Paul II

On social concern Like Pope Paul VI in 1967, Pope John Paul worried about the poor nations and how the rich nations must help them. He warned Western countries against consumerism. He said that the massive amounts of money spent on buying arms and weapons in the world is an injustice to the poor of the world.

1991 Pope John Paul II

The one hundredth year In this letter written on the centenary of the first letter on social justice, Pope John Paul talked about a whole series of issues: capitalism, just wages, unemployment, profit, unions, the family, etc. He also warned against consumerism and showed concern for the environment.

1995 Pope John Paul II

The gospel of life In this letter, Pope John Paul urged Catholics to help maintain the right to life. He talked about abortion, euthanasia, assisted suicide and capital punishment.

(All of these encyclicals can be found on the Vatican Web site.)

golden rule:

The *golden rule* of Jesus ("Do unto others what you would have them do unto you") is one way in promoting cooperation. To live according to this rule is to let *agape*-love interact with justice.

...a common theme in the social encyclicals is the protection of the weak and the poor? In a world ruled by competition, those who cannot compete, for whatever reason, are left behind. They usually suffer through poorer health care, famine, poor or no housing, unemployment, etc. For that reason, one of the main themes of the Scriptures is the jealous care that God has for the poor, for those who are defenceless.

The Old Testament identifies two types of people as being in particular need of care because they are not protected by the structures of the family. Using a concordance, find texts in the sacred Scriptures that refer to the widow and the orphan. What does the Bible call us to do for those who are poor and powerless?

social encyclicals:

Over the past century, the popes have written letters on many issues of social justice. We call these letters *social encyclicals*. They help us as a society to put the golden rule into practice, both in our economy and our social life. The Canadian bishops have also contributed to the Church's teaching on social justice.

Social teaching of the Canadian Catholic bishops

In 1948, the bishops of Canada established the Commission for Social Action. The primary purpose of this commission was to help the bishops and the People of God spread the gospel through actions for justice and the transformation of society. Since it started, this commission has issued many teaching documents. These are a few of the key ones:

- *Words to Action* (1976) This document stressed that the struggle for justice is not optional; it is an integral part of bringing the gospel into the world. To help people take part in this struggle for justice, the bishops suggested a method for reflecting on the gospel, hearing the voices of the victims of injustice, and helping the poor and oppressed.

- *Ethical Choices and Political Challenges* (1983) The bishops continued to reflect on how to struggle for a just society. This document reinforced their stand on the struggle for justice, and offered a refined five-step approach for doing justice. This approach continues to help Catholics fulfill their call to justice.

- *The Struggle Against Poverty* (1996) The bishops criticized governments for neglecting the care of the poorest sectors of society. They called for immediate action to eradicate poverty, with a special awareness of the poverty among women, the young, newcomers to Canada, and Aboriginal people.

- *The Common Good or Exclusion: A Choice for Canadians* (2001) In an open letter to members of the new Parliament, the bishops recalled "that the Church, in its concern for the welfare of each person, is especially preoccupied with defending the poor."

(The more recent documents can be found on the Web site for the Canadian Conference of Catholic Bishops.)

"It will be necessary above all to abandon a mentality in which the poor – as individuals and as peoples – are considered a burden, as irksome intruders trying to consume what others have produced.... The advancement of the poor constitutes a great opportunity for the moral, cultural, and even economic growth of all humanity."

(Pope John Paul II
in *Centesimus annus* [1991] #28)

Theme 18

"Peace be with you"

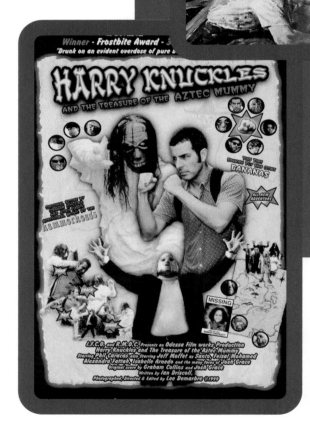

How do you explain the fact that people love to watch violent acts? Is professional "wrestling" anything more than tough talk and acted-out aggression? Why do the fans at hockey games stand up and cheer when a fight breaks out? Why do people pay money to watch horror films where people are stalked and murdered, and even eaten? Why do filmmakers spend millions of dollars to create awesome scenes of destruction?

These questions are not easy to answer. What is even more difficult to understand is when violence crosses the line from entertainment and becomes a lived reality. How do you explain people killing people? Torturing? Abusing? If you have ever been a victim of violence, you know first-hand the senselessness and pain of violence. In this theme, you will explore this issue and see how Jesus dealt with it. Jesus was a peacemaker. He calls us to be peacemakers too.

Focus your learning

- **Aware and Informed**
  What are the roots of violence?

- **Practical and Active**
  How can we overcome violence?

- **Creative and Grateful**
  What would the world be like without violence?

Above: A detail from a World War II movie poster depicts the destruction of a merchant ship while surviving crew members escape from the wreckage.

Left: This poster advertises a movie that uses satire to examine the world of horror movies.

Key terms

peace   violence

Loss of innocence

It suddenly got very quiet. Then someone screamed. A group of boys lunged at someone holding a knife. A student lay bleeding on the ground.

It was John. There had been a confrontation at the smokers' corner at the edge of the school property. Members of a local drug gang had been waiting at Al's Smoke Shop across the street for John's friend. Apparently, John's friend hadn't paid up. John, trying to be the peacemaker, had stepped between his friend and the drug dealer just as the knife came up. He was stabbed four times before the other students overpowered the attacker.

peace:

In common usage, *peace* means the absence of war or conflict. In the Bible, however, peace is something that exists between people or between people and God. It is linked with justice, truth, faithfulness, grace and love. It is God's gift for the future. That is why the Hebrew term for peace, *shalom*, is also a greeting. It is a wish that the future blessing of peace may come upon us now.

Did you know...

...that Jesus' greeting to his disciples after his resurrection was "Peace be with you"? (See John 20.19-21.) We use this same greeting several times in the Eucharist. We pray for peace and offer each other a sign of peace, because we recognize the violence and fear that pervade our culture.

What do you think?

Why do some people use violence to solve their problems?

What difference does it make in situations of potential or actual violence when there is a crowd present?

Is there ever an occasion when violence does solve a problem?

Is there an alternative to violence? What is it?

Why violence?

Aggression among humans is so common that we think it is natural. Television, movies, computer games and newspapers are full of violence. In the so-called action shows, viewers witness on average 20 acts of violence every hour. What is the result? Data from the American Psychological Association reveal that young people who watch violent shows, even cartoons, are more prone to hit their classmates, argue, disobey class rules, leave tasks unfinished and be less willing to wait for things than those who do not. But they also tell us that these same viewers see the world with more fearful eyes. People have a certain fascination with violence. All sorts of reasons have been given for its prevalence in the world. Let us examine just a few:

• People become violent when they want to find *a way out* of a situation that they find intolerable. They want to break out of the frustration of having no voice, of people refusing to listen to them or notice them. This frustration can come from being poor, lacking the money to feed their family or to give gifts to loved ones while seeing so much wealth all around. People can feel trapped, when from early childhood they have been deprived of respect and love or have been physically or sexually abused. When people are put down and

silenced, the moment comes when all the pent-up frustrations turn into acts of violence. Hopelessness and desperation can lead to people using violence rather than language to draw attention to their needs.

At a personal level these intolerable situations are felt as anger. We feel anger welling up inside us as someone makes fun of us, accuses us falsely, or excludes us. Anger is a powerful emotion. It is also a healthy emotion because it is like an inner sensor that helps us to detect

Did you know...

...that the national murder rate in Canada in 1999 was at its lowest point in more than 30 years? The murder rate has generally been falling over the last decade. Check the current statistics to see if this trend has continued. What do you think are the reasons for this decline?

violence:

Violence is the aggressive or unjust use of power or force to hurt others. It is often the result of situations in which people lose the power to act for themselves (because of poverty, injustice, hopelessness, tyranny, etc.). But it is also often used by people to hold on to their power over others, to gain it, or to increase it.

"*I object to violence because when it appears to do good, the good is only temporary; the evil it does is permanent.*"

(Mahatma K. Gandhi)

"*At the center of non-violence stands the principle of love.*"

(Martin Luther King, Jr.)

whether we, or others, are being dealt with fairly and respectfully. Righteous anger is attributed to God in the Scriptures. Anger, however, is an emotion that we are often afraid of. Some people decide to suppress their anger in such a way that they seem to be totally passive. But the suppressed anger is still there, and can be felt by others. People tend to shy away from overtly angry people, but also from those who have suppressed their anger. When people express their anger outwardly, they often direct it at innocent people rather than at the real cause of their anger. They lash out in frustration at those who are innocent because they are afraid to confront the real source of their anger. Anger needs language to find a proper outlet. Not cheap shots or obscenities, but the language of reason and feeling that often reveals to us the real source of anger. As the Letter to the Ephesians counsels: "Be angry but do not sin; do not let the sun go down on your anger, and do not make room for the devil" (4.26-27).

- *We have to compete* to obtain food, housing and clothing. None of these come without a certain amount of struggle. We need to assert ourselves and to compete to get a job, to get a place in college or university, or to make a living. Being assertive is not the same as being aggressive.

- Violence comes from *abuse of power*. When one person seeks to dominate another by physical force, by pushing, shoving or using a weapon, they generally do it in order to force the other person to give them what they want. School bullying, shoving and fighting usually are about power and status in the school. People use violence to gain respect. But it is a grudging respect based on fear. Because of the fascination with violence in our culture, the fear is mixed with admiration to create a dangerous mix.

- Another reason people are violent is because of *envy and jealousy*. Two guys want to go out with the same girl; the rich kid comes to school with his father's sports car; two top students go after the same scholarship; my friend is dating my former boyfriend; a sister is very successful at school while her brother can never do anything right. It is extremely easy for people to become rivals – each one becoming an obstacle to what the other wants. Rivalry, goaded by envy and jealousy, is a frequent cause of violence.

- Some explain violence by proposing that at the beginning of history there was *an act of violence* much like the murder of Abel by Cain in the Book of Genesis. Many countries came into being through wars or revolutions. Canada's history, for instance, was shaped in part by the battle on the Plains of Abraham. Most nations hide the violence of their origin by covering it with cultural expressions. They create heroes and symbols of the new identity that glorify and celebrate acts of violence. But, as we see even in Canada, conflict and violence remain close to the surface. There is a constant fear that acts of violence can destroy the structures our culture has built up. The organization of culture and its institutions are a way of protecting us from this kind of violence. But violence still shows its face from time to time and people find it difficult to face it.

- *Violence fascinates some people* perhaps because they feel it lets them toy with or defy death. They find a sort of ecstasy in violence, the same way they find entertainment in horror. This fascination with violence can be seen in some people's interest in war and battles, or in boxing, wrestling, and other violent sports. It breaks the monotony for those who find life boring.

Select one of the reasons for violence given above. Find an example that illustrates the reason you have chosen. Analyze your example using these questions:

- What happened in the event?
- Who was involved? Who was the aggressor and who was the victim?
- What was the violence about?
- Who took the blame for the violence?
- Why did it happen?
- Could it have been prevented? How?

What do you think?

People like Gandhi and King were powerful leaders who refused to use violence as a means of resisting injustice. Some people think that refusing to fight back in the face of violence is a sign of weakness or cowardice. What do you think?

Let's talk!

Violence is frightening because it makes so little sense. Nothing good ever seems to come from it. It intimidates us. In extreme situations it can lead to amnesia and make us speechless. The intention behind violence is often to make someone shut up – to make the victim cower and become speechless. The perpetrator wants the other person to do his or her will without saying anything back. That is why language is so important to break violence. Not just any kind of language, though, because language too can be violent. To end violence we need a language that does not give up on human dignity, a language that refuses to be intimidated. We need a language that does not return violence with more violence, but confronts it

with reason and love. Violence fears the voice of reason and peace. Our democracies exist because we are allowed to speak and express our opinions. Used peacefully and lovingly, language can be the most powerful tool we have to disarm violence. It actually takes more courage to speak truthfully in the face of violence than to respond with more violence or run away.

This is probably why the vice-principal in school and parents at home will so often say to someone who has gone way out of line, "Let's talk." They are in effect saying, "Let's put some reason into this situation." One African student has a habit, whenever his government or a group in his country has been violent, of writing them to express politely what he thinks has gone wrong. He refuses to give up when he receives no response. That is why our freedom of speech is so important. Because being allowed to speak is our best remedy against violence.

Did you know...

...that until recently young people under the age of 20 were more likely than people in other age groups to commit both violent and property crimes, as well as to be the victims of violent crime? Youth crime in 2000, however, was down more than 7% from 1998, and 21% lower than in 1989. (*Statistics Canada, The Daily, Catalogue 11-001, July 2000*)

- How can language make a difference in a violent situation? What precautions would you take if you were dealing with a violent situation?
- Is the use of language appropriate and safe in every occasion? If so, how? If not, when should language be brought back into the picture?
- How could you make better use of language in situations of violence? What would you like to be able to do?

"Much violence is based on the illusion that life is a property to be defended and not to be shared."

(Henry Nouwen – a priest, writer, and teache[r] who shared his final years with the peopl[e] of a group home for severely disabled people[)]

Violence in the Bible

The Bible is full of stories of violence. Right after the expulsion of Adam and Eve from the Garden we are told the story of Cain and Abel. The first murder! And it does not end there. Violence gets into the blood line of Cain, transmitted from father to son. As the story unfolds from father to son it becomes more and more a story of inhumanity. Lamech, a descendant of Cain, boasts to his wives, "I have killed a man for wounding me, a young man for striking me. If Cain is avenged sevenfold, truly Lamech seventy-sevenfold" (Genesis 4.23-24). It is clear that the nature of violence is to grow and grow until "the earth is filled with violence" and "an end of all flesh" (Genesis 6.13) is brought about. Genesis says that the Lord was sorry to have created humanity because of all the violence. Reading other books in the Old Testament reveals that war and violence of all types are deeply ingrained in the human story. The Chosen People were subject to and committed much violence. Yet there are also plenty of texts in the First (Old) Testament that speak against violence. The most clear is the text of the Ten Words with the injunction, "You shall not murder." But what all these texts reveal is that there is a hidden place in all of us that is the source of violence. The Bible calls it the violence of the heart.

What about the New Testament? Its message is forgiveness and gentleness, but it also tells stories of violence. King Herod, entranced by a young woman's dancing, made an oath to give her anything she asked for. She asked for, and received, the head of John the Baptist on a platter (Matthew 14.1-12). Scribes and Pharisees brought a woman caught in adultery to Jesus, prepared to stone her to death for her sin (John 8.1-11). Jesus' own neighbours became enraged at him and were prepared to throw him off a cliff for what he was saying (Luke 4.16-30). A group of righteous people in the early days of the Church stoned the disciple Stephen for preaching the gospel (Acts 7.54–8.1). But through it all we are given a new way of looking at violence and responding to it. At the centre is the cross of Jesus. Here violence is converted into love through the work of the Holy Spirit.

Read the beatitudes in Matthew's Gospel, chapter 5.

- What is the meaning of the sayings in this passage?
- Each statement presumes that there is violence in the world. What is a disciple of Jesus to do to curb violence? How does each saying change violence?
- Is it easy or difficult?
- Where do you see these sayings of Jesus being put into practice?
- What is Jesus telling us in this passage?

"All of us desire peace, but few desire the things that make for peace."

(Thomas à Kempis – author of *Imitation of Christ*, 1380–1471)

In Michelangelo's version of the great *Deluge*, people make a vain attempt to save themselves by fleeing to higher ground.

The cross of Jesus: Victory over violence

The longest story in all of the gospels is the account of the passion and death of Jesus. Jesus died a violent death. However much he may have preached gentleness and love, Jesus could not avoid violence. The world around him, like ours, was violent. His message was so radical that those who didn't want to listen to him were incensed to the point that they put him to death in a most gruesome manner. So high were their passions, people chose to free a violent man named Barabbas rather than Jesus. Shortly after Jesus' birth, Simeon, a devout man in Jerusalem, made a prophecy to Mary, the mother of Jesus: "This child is destined for the falling and the rising of many in Israel, and to be a sign that will be opposed *so that the inner thoughts of many will be revealed*" (Luke 2.34-35, italics added). Was this why people felt threatened by Jesus – because he revealed their hidden thoughts?

From our earliest childhood we learn to say, "I didn't do it!" when something bad happens. We find it difficult to take the blame for something that we have done. We don't want to be held responsible, even when we are, so we avoid responsibility by pinning it on others. There is always someone around whom we can transform into a

Did you know...

...that the original "scapegoat" was a real goat? A day of atonement was observed in Israel once a year, to atone for the sins of the past year. (See Leviticus 23.27-32.) The sins of the people were symbolically placed on the scapegoat, which was then driven into the wilderness.

They shall beat their swords into ploughshares,
and their spears into pruning hooks;
nation shall not lift up sword against nation,
neither shall they learn war any more.

(Isaiah 2.4)

He will not cry or lift up his voice,
or make it heard in the street;
a bruised reed he will not break,
and a dimly burning wick he will not quench.

(Isaiah 42.2-3)

scapegoat. It is difficult to be honest. Blaming others can happen in our personal lives with smaller things, or in communities when there is a larger crisis: the water supply got contaminated; there was a fight at the school dance; a drug ring got busted. It isn't long before everyone is finger pointing. The scapegoat is made to bear all the guilt – even though he or she may be innocent.

That is what happened to Jesus – he became a scapegoat. Caiaphas, the High Priest, admitted as much at the time that the Jewish leaders were plotting to have Jesus arrested: "It is better for you to have one man die for the people than to have the whole nation destroyed" (John 11.50). Why? Was it because, as Simeon said, he revealed the inner thoughts of many? Yes. If one reads the story of Jesus, one realizes how Jesus revealed everyone's inner violence. No one escaped Jesus' exposure of their inner self, not even his closest disciples. Yet he, the innocent one, remained gentle and meek: "like a lamb he was led to the slaughter." As John said, Jesus loved to the end. With his love and total self-gift he overturned the violence of his enemies and God's Holy Spirit transformed it into a possibility of life and love. When, in a final act of violence, the soldier pierced his side, blood and water flowed out. The Holy Spirit transformed this blood and water into the baptism and Eucharist of which we all partake. It is true: The gentle and the meek do inherit the earth.

> Read the account of the passion and death of Jesus according to Luke (chapters 22-23).
>
> 1. Identify all the characters in the story.
> 2. Take one of the characters in the story (Peter, Herod, the other disciples, Pilate, etc.) and answer the following questions about this person:
>   - What is this person's role in the story?
>   - What did this person do in the face of violence?
>   - Did the person become aware of the violence in their heart?
>   - How did Jesus act? How did he make them aware?

---

from an interview with Desmond Tutu...

"At the end of their conflicts, the warring groups around the world… will sit down and work out how they will be able to live together amicably. They will, I know it. There will be peace on Earth. The death and resurrection of Jesus Christ puts the issue beyond doubt: ultimately, goodness and laughter and peace and compassion and gentleness and forgiveness will have the last word."

("My Idea of Heaven" by Gyles Brandreth
for *The Sunday Telegraph*.
Reprinted in *The Ottawa Citizen*,
April 16, 2001, Section A–10)

Theme 19

Power and service

One reason that young people sometimes find themselves in conflict with their parents, teachers, or other people who have authority is that they themselves are learning how to use power. Power is a good thing. Consider its absence – powerlessness. Powerless people are unable to do anything, even to care adequately for themselves. Power is our ability to act on the world, and to interact with other people in a way that achieves results. Using it appropriately, for positive ends, moves us and our communities forward. Abusing it, on the other hand, is destructive. Often, we live in a "grey area" where our use of power may drift from being positive to being negative. You have probably experienced this in your relationships with your parents and teachers when, all of a sudden, they let you know that you have "crossed the line" and are misusing your power.

Canada's Parliament Buildings symbolize the responsible use of power that benefits the nation.

Focus your learning

- **Aware and Informed**
  What is power?

- **Practical and Active**
  How are Christians expected to respond to civil authority?

- **Creative and Grateful**
  What does it mean to be a person of service?

In this theme, you will explore the nature of power, both as our culture understands it and as Jesus used it. Jesus calls us to be powerful in the same way that he was powerful. He defined his power through service. As Christians, we are called to exercise our power privately in our religious practice. But most importantly, we are to use it to be of service in our day-to-day lives. In this way, power benefits us personally, but also society and the world at large.

Key terms

power	violence
authority	symbols of power
service	state

A call from the VP's office

The beige phone near the door of the classroom rang a few minutes before the end of class. The teacher picked it up and spoke in that hushed and guarded way that always makes it clear something secret is going on. It is usually chatty at that point in the period, but when the phone rings, it gets quiet. Everyone wants to know who's in trouble now.

"James, could you go to the office please and speak to the vice-principal. You may as well take your books with you, class is almost over," the teacher said matter of factly.

"You may as well take your books with you." That's a loaded one! It can mean anything from a day to a week's suspension, or simply that the class is almost over. I packed up my stuff kind of slowly and caught the eyes of a few kids – they were looking at me with a mixture of pity and support, but also probably relief that it wasn't them being called to the office. As I made my way to the office I wondered why it had taken him so long to call me in. Being new to the school I hadn't met him yet, although I had seen him around. Everybody said he was – well, you know what they say about VPs!

When I got to the office, he was waiting for me. "Hello James, I'm Mr. Kerwin, the vice-principal. I don't think we have had a chance to meet yet."

Then he shook my hand, which I thought was kind of weird. I followed him into his office and put on my "who cares" grin. He started asking me about my attendance and why I had been away so much. I shrugged and told him I didn't know why I skipped school, keeping my grin intact.

I waited for things to get ugly (they usually do at this point – you know the drill, with the threats, consequences, and phone calls home), but he just stopped talking for a

minute. Then, he said kind of quietly, "James, there are two of us here and one of us knows why you're not coming to school. Help me understand what's keeping you from school."

I could feel the grin abandon me and the corner of my mouth start to shake a bit. I didn't want to speak so I just sat and tried to find my grin. A full minute went by while we just sat there in silence. I could see the wall clock out of the corner of my eye, and the second hand seemed to take forever to make that circle. Then he said, "Look, James, just take your time. You don't know me and I can see that something's going on in you. You don't have any reason to trust me, but I can tell you that whatever is happening to keep you away from us, I'll do what I can to help."

He said "us" – that just about did it. There was another silence, while I thought, "Does this guy really care about me?" I swallowed hard and could feel tears (just a couple – honest!) start to form. I decided I felt okay to talk to this guy and it all came tumbling out... I told him I was having a hard time because I was new and really didn't have any friends. This was my fifth school in the four years since my parents split. Then I told him about Dad and why I had to move back in with Mom because of his girlfriend...

He shook my hand again when I left. It didn't seem weird any more.

- James had never met the VP before, but he understood that he had power and authority in the school. How did James first react to Mr. Kerwin?
- What is our usual reaction when we are called in by someone who has power and authority over us?
- Why do we feel this way? What do you think James expected to happen?
- Was the vice-principal's intervention a good use of power? Why? Why not?
- Where does the vice-principal's power and authority come from? Is there a difference between the person of the vice-principal and his role? What is the difference?

Distinguishing power and authority

Power is everywhere. Power is found in every relationship – between parent and child, between teacher and student, between friends, between members of society, and between nations. What is it in us that allows us to influence what others do? What is this force we call power?

Power: Power has to do with the ability of human beings to act. When humans act, they almost always interact, that is, they act upon other people. Power is a mysterious force or energy that is part of all our human relationships. For example, a singer has power when, through her songs, she can move others to listen to her music and buy her CDs. Power shows itself through one person's ability to change what another person is doing. It also shows itself in helping others.

- Identify situations in the world where power is at work.
- Consider your own various relationships and how all of your interactions involve the use of power; for example, you express a strong preference for a certain movie, and the other person goes along; or a coach tells you to play harder, and you do. How have you influenced others? How have others influenced you?

Authority: Authority adds something to, or complements, power. I may have the power (ability) to do something, but not necessarily the authority to do so. In order for my power to be effective, I need others to accept it. If someone claims the right to wield power within a community without the agreement of the community, that person is using power in an illegitimate way, and without authority. For example, dictators, vigilantes and terrorists all use power without authority. Society recognizes the danger of power without controls, which results in anarchy. For this reason, one must be authorized to exercise power in society. Think of the government and justice system. Voters elect Members of Parliament and grant them authority to create laws that will protect the common good. Judges are granted the authority to make sure these laws are applied fairly. The police force is given authority by society to enforce these laws. In other words, society recognizes the legitimate use of power by creating institutions, such as the structures of government, that have built-in checks and balances. Elected politicians, duly appointed civil servants, ordained ministers, and teachers have all been given the authority to use their power. But they have to use it within a carefully prescribed framework, and with the approval of the members of society. Authority is given by others, by institutions, by the Church or by the state.

- Recall the story of the vice-principal. How did Mr. Kerwin become vice-principal? What gave him the authority to call James to his office?
- Name other individuals who have authority and describe how or from whom they received this authority. (Examples: parents, judges, bishops, prime minister, etc.)

violence:

Violence is the aggressive or unjust use of power or force to harm others. It is often the result of situations in which people lose the power to act for themselves (because of poverty, injustice, hopelessness, tyranny, etc.). But it is also often used by people to hold on to their power over others, to gain it, or to increase it.

Service: Some people seek power because they want to feel important; they believe others will respect them for their power. As Christians, we are all called to use whatever power we have for the common good. Service is using our power to help others. Service is giving of our time and energy to help others fulfill their needs.

- Give examples from the news of people who seek power for themselves.
- Give examples of people who are dedicated to helping others.

Symbols of power: Power needs to be recognized by others. That is why power in a community or a state is always surrounded by symbols and rituals. To receive power and authority, people go through rites of ordination, swearing-in ceremonies, initiation, calling to the bar or graduation ceremonies. These rituals symbolize their new role in society. A community uses symbols (robes, rings, mitres, diplomas, certificates, insignia, medals, maces, etc.) to show its recognition of power.

> Recall your study of symbols and rituals of the Catholic Church in Theme 5 (see especially pages 44-45). For the Church, the sacraments are symbols and rituals of the power of the risen Christ active in our midst.
>
> Using the example of the sacrament of the sick:
> - What sort of power is called upon in the sacrament of the sick?
> - Who has the authority to call upon this power?
> - How was this power conferred upon this person? By whom? In whose name?
> - How is this power symbolized and ritualized?

The power of the state and the authority of the Church

One of the highest forms of power and authority is the state. The Canadian Parliament enacts laws to govern our lives as citizens of Canada. The state has the power to enforce these laws. If we do not obey the laws, the state can punish us. It is no wonder that we consider the state, the courts and the police to be so powerful.

> - Give an example of how the state exercises power over its citizens.
> - How is the power of the state held in control?
> - Why is it important that institutions like the Catholic Church, as well as individual citizens, participate in public discussions about the decisions that are made by governments?
> - Are you aware of any laws in Canada that Catholics would find unjust or immoral? What are they? What actions should Catholics undertake to show their disagreement?
> - Why are unjust or immoral laws not binding in conscience? (See *Catechism of the Catholic Church*, #1903.)
> - What does it mean when Catholics assert that God's power and authority is higher than any earthly authority?
> - What should Catholics do when they experience a conflict between the authority of the state and the teaching of the Church?

state:

The *state* is one of many institutions that wield power in society. In politics, the relationships of power in a community reach their greatest intensity. As Catholics, however, we believe that there is a higher power than the state: namely God. Consequently, there is often tension between the state and the Church.

But is there no higher power than the state? Because we are part of a global community, we recognize that there are institutions that limit Canada's power. One might point to the United Nations or international law, to other powers such as the United States or Europe, or even to multinational companies. But one might also point to the power of God. After all, Jesus said, "All authority in heaven and on earth has been given to me" (Matthew 28.18). Where can we see the power of Christ? What sort of power is it?

Jesus sent his Holy Spirit upon the disciples at Pentecost and anointed them with his power. The Church is the community of Jesus' disciples even today, filled with the power of the Holy Spirit. This power is a spiritual power. It shows itself in daily life and in the teaching of the Church. In Canada, the Church and the state are officially separated. Because ours is a multicultural society, the government listens to many voices. The voice of the Church is one among many. And so the Church must work with its moral authority, using this authority whenever it feels that laws are unjust or immoral. The Church holds that God's power and authority are higher than the laws of the state. And whenever the state enacts unjust laws, the Church feels bound to protest because of God's concern for the people who suffer injustice or who are too weak to defend themselves.

The duties of government

What are the duties of governments, and how should Catholics respond to governments? The following list of duties is taken from the *Catechism of the Catholic Church*. (The numbers refer to the paragraphs in the *Catechism*.)

1. Respect for the dignity of the person

Society must give priority to the basic rights of the individual over the desires of the community. The fundamental rights of the individual may not be sacrificed, except in exceptional situations, to the needs of the whole. It is the government's task to respect the fundamental rights of individuals. Everyone should look upon the neighbour as another self and take into account the word of Jesus, "Just as you did to one of the least of these who are members of my family, you did to me" (Matthew 25.40). The state does this by building up a spirit of truth, justice, solidarity and freedom in society. (#1907, 1925, 1929-1932, 1944, 2254)

2. Accept the rule of law

Governments should accept the "rule of law," in which the law is sovereign, over the day-to-day preferences of leaders. Government rule must not be arbitrary. (#1904)

3. Promote the common good and good order

The state must defend and promote the common good of society. For this reason it must grant political rights to all its citizens. Government must also work to strengthen the values that promote life and encourage people to put themselves at the service of others. (#1910, 1917, 1927, 2237)

4. Protect the family

"The family is the original cell of social life." Therefore, the state should do everything in its power to promote, aid and defend the family. (#2207-2211)

5. Safeguard the right to life of every innocent person

One of the most sacred duties of the state is to protect the right to life of every innocent human individual. This right exists from the moment of conception. The state must place its power at the service of the rights of each citizen, particularly the most vulnerable. (#2273)

6. Be responsible for the economy and the well-being of citizens

The state is responsible for the economy and for the well-being of its citizens. It must provide stability and security so that those who work can enjoy the fruits of their

Canada's House of Commons

labours. The state is also responsible for ensuring respect for human rights in the economic sector. (#2372, 2431)

7. Give access to work and a just wage

The government should help citizens find work and employment. (#2433)

8. Ensure religious freedom

The state must not put constraints on the practice of religion. It is a natural or civil right to practice one's religion in private or in public. (#2104-2108, 2137)

9. Look after the health of citizens

Governments must help its citizens to attain living conditions that allow them to grow and reach maturity. For this they need clothing, housing, health care, basic education, employment and social assistance. (#2288)

10. Defend the country

Governments must to do everything in their power to avoid war. Only under strict conditions may a state use military force to defend itself or to come to the defence of other nations. It may impose military duty on its citizens to protect the country and to secure the freedom of nations. But it must respect those who object to bearing arms for reasons of conscience, and give them other duties to serve the community. (#2308-2311, 2265)

Duties of Catholics to the state

The following are some of the duties of Catholics as citizens of a country:

1. Obey civil authority

We must obey and honour civil authority. We should treat those who have been given authority with respect, and, when warranted, with gratitude and goodwill. We should pray for those in authority so that, in the words of St. Paul, "we may lead a quiet and peaceable life in all godliness and dignity" (1 Timothy 2.2). (#1900, 2240) But what about when governments act unjustly, not respecting the moral order, the fundamental rights of persons or the teachings of the gospel? In these cases we are obliged in conscience not to follow their directives. Jesus said, "Give to the emperor the things that are the emperor's, and to God the things that are God's" (Matthew 22.21). (#2242-2243) Armed resistance to oppressive political authority is allowable only as a last resort, and only when strict conditions have been met.

2. Vote

We should exercise our right to vote. (#2240)

3. Participate in public life

As far as possible, we should take an active part in public life. We should promote institutions that improve the living conditions of all. It is our duty as citizens to work with civil authority to build up society in a spirit of truth, justice, solidarity and freedom. (#1915-1916, 2255)

4. Pay taxes

We must accept the authority of the state, but also share in its responsibility for the common good. For this reason, we are morally obliged to pay taxes. Here is what St. Paul had to say about taxes: "Pay to all what is due them – taxes to whom taxes are due, revenue to whom revenue is due, respect to whom respect is due, honour to whom honour is due" (Romans 13.7). (#2240)

5. Welcome immigrants and refugees

As a prosperous nation, we are obliged, to the extent that we are able, to welcome foreigners searching for security and the means of livelihood that they cannot find in their country of origin. For each of us, this welcome and hospitality becomes our personal responsibility as a citizen. (#2241)

6. Defend our country

We must, as citizens, accept the duty to defend our country. (#2240)

St. Peter's Basilica in Rome has become a symbol of authority in the Catholic Church.

Did you know...

... that the meaning of the word "minister" is derived from the call to service of Jesus? The word minister, whether it is used for "ordained minister" or "Prime Minister," is the same word. Also the word "deacon" in the Catholic Church, which comes from the Greek *diakonia*, refers to table service. The Church wanted to follow the example of the master.

service:

Jesus set the example of service. He came among us, not for himself, but for others. *Service* is using our power for the benefit and well-being of others, for the common good. It does not seek honour and privilege, but rather seeks to uphold the dignity of all. That is why governments have ministers and why the Church has ministers of the gospel: they are there to serve others, not advance themselves.

"It will not be so among you"

<table>
</table>

Did you know:

…that there are two different views of the state in the Bible? One view is that rulers of nations need to be constantly reminded of their duty to act justly on behalf of the weak and the lowly: "Rescue the weak and the needy; deliver them from the hand of the wicked" (Psalm 82.4). The writer of the Book of Revelation (Chapter 13) must have experienced injustice at the hand of the Roman Empire. He compares the state with a "beast," a great blasphemer of God, who seduces people with power. For this writer the state is a dangerous power.

On the other hand, St. Paul urges Christians "to be subject to rulers and authorities" (Titus 3.1) and not to look down on them (2.15). In his letter to the Romans he writes, "Let every person be subject to the governing authorities; for there is no authority except from God, and those authorities that exist have been instituted by God" (13.1). Christians reflect these two different views of power and authority in their own attitudes toward the state.

Jesus understood the passion for power that is in us. He had seen it among his own disciples. One day when two of his disciples had been less than discreet about their desire for power, Jesus said, "You know that the rulers of the Gentiles lord it over them, and their great ones are tyrants over them. It will not be so among you; but whoever wishes to be great among you must be your servant, and whoever wishes to be first among you must be your slave" (Matthew 20.25-27). Now that is turning the tables upside down! Jesus does not say, "Let's do without power because all power is corrupt." He recognizes that power is essential, but also dangerous when the desire for power rules the human heart. Jesus wants it to be different among his followers.

Jesus encourages those who have power and authority to serve those who have no power. It is the powerless, not the rich and the powerful, who need help! Paul understood this when he wrote, "God chose what is foolish in the world to shame the wise; God chose what is weak in the world to shame the strong" (1 Corinthians 1.27). Jesus set the example of service. In fact, on the night before he died, he said to his disciples, "Who is greater, the one who is at the table or the one who serves? Is it not the one at the table? But I am among you as one who serves" (Luke 22.27). Jesus, who is rightfully the Lord and master, chooses to act as the servant of all.

The Gospel of John gives the same message: On the night before he died, Jesus took off his outer robe, tied a towel around himself and began to wash the feet of his disciples. After he had washed their feet, he said, "Do you know what I have done to you? You call me Teacher and Lord – and you are right, for that is what I am. So if I, your Lord and Teacher, have washed your feet, you also ought to wash one another's feet. For I have set you an example, that you also should do as I have done to you." Then he added, "If you know these things, you are blessed if you do them" (John 13.12-17).

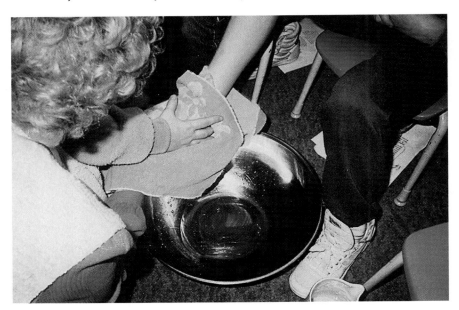

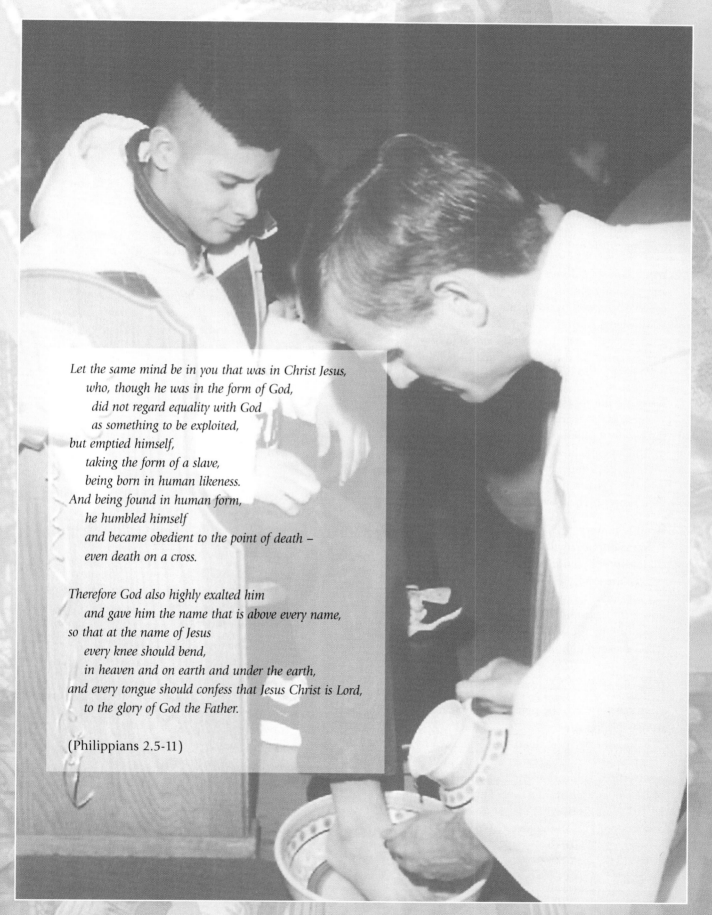

Let the same mind be in you that was in Christ Jesus,
    who, though he was in the form of God,
      did not regard equality with God
      as something to be exploited,
but emptied himself,
    taking the form of a slave,
      being born in human likeness.
And being found in human form,
    he humbled himself
    and became obedient to the point of death –
      even death on a cross.

Therefore God also highly exalted him
    and gave him the name that is above every name,
so that at the name of Jesus
    every knee should bend,
    in heaven and on earth and under the earth,
and every tongue should confess that Jesus Christ is Lord,
    to the glory of God the Father.

(Philippians 2.5-11)

Unit 6 review

In this unit, you explored your relationship to civil society from a Catholic perspective.

Aware and Informed

What is time for?

Christian time celebrates the focal point of human time: the story of God with us. Jesus is the beginning and end of time. Time is for living in a covenant relationship with God.

When is justice done?

The generally accepted definition of justice is to render to others what is their due. To do justice means to acknowledge our responsibility for our neighbour. Jesus reminds us that we would encounter him whenever we cared for the sick, the thirsty, the hungry and the naked.

What are the roots of violence?

Violence is the aggressive or unjust use of power or force to hurt others. It is often the result of situations in which people lose the power to act for themselves (because of poverty, injustice, hopelessness, tyranny, etc.) But it is also often used by people to hold on to their power over others, to gain it, or to increase it.

What is power?

Power is our ability to act and to cause or influence change in our world. Jesus defines power as service, and set the example of service. He came among us, not for himself, but for others. Service is using our power for the well-being of others, for the common good. It does not seek honour and privilege, but rather seeks to uphold the dignity of all.

Practical and Active

How can the Catholic perspective on time help me to live a fuller life?

The Catholic perspective on time is shaped by its calendar of celebration, centred on Jesus' life, death and resurrection. Living the year around the central feast of Easter, and celebrating every Sunday as a "little Easter" reminds us what the centre of our life is. Jesus anchors our lives in the love of God.

How can the golden rule lead to a more just society?

"Do to others as you would have them do to you." This is how Jesus urges us to do justice. Don't consider only yourself; keep in mind the other, even in your use of money and property. Following this rule would ensure the equitable distribution of goods in society.

How can we overcome violence?

The senselessness of violence must be confronted with language of reason and love. Used peacefully and lovingly, language can be the most powerful tool we have to disarm violence. Peace is linked with justice, truth, faithfulness, grace and love.

How are Christians expected to respond to civil authority?

The duties of Catholics to the state are:

1. Obey civil authority
   Jesus said, "Give to the emperor the things that are the emperor's, and to God the things that are God's" (Matthew 22.21).

2. Vote

3. Participate in public life

4. Pay taxes "Pay to all what is due them – taxes to whom taxes are due, revenue to whom revenue is due, respect to whom respect is due, honour to whom honour is due" (Romans 13.7).

5. Welcome immigrants and refugees

6. Defend our country

Creative and Grateful

You can answer these questions for yourself. The answer is found in your relationship with God.

How do we "keep the Lord's Day holy"?

Who advocates for justice in our lives?

What would the world be like without violence?

What does it mean to be a person of service?

Unit 7

Relating to the Church: We are the Church

Aim: to understand how the work of Jesus continues in the world through the Catholic Church

Theme 20

The Catholic Church – sacrament of Christ

When you walk into a Catholic Church, you will almost always see a large crucifix placed front and centre. The image of the crucified Lord reminds us of God's complete love for us. It reminds us of the presence of hope even within the depth of human suffering. We, as the Church, witness to the crucified and risen Christ within our culture.

In this theme you will explore the Church as a sign of salvation in the world. As a sacrament, the Church is visible. It is made up of people like you. It has a structure similar to other cultural institutions. The Church celebrates Christ's saving actions through its official worship, the seven sacraments. It offers the world the sacred Scriptures and its teaching, especially on justice and mercy. The Catholic Church is a sign of Christ's continued activity among us in the power of the Holy Spirit. What is visible is the material dimension of a spiritual reality.

In the Bible we find many stories of how God chooses the least likely people to help sow the seeds of the kingdom. When we look at the Church, we may think that, surely, God could have done better. And yet, we are part of this Church. God has chosen each of us to help in the mission of Christ. Each of us, as a member of this Church, with all of our faults and weaknesses, as well as our talents and strengths, is called to reveal Christ to the world.

Focus your learning

- **Aware and Informed**
  How is the Church an effective sign of Christ in today's world?

- **Practical and Active**
  How does God work through us?

- **Creative and Grateful**
  What difference does our participation in the Church make?

Key concepts

Church	sign
sacrament	salvation

The Catholic Church at the beginning of the twenty-first century

Our culture is increasingly indifferent toward religion. Many people see the Catholic Church as an institution in serious decline. They believe that what it has to say about contemporary issues is irrelevant. Midway through the last century, Pope John XXIII could see this coming. He asked: "What will the church do? Should the mystical bark [another word for boat] of Christ remain tossed about on the waves and allow itself to be dragged along in their wake? Do we not expect the light of a bold example rather than simply another warning? What might this light be?" (See G. Lafont, *Imagining the Church*, Liturgical Press, 2000, p. 1.) In answer to his concerns, he called a council of the whole Church. The Second Vatican Council, as it became known, lasted from 1962 to 1965. No other religious event of the twentieth century so shaped Church and society. One document produced by the bishops attending this council is called the Pastoral Constitution on the Church in the Modern World.

The preface of this document states clearly what the Church is about. It talks about the "joys and hopes, the griefs and the anxieties" of people in our time. And it describes how these joys and griefs, especially those of the poor or afflicted, are shared by the followers of Christ. All of human experience finds an echo in the hearts of believers. That is because ours is a community "united in Christ." Within this community, we are "led by the Holy Spirit" in our journey toward our Father's kingdom. And we are bearers of the news of salvation for all humanity.

Did you know...

...that the Catholic Church has taken part in many key debates on social issues in Canada? It has made presentations on Parliament Hill and at the Supreme Court. It has spoken out on abortion, employment, poverty, bioethical issues, and much more. As a symbol of Christ, the Church continues to speak in the name of truth, even when opposed.

The council also explains how it understands the presence and activity of the Church in the world of today. The council has in mind "the whole human family," seen in the context of the culture in which it lives. (See Pastoral Constitution on the Church in the Modern World, #1, 2.)

Other changes, besides the Second Vatican Council, have shaped the twentieth-century Church. More than at almost any other time in its two-thousand-year history, the Catholic Church has sought to be a minister and servant. It has tried to be an increasingly effective sign of Christ in the world. It has been tireless in bringing the gospel everywhere; it has known courageous leadership; it has contributed significantly to knowledge and the sciences; it has prompted study of the Scriptures and has applied the human sciences to its ministry; it has, through dialogue, helped build friendlier relations between other religions and the Christian Churches. So why is it that so many people say "yes" to Jesus and the Bible or to spirituality, but "no" to the Church?

What do you think?

How would you assess the state of the Church at the beginning of this new century?

Do you think that the Church is in a state of decline? Explain.

The Church has been around for two thousand years, and over those 20 centuries has, for the most part, been at the forefront of human development and spiritual leadership. What do you think empowers the Church to move forward, even during its darkest days?

The Catholic Church as an institution

The Catholic Church took shape slowly with the first disciples bringing the message of God's kingdom to the communities around the Mediterranean Sea. We have some idea of how these early communities were structured, and an even clearer picture after the first few centuries. The world around the Mediterranean Sea was dominated by Greek culture. As a result, the early Church took over many ideas and images from that culture. This had a big impact on how the Church as a new institution understood its mission of spreading the gospel.

After he became the emperor of Rome in AD 312, Constantine the Great declared that Christianity was to be the official religion of the Roman Empire. In many ways, the Church took on the structures of the government at that time. After all, the Church interacts with and transforms culture. But it also adapts elements of culture for its own use, according to the vision of the time.

When we refer to the way the Church is organized, we often use the term "hierarchical." Christ is the head of the Church. By baptism all Christians belong to the Lord and all have the task of being priests, prophets and rulers. But in a special way this office is entrusted to those called by Jesus to be the successors of the twelve apostles. These are the bishops. Chief among them is the bishop of Rome, who is the Pope, the successor of Peter. When we speak about the hierarchical Church, we usually mean the bishops' role of teaching, sanctifying and governing. The hierarchy also includes the role of the priests and deacons, who are also called ministers of grace. All of these need to receive their authority from Christ, for only Christ is the head of the Church.

Church:

We have many names for Church – names found in the Scriptures and in sacred tradition. It has been called the people of God, communion with God, the body of Christ, the sacred assembly, and the eucharistic community. It is also called the sacrament of Christ, the temple of the Holy Spirit, the new people, the new Israel, and the saints. But whatever its name, the Church, in the power of the Holy Spirit, makes the risen Christ alive in history until he comes again.

Did you know...

...that nearly all institutions are hierarchical? The Catholic Church, like most institutions, is organized according to different levels of authority.

As we entered the new millennium, the President of the Canadian Conference of Catholic Bishops, Most Reverend Gerald Wiesner, shared these hopes and prayers for our Church and our world:

December 8, 1999

My dear brothers and sisters:

With the close of this century and a new millennium approaching, I address my message to Canadians of all traditions and races as well as to those of other nationalities living in our country. Let me first underline why this time is important for all of us who are Christian. It marks two thousand years since Jesus of Nazareth graced our planet and set in motion a movement of love that never ceases to blossom, even though there have been times when we Christians have been inept in showing and sharing that love.

Our sentiment is primarily one of gratitude. We thank our Creator for the wonderful country and the bounties of nature that we share. We thank the multitude of pioneers who came from distant shores, and with courage and perseverance brought about the democratic society that we call Canada. We thank the people of the First Nations for their many sacrifices in the process of building the country that we cherish. We thank as well not only Catholic clergy and religious but also the leadership of all other faith traditions. We also have gratitude in our hearts for the men and women who gave their lives on the battlefields of history to defend our heritage. Finally, we thank all people who have contributed their lives and resources to the common good: teachers, health-care workers, labour leaders, politicians, government employees, volunteers and activists.

It is a proper time to ascertain what is truly important and what our petitions to God should be emphasizing. Indeed, such are our prayer intentions for the new millennium:

We pray for growing unity that respects diversity and enhances the well-being of all the inhabitants of our country.

We pray for the eradication of poverty and want everywhere in Canada, but especially among children and the First Nations.

We pray for our young people that they may find solid mentors leading them to creative and satisfying lives.

We pray for marginalized people, including immigrants and refugees, that they be welcomed to take their rightful place within society.

We pray for the development of restorative justice, that thereby we may find lasting solutions to the blight of crime as well as to the sorry situation of penal institutions.

We pray for all health professionals that their respect for life be foremost in their endeavours to bring the best of science to bear in the care they exercise.

We pray for all scientists and all technicians that their work be profitable for all segments of society and the good of the whole planet.

We pray for all who are engaged in volunteer work that it may lead them to deep spiritual peace.

We pray for our government leaders that they may have the courage and wisdom always to decide what is best for the common good.

We pray for ourselves and for all religious leaders that we may always preach what is true and good and live accordingly.

Our list is not exhaustive, yet through it we wish to express our dedication to the building of a society wherein it will be easier to live virtuously, where joy will be the lot of many, where all children will be surrounded with love, where prejudice will have no place and where God will be more evident to all.

In the spirit of the birth of Jesus two thousand years ago, and in the spirit of the Great Jubilee, proclaimed by Pope John Paul II, let us be open to new beginnings – opening our doors to all God's people and our hearts and homes as well.

Your brother in Christ,

+ *Gerald Wiesner, OMI*

Most Reverend Gerald Wiesner, OMI
Bishop of Prince George
President
Canadian Conference of Catholic Bishops

Images of Church

Institution · Advocate · Teacher · Community · Servant · Transformer

Our Church

The Church is a sacrament of Christ

We think of Church as many things: a building; the things that happen in that building; priests, bishops and popes; and the people who are baptized and follow the teaching of its spiritual leaders. And we are right! Each of these things embodies some part of Church. Through each of them, something spiritual happens – the dying and rising of Christ. When Christians gather on Sunday morning, the Holy Spirit makes alive among them the mystery of Christ. Jesus said, "Where two or three are gathered in my name, I am there among them" (Matthew 18.20). Or as he said on another occasion, "Truly I tell you, just as you did it to one of the least of these who are members of my family, you did it to me" (Matthew 25.40). The gathering of God's people on Sunday is a sign that Christ is there. The bishop or priest who acts among the faithful or the poor, who presides over the Sunday Eucharist, or who forgives sins, is acting as the person of Christ. They all continue what Jesus began.

Jesus began the Church by preaching the good news of God, telling parables, healing, and casting out evil spirits. When he died and rose he poured out on his disciples the same Spirit that had been with him. The Spirit passed the gifts of Jesus on to the disciples. They were to take on the mission of proclaiming and establishing the kingdom of God. This became the Church – the people gathered by Christ who believed Jesus and who are now the seeds of God's kingdom. Christ is present in the world through the Church.

- How is the Church a sacrament? What is the material aspect of the Church? What is the spiritual aspect of the Church?
- When are we the Church? How are we an effective sign of Christ to the world?
- What happens if members do not participate in the actions that make Christ present?

sacraments:

Sacraments are effective signs of grace. They have been instituted by Christ and entrusted to the Church. Through them we show and communicate our communion with God. The purpose of the sacraments is to make us holy, to build up the body of Christ, and to give praise and worship to God.

The body of Christ

In the Scriptures there are many images and symbols that express the close relationship between Christ and his followers. None says it more graphically than "body of Christ." As Church we are called the body of Christ. That means our relationship with Christ is not only spiritual, but also physical. Our relationship with Christ involves our bodies at every turn. Think of the sacraments and rituals of the Church: we gather, listen, sing, greet one another, stand, sit, kneel and bow. Each of these actions gets the body involved and changes it, however slightly and gradually. The body, or the community, is gradually recreated in the image of Christ through the action of the Holy Spirit.

When the Church gathers to celebrate the sacred mysteries in the liturgy, the Holy Spirit works through that gathering to bring about reconciliation. Through the sacraments, Christ gives himself to the community. The Holy Spirit inspires and moves us to try to live as Jesus lived, to serve as Jesus served, to love as Jesus loved. In the sacraments we encounter the physical and spiritual presence of the risen Lord. Through these acts the Holy Spirit shapes a community in the image and likeness of Christ. What better way to describe this community than to call it the body of Christ? The Church is indeed the body of Christ.

- Turn back in your books to pages 13 and 45, and reread Principles #1 and #5. What do they say? How do they relate to this theme on Church?
- Where else in our daily speech do we use the term "body" to represent a community?

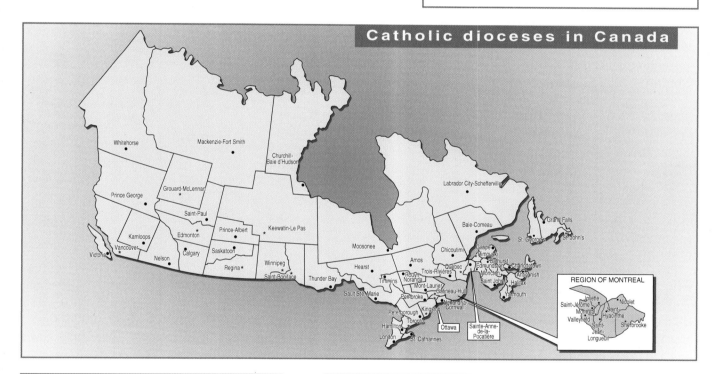

Catholic dioceses in Canada

sign:

Signs are objects or gestures that express a specific message or meaning. Sacraments, as "effective signs," bring about what they signify. For example, Eucharist *is* the body of Christ, and also *creates* the body of Christ, the Church.

salvation:

The Church proclaims that we are made whole through faith in God. The Church believes that through our devotion to and trust in God, particularly through our faith in Jesus Christ, human beings are set on the path of fullness of life. Belief in salvation is at the heart of religion. The Church is an effective sign of salvation for us.

Liturgy

All the way to Elizabeth
and in the months afterward,
she wove him, pondering,
"This is my body, my blood!"

Beneath the watching eyes
of donkey, ox, and sheep,
she rocked him, crooning,
"This is my body, my blood!"

In the moonless desert flight
and the Egypt days of his growing,
she nourished him, singing,
"This is my body, my blood!"

In the search for her young lost boy
and the foreboding day of his leaving,
she let him go, knowing,
"This is my body, my blood!"

Under the blood-smeared cross,
she rocked his mangled bones,
re-membering him, moaning,
"This is my body, my blood!"

When darkness, stones and tomb
bloomed to Easter morning,
she ran to him, shouting,
"This is my body, my blood!"

by Irene Zimmerman, OSF
(*Woman Un-Bent*. Winona:
Saint Mary's Press, 1999, p. 70)

Annunciation (1489-90)
by Sandro Botticelli
Uffizi Gallery, Florence

Day of Pardon

The First Sunday of Lent, March 12, 2000, Pope John Paul II declared to be a Day of Pardon. The year 2000 was to be a Year of Jubilee, a year in which the Pope hoped the Church could begin to purify its memory. The Church was weighed down by the memories of sins committed long ago. But even more troubling, some of these deeds were being repeated in the present by what Catholics continued to do. As long as these memories persisted, they continued to harm the body of Christ. The Pope said the Church needed to kneel before God and beg forgiveness for the past and present sins of her sons and daughters. He said, "While we praise God who, in his merciful love, has produced in the Church a wonderful harvest of holiness, missionary zeal, total dedication to Christ and neighbour, we cannot fail to recognize the *infidelities to the Gospel committed by some of our [brothers and sisters]*."

What were these sins of the Church? He mentioned four:

The first sin was the division of Christians. The Church proclaims one Christ and yet there is no unity among the churches. They are divided in their worship and in their beliefs. This is one of the greatest scandals of the Church. The Pope asked for pardon especially for those who do things that make this division worse.

The second sin was the use of force and intolerance in the service of truth. The gospel is not served by violence or force. Catholics have not always been quick enough to denounce injustice and violence. For this too he sought pardon.

The third sin was the sin against the Jewish people. As Catholics today, we cannot be held responsible for what was done to the Jews in the Shoah – the attempt by the Nazis in the Second World War (1939-1945) to exterminate the Jews. But the Nazis could never have murdered so many Jews if there had not been anti-Semitism in the countries from which the Jews were deported. The Pope asked pardon for those who even today persist in anti-Semitism.

The fourth sin concerned the responsibility of Catholics for the evils of today. What are these evils? Many of them we have touched on in the previous themes: the death or eclipse of God in our culture; religious indifference; the widespread loss of a higher sense of human life; the climate of secularism and of the loss of ethical commitments; the denial of the right to life of the unborn child sanctioned by laws; and the great indifference to the cry of the poor in entire sections of the human family.

All of us probably need to admit that we are guilty as charged for some of these sins. As Pope John Paul II prayed: "We humbly ask for forgiveness for the part which each of us has had in these evils by our own actions, thus helping to disfigure the face of the Church."

- What does it mean to ask pardon?
- What does it mean for the Church to ask for pardon?
- How are we implicated in these sins of the Church?
- What does it mean to be reconciled?

Consider your own call, brothers and sisters:
not many of you were wise by human standards,
not many were powerful,
not many were of noble birth.
But God chose what is foolish in the world to shame the wise;
God chose what is weak in the world to shame the strong;
God chose what is low and despised in the world,
    things that are not, to reduce to nothing things that are,
    so that no one might boast in the presence of God.
He is the source of your life in Christ Jesus, who became for us
    wisdom from God,
and righteousness and sanctification and redemption,
in order that, as it is written, "Let the one who boasts, boast
    in the Lord."

(1 Corinthians 1.26-31)

Theme 21

The presence of God's Spirit in the Catholic Church

In this theme you will find a quotation that says if you don't care about other people, then you have no reason to go to church, or even to live. Another quotation says that Jesus is the vine, and you are a branch on that vine. God prunes off the branches that bear no fruit. Should you worry?

Sometimes we think of the Church as a "spiritual gas station." We find ourselves going to church in order to get something. Often people who don't go to church use the excuse, "I don't get anything out of it."

Focus your learning

- **Aware and Informed**
  What is the mission of the Church?

- **Practical and Active**
  As a member of the Church, what am I supposed to do?

- **Creative and Grateful**
  How does Jesus work through me and the Christian community?

In this theme we are reminded that the Church is about loving others, and that love is not just a warm feeling that we have when somebody likes us. Love moves us to contribute our time, talents and treasures for the good of the community. Love is, as John's Gospel puts it, "bearing fruit" (John 15.1-5).

Key terms

one	catholic
holy	apostolic

The Church is one, holy, catholic and apostolic

In the Creed, Catholics profess that the Church is one, holy, catholic and apostolic. These words are very important to understand what the Church is about. They are not tasks, but four essential traits of the Church and its mission. The Church is one already because of the presence of Christ in the Church. We are all one in Christ. The risen Christ also makes the Church holy, catholic and apostolic. These four traits direct us toward Christ and remind us of him. The Church's unity, holiness, catholicity and apostolicity are gifts of the Holy Spirit. It is our task to work together with the Holy Spirit to make them more visible. (See *Catechism*, #811.)

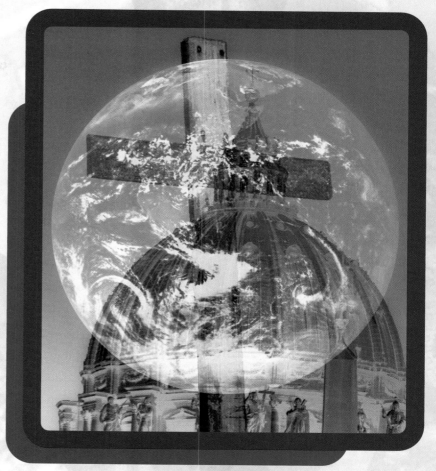

One The Church is one because it is the sacrament of the risen Christ. The Holy Spirit works in us to make us more like Christ, to be one with him. The Holy Spirit joins all believers into a unified community. Unity here does not mean that the Church is without diversity. It is a union with and in Christ among a wide variety of peoples and cultures. (See *Catechism*, #813-814.)

Holy The Church is holy because it embodies the love of God that Jesus revealed in his life, death and resurrection. "I am with you always, to the end of the age" (Matthew 28.20). The Church is holy because it is the body of Christ. We are a holy people. Holiness arrives as a gift through the waters of Baptism, and is nourished through the Eucharist. Paul calls the members of Christ's body the saints. Our holiness is obviously not perfect but it is still real. The source of holiness in the Church is *agape*-love or charity. The Church is holy despite having sinners in its midst. (See *Catechism*, #823-827.)

Catholic The Church is catholic (that is, "universal" or "in view of the whole") in two senses. It is universal because the fullness of Christ's body and his life dwells in it. Christ is the beginning and the end of everything. Where Christ is, all creation is. The Church is catholic also in the sense that it has been sent out to all nations. Wherever the Church is, Christ is. And so in every parish on every Sunday, the whole Church is present. Every community where the gospel is preached and the Eucharist is celebrated is catholic. (See *Catechism*, #830-852.)

Apostolic Apostolic means that the Church is founded on the apostles and their mission. Jesus said that he would build his Church on Peter because of Peter's faith. The Catholic Church is built upon the faith of the apostles. As successors to the apostles, all bishops throughout history have retained a link with the apostles through the sacrament of Holy Orders. Each bishop passes on the one, holy, catholic and apostolic tradition. In other words, the teaching of the Church today is the continuation of the teaching of the apostles. To this day, the college of bishops, assisted by priests, in union with the successor of Peter, the pope, continue to hand on the Catholic tradition. (See *Catechism*, #857-865.)

Understanding the beginning of the Church

Jesus never left a clear plan to organize the Church. That was the work of the Holy Spirit through the men and women who were the first followers of Jesus. The Spirit formed them into the body of Christ. The disciples had been with Jesus, many of them from the beginning. They had heard his words and seen his deeds; they had witnessed his death and their own shameful behaviour at the time of his arrest and crucifixion. But more important, on the third day after his death, they had seen the Lord, the risen one. Upon seeing the Lord, they had a powerful experience of God's Spirit, so powerful that people thought they were drunk with wine. Through the Spirit, Jesus Christ would remain with them until the end of time.

So what were the apostles to do? They began to preach that Jesus was the Messiah, God's anointed one; that he was risen from the dead; and that his followers would share eternal life by believing in him. They urged people to accept Jesus. Many Jews, as the Acts of the Apostles tells us, joined the way of Jesus and were baptized. The first members of the early Church were the Jewish disciples of Jesus. They still saw themselves as faithful Jews. They kept Torah; they urged the followers of the way to accept circumcision, to worship in the temple, to observe the Jewish food (kosher) laws, and to keep Jewish practices. At first, the disciples and the Twelve understood their mission as being only to their own people. The only practice they added to their Jewish traditions was "the breaking of the bread," a gathering of the disciples in which they remembered the life, death and resurrection of Jesus on the first day of the week.

Because of their importance in the early Church, saints Peter and Paul have always had prominent places in Christian art. Mosaics of Peter (illustrated above) and Paul (opposite page) can be found in the northern Italian city of Ravenna, which was the capital of the western Roman Empire during the fifth century AD.

Not all early Christians who kept Jewish practices (see above) were able to worship at the Temple in Jerusalem. Those who lived elsewhere gathered in synagogues to worship. The building ruins pictured here are from a synagogue in the town of Capernaum on the north shore of the Sea of Galilee. This building dates from around AD 200 and may be built on the foundation of the synagogue that was there during the times when Jesus visited the town.

"They devoted themselves to the apostles' teaching and fellowship, to the breaking of bread and the prayers" (Acts 2.42).

Did you know...

...that the Acts of the Apostles was written by Luke, who also wrote a gospel? In the first part we find an account of the life of the first community of Jesus' disciples in Jerusalem. They were initially known as the followers of "the way." The second part of Acts is about Paul and his ministry to spread the gospel to the Gentiles. It ends with his arrest and trial, followed by his preaching in Rome.

Opening the doors to the Gentiles

The followers of the way of Jesus were creating quite a stir in Jerusalem. The Jewish leaders were enraged by their boldness and by the number of Jews who were attracted to the way of Jesus. They persecuted the apostles and tried to force them not to speak in the name of Jesus. However, those who only a short while earlier had fled and denied they knew Jesus, now would not back off. For them, the truth of Jesus could no longer be hidden.

The Holy Spirit works in wondrous ways. There were at the time a number of Greek-speaking Jews known as the Hellenists. Hellenists were Jews living in other countries or in the Holy Land who spoke Greek. They joined the way of Jesus in large numbers. Over time it became clear that they were being treated differently than the Hebrew followers. When they complained that their widows were overlooked in the daily distribution of food, the community met and appointed seven men to serve their needs. Over time, the community would make many more decisions in response to events and to needs of people. By laying hands on these men, the community expressed its faith that this was an action of the Holy Spirit. It was the Holy Spirit guiding the community to an ever deeper understanding of the person of Christ in their midst.

This was only the beginning of many more changes. They did not all come easily. The greatest challenge came through several events that pushed the community to also welcome the Gentiles into their midst. Historically it is hard to figure out who pushed the hardest. Scholars credit the Hellenists, who had fled to Antioch in Syria (see maps on page 182) because of persecution. Luke's account in Acts tells several stories that led to the change: Philip and the Ethiopian eunuch; Peter's dream and his visit to the household of Cornelius; and the Hellenists in Antioch and Paul.

Paul, the Apostle to the Gentiles

We first hear of Paul (still named Saul) as he was overseeing the killing of Stephen. (Stephen was among the first group of Christians to be ordained by the apostles. See Acts 6.5-6. He was also the first to be martyred for proclaiming the gospel.) Saul persecuted the Church in Jerusalem "by entering house after house, dragging off both men and women" and sending them to prison. (Acts 8.3) "Breathing threats and murder" (9.1), he asked the high priest for permission to go to Damascus to round up anyone belonging to the way of Jesus and bring them back bound to Jerusalem. But after he was converted on the road to Damascus, no one had a greater influence on the direction of the early Church.

After his conversion, he became a thorn in the side of the Church in Jerusalem in a different way, challenging it again and again to broaden its mission. He spoke with authority, based on his own experience of the Holy Spirit. Paul had never known Jesus in person. As Saul, he knew enough about him, or so he thought, to persecute his followers. On the road to Damascus, though, he had a mystical experience of the very Jesus whom he had been persecuting. What he once had not been able to accept became the guiding light of his life after his conversion experience. Jesus was God's Messiah. Jesus' way was God's way. What he had found impossible to accept before – namely, the death of a Messiah on the cross – now became the heart of his teaching: the dead messiah is risen. This changed everything in his life.

Paul wanted to preach this truth, but obviously no one trusted him at first. Everyone was against him. The apostles he had persecuted could not accept him as a true witness of Jesus since he never knew Jesus. When he tried to preach in the synagogues, the Jews wanted to kill him. As he tells us in one of his letters, he went back to Tarsus for several years to come to grips with his discovery of Jesus Christ. Only then did some members of the Church →

…that St. Paul's letters were written between AD 50 and 64, before any of the four gospels? His letters provide the first glimpses of what Christian life was like some 20 to 30 years after Jesus' death. These letters are call epistles.

call him back to preach the gospel to Jewish communities in the Roman Empire. The rest of his life Paul fought for Christ, for the Church, and for the gospel. He claimed to be an apostle in the same right as the others because he too had seen the Lord. But his vision of the Lord led him further and further away from the Jewish Christians in Jerusalem. They had kept the Jewish customs as Jesus had done. Paul's experience in the towns and cities of the Roman Empire was different. Whenever he tried to preach to the Jews, he was rejected. But he was accepted by the pagans. He saw how they received the Holy Spirit. The question was whether these former pagans could express their faith through their own Hellenist customs and culture. Or should Paul ask them to accept Jewish ways, such as circumcision, eating kosher food, and following all the rules and customs of the Torah? He knew full well that Jewish traditions were sacred to the Church in Jerusalem. Paul's personal experience of Christ in his ministry, though, led him to fight for those who were not Jewish (Gentiles) to be set free. Paul's view prevailed. He convinced the Church in Jerusalem that the way the Gentiles lived out their faith in Christ would be different from the Jewish Christians. The essentials were the same, just the way of living and expressing it was different. More than anyone else he opened the way of Jesus to other nations.

Since the early days of Christianity, artists have searched for ways to express the role that Jesus plays in revealing the mysteries of human life. One of the oldest and most often used images is that of the philosopher-teacher, an image that was borrowed from Greek art. The photo above shows a contemporary version of that image. Here, Jesus sits on the teacher's chair and holds the book of the Law, which symbolizes the truths he is engaged in revealing.

Paul's missionary journeys

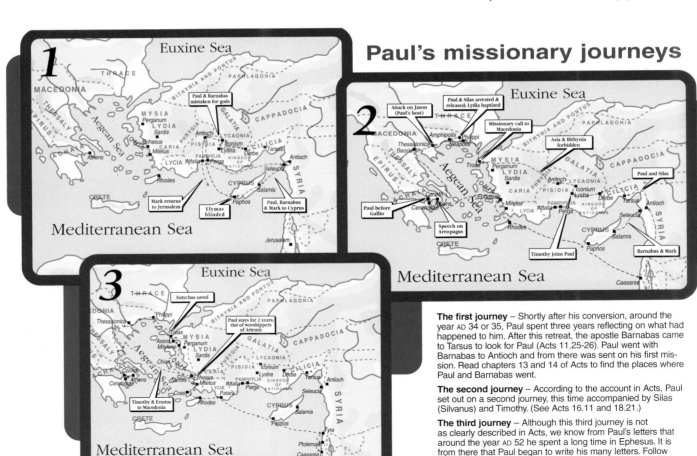

The first journey – Shortly after his conversion, around the year AD 34 or 35, Paul spent three years reflecting on what had happened to him. After this retreat, the apostle Barnabas came to Tarsus to look for Paul (Acts 11.25-26). Paul went with Barnabas to Antioch and from there was sent on his first mission. Read chapters 13 and 14 of Acts to find the places where Paul and Barnabas went.

The second journey – According to the account in Acts, Paul set out on a second journey, this time accompanied by Silas (Silvanus) and Timothy. (See Acts 16.11 and 18.21.)

The third journey – Although this third journey is not as clearly described in Acts, we know from Paul's letters that around the year AD 52 he spent a long time in Ephesus. It is from there that Paul began to write his many letters. Follow Paul's journey as he went from Ephesus in chapters 19 and 20 of Acts.

With Paul's missionary work, Christianity began to spread to people who were not Jewish. As their new faith penetrated all aspects of their lives, these Gentiles began to express it in ways that were rooted in their own traditions and customs. This statue of the Good Shepherd, from the third century AD, is a good example. Figures of peasants carrying calves or sheep to market were often found in Greek and Roman sculpture. Because of the importance of agriculture, images like this were quite popular even *before* the spread of Christianity. As they reflected on Jesus' description of himself as a shepherd, it was only natural that early Gentile Christians would use an image and a style already familiar to them to express the idea in visual form. In this way, the idea of Christ being truly present to them in their everyday lives (i.e., their culture) was given concrete expression. The challenge was to express who Christ was to them in their lives and their world rather that what he looked like when he was alive.

Five important actions of the Catholic Church

The Church has a mission in the world, a mission in which Jesus Christ plays a central role. The Catholic Church believes that the meaning of the life, death and resurrection of Jesus is essential for the future of the world. How does the Catholic Church accomplish its mission? It does five basic things:

1. The Catholic Church proclaims Jesus Christ

The Church keeps alive the memory of Jesus, proclaiming that Jesus is present in people's lives and in history. The Holy Spirit dwells in the hearts of believers. How do we remember Jesus in all cultures in every age? By preaching. The Church preaches the good news of Jesus in all new circumstances of life. The Church must continually find new ways of telling Jesus' story and living it. The world needs people of faith, hope and *agape*-love.

2. The Catholic Church worships Christ through the sacraments

The Church celebrates life and love through the sacraments. The liturgy, or official worship of the Church, expresses the faith of the people and also builds up the Church. Through baptism and confirmation, it makes Christ present by initiating people into his life, death and resurrection. As Church, we celebrate the memory of Christ each Sunday in the Eucharist. In the name of Christ, we forgive when forgiveness is needed, heal when healing is needed, call people to represent Christ when leaders in the faith are needed, and preside when Christians seek to place Christ in the centre of their married life together.

3. The Catholic Church forms a communion of people

The Church gathers us so that we can build communion with God, in Christ, through the Spirit. The original meaning of Church comes from the Hebrew word *qahal*, which means a religious assembly of people. The Church is made up of God's holy people. As Church, our main task is to bring about a spiritual and physical communion of all people with God. As a community, we are to maintain a close friendship with the Lord. The Spirit transforms us into a community of love, justice, compassion and courage. The community is then a sign of the presence of Jesus and the Spirit in the world.

→

4. The Catholic Church gives witness

The message of salvation, healing, forgiveness and love must be conveyed to the world by what the Church does as well as what it says. This is a difficult task that takes a lifetime to accomplish. To be faithful to the gospel means that we must live it. Catholics must always ask how we can best live the reality of Christ in our daily lives.

5. The Catholic Church serves

The Church follows the example of Jesus, who came not to rule but to serve. The Church exists for the sake of the kingdom of God – that God's Name be holy. By serving the people of the world, we draw nearer to the kingdom. We, as the Church, are expected to serve especially those who are most in need of help.

"If the hunger of others is not my own;
If the anguish of my neighbour in all its forms touches me not;
If the nakedness of my brother and sister does not torment me,
Then I have no reason to go to church or to live."

(Javier Torres, Nicaragua)

"I am the true vine, and my Father is the vine-grower. He removes every branch in me that bears no fruit. Every branch that bears fruit he prunes to make it bear more fruit.... Abide in me as I abide in you. Just as the branch cannot bear fruit by itself unless it abides in the vine, neither can you unless you abide in me. I am the vine, you are the branches. Those who abide in me and I in them bear much fruit, because apart from me you can do nothing."

(John 15.1-5)

The *Catechism of the Catholic Church* and the mission of the Church

"'This is the sole Church of Christ, which in the Creed we profess to be one, holy, catholic and apostolic.' These four characteristics, inseparably linked with each other, indicate essential features of the Church and her mission. The Church does not possess them of herself; it is Christ who, through the Holy Spirit, makes his Church one, holy, catholic and apostolic, and it is he who calls her to realize each of these qualities." (#811)

Theme 22

Encountering Christ in the sacraments

What do you do when Sunday morning comes around? Most people in our culture come up with quite a list of things that they consider to be more important than going to church. That is clear from statistics on church attendance, and by simple observation.

And yet, millions of people *do* go to church. They do give up their time for sleeping in or taking in some other activity because they believe it is important to do so. Faithful Christians have been doing so for two thousand years, and they will continue until the end of time. The fact that they go to church is a sign to the world that there is something going on in this weekly gathering.

The Church, the people of God, are saying that God is encountering them through their gathering and through the religious symbols and rituals of their tradition. Through the Church and the sacraments, God embraces all of creation in a personal way. When you go to church and take part in the life of the Church, you are part of that living sacrament. In this theme you will explore what this means.

Focus your learning

- **Aware and Informed**
  What is the meaning of "sacred mysteries"?

- **Practical and Active**
  How can the sacraments that I have celebrated become more meaningful for me?

- **Creative and Grateful**
  How can we encounter God in the Church?

Key terms

sacraments, or sacred mysteries

sacraments of initiation

sign

salvation

grace

Eucharist

liturgy

grace:

Grace describes God's kind, merciful and absolutely generous love for us. Grace shows itself in God's gifts of creation but particularly in the person of Jesus Christ. It is shown in the offer of a free and joyful new way of life opened up for us by Jesus Christ. As Paul writes in the Letter to Titus, in Jesus "the grace of God has appeared, bringing salvation to all" (2.11).

I remember it was hot

I was confirmed in Grade 6. My cousin George was my sponsor. I don't remember much about the experience, except that George drove in from out of town in his new car, that my parents bought me a nice new dress, and that we had a party after Mass. During the service, I remember the bishop smearing a lot of oil on my forehead. The cathedral was packed with people. I remember that it was very hot, and that the bishop and those helping him out at the altar looked uncomfortable in their heavy vestments. My cousin George didn't last long in his suit jacket either. I remember my dad preparing me and two of my friends for confirmation every Thursday evening for about four months. We would read stories from the Bible and talk about stuff. I don't remember my confirmation as being some great spiritual experience. I haven't really thought about it much, until you asked me.

What do you think?

When you think back to your confirmation, what do you remember?

How do you feel about your experience of confirmation?

How does your confirmation have ongoing bearing on your life? Explain.

Experience the mystery

When you go to the movies, you don't want to see the ending before the movie starts. When you watch a game on TV, you don't want to know the final score before the game ends. When you read a mystery novel, the fun of reading is all about being wrapped up in the mystery. Life is like that – a mystery to be experienced, day after day. Relationships are like that too – we continue to learn new things about the people we love year after year. And our faith is like that – we continue to deepen our sense of God as we bring our lives to God in prayer and worship.

We may have been confirmed a year or two or three ago, and our memory of the event may be fuzzy. The event itself may or may not have been memorable. However, it is part of our history, part of our experience, and we come to understand its meaning throughout the course of our lives.

The Church uses a word to describe the time after receiving a sacrament as *mystagogy*. Basically, the word means "living with the mystery." As you know, the sacraments are special moments in the life of the Church in which we encounter Christ. God reaches out to us through the signs, symbols and rituals of our religious tradition, and speaks to us through the Scriptures.

Remember the stories of Jesus and his disciples? Jesus taught his disciples for about three years, living and eating with them, and still they had trouble understanding his message. Only after Pentecost, when they received the Holy Spirit, did they begin to understand the significance of their relationship with Jesus. Then in the Acts of the Apostles, we read that they had to figure out a lot of things in the early days of the church. You could say they "lived their way into the answers." How? By accepting the mysteries of their faith, reflecting on them in the context of their lives, and praying together as a community. As Church, we continue to "live our way into the answers" – working to discern what the good news of Jesus means in our world today.

Think back to your confirmation, or to your first Communion or sacrament of reconciliation, or to the last time you went to Mass. What do you remember about the experience? Probably not a lot. The important thing to realize is that each time you celebrate a sacrament, you take a step deeper into the mystery of life with God. We experience the sacred mystery, in whatever capacity we are able, and spend the rest of our lives growing in it.

sacraments (sacred mysteries):

Sacraments are effective signs of God's saving actions in the world through the risen Lord, Christ Jesus. They have been instituted by Christ and entrusted to the Church. The purpose of the sacraments is to make us holy, to build up the body of Christ, and to give praise and worship to God.

- What does the word *mystagogy* mean?
- What are sacred mysteries?
- Why does the Church recognize that the time after receiving a sacrament is just as important as the sacramental ritual itself?
- If we are to grow in the appreciation of the sacred mysteries, what must we do?

sign:

Signs are objects or gestures that express a specific message or meaning. Sacraments, as "effective signs," bring about what they signify. For example, Eucharist *is* the body of Christ, and also *creates* the body of Christ, the Church.

We celebrate Jesus Christ in the sacraments

The section of the *Catechism of the Catholic Church* that deals with sacraments is called "The celebration of the Christian mystery." This means that we recognize that the life of the Church is a gift from God, a gift worth celebrating. But we do not and cannot understand it fully, because God is so much greater than we can imagine. We *celebrate* this mystery in the sacraments. It is in our nature to celebrate, especially key events of our lives. We celebrate birthdays, holidays, the end of school, marriages, etc. These events mean something to us, and by celebrating them, we share our stories and build community ties; we recognize and announce what is important in our lives and what gives us life and joy for living.

The way we celebrate the mystery of God in our lives goes back to the early Church. When they received the gift of the Holy Spirit at Pentecost, the disciples of Jesus recognized him as the human face of God. They saw that his actions and words revealed God to them. They had heard Jesus say, "Do this in memory of me." And so, from the beginning, the disciples baptized in the name of Jesus; they anointed new members of the community with oil as a sign of the Holy Spirit; they laid their hands on the heads of those who were chosen to be leaders in their communities and prayed over them; and they celebrated the Lord's supper, taking bread and wine, giving thanks, blessing, breaking, and sharing it among the members of the community. In other words, the early Church continued to do what Jesus had done. Jesus continued to be present to the community through these actions and words. Over time, these actions and words became formalized in symbols and rituals, and came to be called sacraments. The core of these sacraments continues to be Christ himself, acting in our lives today.

Can a celebration ever be bad?

Have you ever been bored in church? If a sacrament is a celebration of the mystery of God, can it ever be a bad celebration? Sometimes we do a really poor job at celebrating the mystery of God. However, does this mean that the sacraments "don't work" when they are poorly celebrated?

Think back on the life of Jesus. Can you think of a time when he turned anyone down? Did he ask for the best dishes and finest food when he visited with people? Did he spend his time only with the most gifted and most honourable people in his society? We know that Jesus was present to all who approached him. He even went looking for those who were outcasts. Do you think that Jesus would choose not to be present today, even in a celebration that we conduct poorly? Jesus promised his disciples, "where two or three are gathered in my name, I am there among them" (Matthew 18.20). While celebration is a human activity, God's presence in the sacraments is not a product of our ability to celebrate. It is not contingent upon the priest's ability to speak well, or the musicians' ability to play well. God's presence is a gift of the Holy Spirit.

So why have a lousy time when you can have a good time? What we bring to celebrations with our family and friends is no different from what we can bring to the celebration of the sacraments. When you are in a position of helping to prepare a celebration of the Eucharist, or when you celebrate prayer times throughout the year, perhaps you will have the opportunity to help make the celebration truly meaningful for those taking part by using the given rituals and symbols and readings in a way that really speaks to you. In fact, the *Catechism* says, "It is fitting that liturgical celebration… express itself in the culture of the people where the Church finds herself, though without being submissive to it. Moreover, the liturgy itself generates cultures and shapes them" (#1207). Most of the time, however, we come to church and take part in what has been prepared for us. Sometimes the liturgies are fantastic. Sometimes they lack imagination. But in all cases, we are invited to the celebration not to watch as outsiders, but to take part as valued members of the community.

- What makes for a good celebration at church?
- How do you think that Jesus would want to celebrate the sacraments with you? What do you think are the symbols and rituals that would not change? What do you think could change?

---

liturgy:

Liturgy is the common ritual prayer of the people of God, the official act of worship of the Church. The word "liturgy" originally meant a "public work." In Christian tradition it means the participation of the people of God in the "work of God." (See *Catechism* #1069-1075.)

Why seven?

God is present all the time. Whenever we turn to God in prayer, God is there. Even when we are not aware of it, God keeps us in existence. So why do we have seven sacraments?

Some things in life are landmark occasions, like being born. It is a unique and unrepeatable experience. The same goes for marriage. When you meet the love of your life, and pledge to love that person and to be faithful forever, that is a life-altering experience that we want to celebrate and share with the community. Sometimes we or someone close to us gets really sick, and we are reminded of our mortality in an up-close-and-personal way. Sometimes we sin, and sorely need reconciliation. Our life needs turning around. Some of us are called by God to be spiritual leaders in the Church. That too is a significant life experience. We all hunger, every day. This, as well, is significant. God has chosen to encounter us in a sacramental way in all of these significant events when the love and support of the community matters. In the Bible, the number seven is symbolic. It is often used to symbolize wholeness or completeness. In a way, having seven sacraments says that we encounter the love of God in all aspects of our lives. Jesus reveals God's love to people in the significant moments of their lives. By celebrating the seven sacraments, we do as Jesus did, proclaiming and celebrating God's total and unfailing love.

The seven sacraments

Baptism
Confirmation
Eucharist
Reconciliation
Anointing of the sick
Marriage
Holy orders

God communes with his people in particular ways, called sacred mysteries. And in each of these ways, Christ shares his life with us. For example, Christ offers to share his eternal life through the saving waters of baptism. He offers to share his life in the Spirit through his gifts in confirmation. He nurtures his life within us through the Bread of Life, the Eucharist. When we are broken spiritually or physically, he heals our lives through the sacraments of reconciliation and anointing of the sick. He offers us true freedom through our commitment to marriage or to the priesthood or to consecrated life. Just as Christ communes with each of us through these sacraments, he also brings us into communion with each other. In him, we all share one life, and one Spirit. As God communes with us in the sacred mysteries, we are brought into communion with each other.

sacraments of initiation

The sacraments of baptism, confirmation and Eucharist are known as the *sacraments of initiation*. They initiate us into the mysteries of Christ. Through them, we become full members of the Catholic Church.

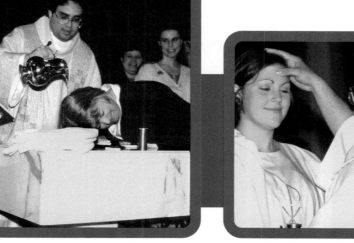

The Eucharist

The *Eucharist* is at the centre of Christian life. "In the blessed Eucharist is contained the whole spiritual good of the Church, namely Christ himself…" (*Catechism*, #1324). To understand what this means, it may be helpful to recall a scripture story that takes place after Jesus' death and resurrection. *Read Luke 24.13-35.*

"Were not our hearts burning within us?"

"Jesus is not here, he is risen!" On that Sunday when the message of Easter was heard for the first time, two disciples of Jesus were on their way to Emmaus. Cleopas and his companion had heard the message from the women who visited the tomb, but they could not accept this astonishing news. Their day and their journey were engulfed by sadness. Jesus, the one they had hoped for as the way to God, had died gruesomely on a cross. In despair, they were leaving Jerusalem, their hearts heavy with snuffed-out hopes and memories of the events of the last few days. For them, the dream had ended. They were returning home to Emmaus, probably to pick up the pieces of their lives. They were hardly expecting what was to happen to them next.

Without them knowing what was taking place, the risen Jesus met them on their way. They thought they knew Jesus. After all, they had walked with him from his baptism in the Jordan to the cross in Jerusalem. As they made their way to Emmaus, this "stranger" revealed himself in word, explaining the Scriptures to them. The two disciples were clearly searching for God. They looked for God in their holy books, in the same way we do today. Jesus gave them a key to understanding the sacred Scriptures in a new way. He showed how God had been involved in the story of their past. Jesus told them the story of Moses and the prophets, and how Jesus was part of that same story of God in our world. At the end of their journey, they saw Jesus in a new light. At the end of the day, they invited the supposed stranger to share a meal with them. During the meal, Jesus "took bread, blessed and broke it, and gave it to them" (Luke 24.30). In the time of Luke, the "breaking of the bread" was the name for Eucharist or the Mass. In that action, the disciples recognized Jesus.

Jesus walks with us on our road through life too. Sometimes, like the disciples, we don't recognize him. But like the disciples, we can meet him in the Eucharist. This is why the Eucharist is the central sacrament of our Church.

salvation:

The Church proclaims that we are made whole through faith in God. The Church believes that through our attachment and trust in God, particularly through our faith in Jesus Christ, human beings are set on the path of fullness of life. Belief in salvation is at the heart of religion. The Church is an effective sign of salvation for us.

Stop and reflect

- In what way do the events in this story mirror the different events or parts of the Mass: gathering; being reconciled to one another; reading of the Scriptures; blessing, breaking and sharing the bread and wine; being sent out to serve?
- What does this story tell you about Christ being really present in the bread and wine of the Eucharist?

Celebrating Eucharist today

Every Sunday we do as Jesus commanded his disciples: "Do this in memory of me." We listen to the Scriptures and say a prayer of praise. Over the gifts of bread, the priest repeats the words of Jesus, "Take this, all of you, and eat it: this is my body which will be given up for you." And taking the cup of wine, "Take this, all of you, and drink from it: this is the cup of my blood, the blood of the new and everlasting covenant. It will be shed for you and for all so that sins may be forgiven. Do this in memory of me." This has been done for two thousand years. Every day for two thousand years, Jesus Christ has been present to his followers in the Eucharist, and through his followers to the whole world.

In the celebration of the Eucharist, we listen to the Scriptures. As one of the ancient prophets wrote (see Ezekiel 3.1-3), we "eat" the Word of God so that it can become part of us. We want the Word to enter into our every cell. We bring gifts of bread and wine, money for the poor and for the community. We give praise and thanks to God for the gifts of creation, for God's covenant with people everywhere, and for giving us Jesus and the Spirit to make us holy. We eat and we drink the Lord in the gifts that the Spirit transformed into the body and blood of Christ. Each time that we celebrate the Eucharist, the Holy Spirit draws us more deeply into the mystery of Christ.

Our eucharistic celebration

Gathering

The opening rite is a gathering and welcoming rite. We come together from our workplaces, our homes and our day-to-day activities to worship. We celebrate that we are one because of what God has done in Christ Jesus.

Thus we welcome one another in the name of God who gathers us. Only after we are properly welcomed in God's name are we ready to hear the word of God. The faithful take on the form of a worshipping community.

In planning and preparing for the gathering, we must ask ourselves some questions: How can we make people feel welcome? How can we encourage them to welcome one another? How can we help them to be aware of God's presence as the one who gathers us together?

RITUAL ELEMENTS	MEANING AND FUNCTION
Opening Song	Opens the celebration and leads our thoughts to what we are celebrating. It helps those gathered feel more united.
Entrance Procession	The entrance procession may involve all those with a special role in the liturgy. Special objects to be used in the celebration (e.g., a cross, the lectionary, incense, candles, banners, flowers) may be carried in the entrance procession. Symbols which represent the community which is gathering may also be carried in. On special occasions, such as Passion (Palm) Sunday and the Easter Vigil, the entire assembly may take part in the procession. The entrance procession helps set the tone for the celebration. It is also a visible reminder that coming together in one place is part of our worship.
Sign of the Cross/Amen	All Christian worship is done in the name of the Father, Son and Holy Spirit. All make the sign of the cross.
Greeting/Response	This greeting can take one of several forms. In each form, we are reminded that God is with us and always will be. →

RITUAL ELEMENTS	MEANING AND FUNCTION
Penitential Rite and the Lord Have Mercy or the Sprinkling Rite	The community seeks reconciliation with one another and with God. This rite can take one of several forms. We may name our sins and ask for the prayers of those around us; we may praise God because we know that God is merciful and then ask for God's mercy; or we may use the rite of blessing and sprinkling holy water to celebrate the new life we have in Christ that is free from sin. The sprinkling rite is a reminder of our baptismal call. God cleansed us from sin when we were baptized. God cleanses us from sin each time we truly repent and seek forgiveness. Each option ends with a prayer of forgiveness.
Gloria	An ancient Christian hymn of praise and thanksgiving. Singing the Gloria adds to the spirit of the season. It is especially appropriate at Christmas, Easter, feast days and special occasions.
Opening Prayer Silence/Amen	This is the "collect" or gathering prayer. Some people say that this is the only part of the introductory rites that can't be left out. After a moment of silent prayer in which the whole community prays for its concerns, this prayer gathers these concerns and presents them to the Father through Jesus' name in the Holy Spirit.

The Liturgy of the Word (Listening)

During the Liturgy of the Word, the Church proclaims the word of God in the midst of the assembled people. The people listen attentively. In a sense, they huddle around God's story.

As liturgy planners, our prime goal here is to help the gathered community hear God's call, to provide a setting in which God's word can enter into us and begin to call up its own response.

RITUAL ELEMENTS	MEANING AND FUNCTION
First Reading	A proclamation from the Old Testament. This reading is chosen to shed light on the gospel. During the Easter season, the readings are from the Book of Revelation and the Acts of the Apostles.
Responsorial Psalm/Refrain	A psalm that reflects the spirit of the first reading. The psalm is best sung.
Second Reading	A proclamation from the letters of the New Testament. The New Testament reading is part of a continuous reading of a particular book.
Gospel Acclamation/Alleluia (or alternative) The Lord be with you...and also with you	We welcome the word of God joyfully by singing an alleluia or other acclamation.
Gospel	A proclamation from one of the gospels as word of God.
Homily	The homily is a key part of the liturgy and is necessary for the nurturing of Christian life. The homily interprets the word of God for today and leads the community to give praise and thanks to God.

→

RITUAL ELEMENTS	MEANING AND FUNCTION
Profession of Faith	The Creed or profession of faith helps the people respond and agree to the word of God. It forms them to call to mind the truths of faith. The Creed is a remembering of God's acts in history.
General Intercessions or Prayers of the Faithful	This is an act of the whole community. It offers to the Lord the world, which the community is sent to serve. Petitions are usually offered in this order: 1. for the needs of the Church 2. for public authorities and the salvation of the world 3. for those oppressed by any need 4. for the local community.

The Liturgy of the Eucharist (Giving Praise and Thanks)

The basic pattern of the Liturgy of the Eucharist, inherited from the Lord himself at the Last Supper and from the apostolic Church, consists of four parts:

- the Lord took bread and wine – we take bread and wine (presentation of gifts)
- he said the prayers of blessing – we pray the prayer of thanksgiving (eucharistic prayer)
- he broke the bread – we break bread (in preparation for communion)
- he gave the broken bread and the cup to his disciples – we share the one bread and the one cup (communion)

The eucharistic prayer is the centre and high point of the whole celebration. It is a prayer of thanksgiving and sanctification.

RITUAL ELEMENTS	MEANING AND FUNCTION
Preparation of the Altar and Presentation of the Gifts	Before beginning the eucharistic action, we prepare the table. The gifts are then brought forward. A collection for the poor and for other needs is taken up at this time. We prepare for the eucharistic prayer and pray that the Lord will accept the prayer and the gifts, to the glory of God's name. The simple prayers over the gifts are modelled on Jewish blessings.
The Eucharistic Prayer	There are nine different eucharistic prayers: four that may be used for any occasion, two for Masses of reconciliation, and three for Masses with children. All of the eucharistic prayers begin with a preface addressed to God the Father. The preface praises God for what has been accomplished in Christ. Following the preface, everyone sings the Sanctus (Holy, Holy, Holy). This hymn reflects Isaiah 6.3 and Psalm 118.26. The whole community joins in the praise of God. In each eucharistic prayer, we ask God to bless the gifts we offer, and recall what Christ did at the Last Supper. The different eucharistic prayers focus on different aspects of the mystery of salvation. It would be impossible to tell in a short time all that God has done for us. Each eucharistic prayer looks at one or two aspects of what God has done for us.

→

RITUAL ELEMENTS	MEANING AND FUNCTION
The Eucharistic Prayer (continued)	The choice of eucharistic prayers depends on the aspect of salvation and our relationship with God that is being looked at during the Mass.
	Eucharistic Prayer I emphasizes the unity of the Church throughout the world and through history. This prayer reminds us of and celebrates our taking part in the community of saints.
	Eucharistic Prayer II sums up all that God has done for us in the person of Jesus. It is a good reminder of the importance of Jesus and how what he has done affects our lives.
	Eucharistic Prayer III focuses on our relationship with Jesus and on how Jesus' sacrifice helps us to reconnect with the Father. When we use this prayer, we call to mind our dependence on God.
	Eucharistic Prayer IV offers the most complete summary of salvation. It reminds us of God's faithfulness and love throughout history. This prayer stresses the hope that God offers to those who need it the most.
	The two eucharistic prayers for Masses of reconciliation stress God's healing and forgiving love. The first talks about healing our broken relationship with God. The second focuses on how God helps us to end divisions among people and to restore peace.
	The three eucharistic prayers for children use simple language to summarize what God has done for us and what God calls us to do. The first of these three prayers focuses on how Jesus acted when he was on earth. The second looks at what Jesus taught us about how we should act. The third stresses that God will help us to get along with each other and to make the world a better place.
	After the priest proclaims the words that Jesus spoke at the Last Supper, the community responds with a proclamation of assent called the memorial acclamation. There are several choices for this acclamation.
	The eucharistic prayer ends with praise to God, through Christ, in the Spirit. This is one of the high points of the eucharistic prayer. That is why it is important for the community to listen to the doxology and then give assent by singing Amen (So be it).

Communion Rite

RITUAL ELEMENTS	MEANING AND FUNCTION
Lord's Prayer, Rite of Peace	Before we break bread together and eat and drink of the same loaf and cup, we express unity with one another. For that reason we pray the Lord's Prayer and exchange peace. These are acts of communion.
Breaking of the Bread	This is a key action of the celebration: we all eat from the one bread which is Christ. During the breaking of the bread, the "Lamb of God" is sung.
This is the Lamb of God... Lord, I am not Worthy	Priest and people prepare themselves to receive Christ's body and blood. We respond to the invitation to communion with a prayer of humility and hope.
Communion	We receive the body and blood of Christ. During this time we meditate in song and silence.

Dismissal Rite (Going Forth)

The dismissal or concluding rite consists of

a) the priest's greeting and blessing;

b) the dismissal of the community, which sends each person back to doing good works, while praising and blessing the Lord.

RITUAL ELEMENTS	MEANING AND FUNCTION
Blessing/Amen	The final blessing can be given in a simple or more complex form. The more complex form reminds the assembly of some of the things God has done for them and names a particular hope connected with the focus of the day's Mass.
Dismissal/ Thanks be to God	The liturgy always concludes with the trinitarian blessing. (We are blessed in the name of the Father, and of the Son and of the Holy Spirit.) We are reminded to go forth and live according to the words and actions we have celebrated.
Closing Song	The closing song and procession remind us that we are sent out into the world to share the Good News we have received.

Stop and reflect

- How does Jesus feed me in my life?
- How has Jesus' gift of himself strengthened me to give of myself to others?

For I received from the Lord what I also handed on to you, that the Lord Jesus on the night when he was betrayed took a loaf of bread, and when he had given thanks, he broke it and said, "This is my body that is for you. Do this in remembrance of me." In the same way he took the cup also, after supper, saying, "This cup is the new covenant in my blood. Do this, as often as you drink it, in remembrance of me." For as often as you eat this bread and drink the cup, you proclaim the Lord's death until he comes.

(1 Corinthians 11.23-26)

Unit 7 review

In this unit, you explored how the work of Jesus continues in the world through the Catholic Church.

Aware and Informed

How is the Catholic Church an effective sign of Christ in today's world?
Jesus proclaimed the good news of God by his parables, by healing those who were ill, by forgiving sins, and by casting out evil spirits. When he died and rose, he poured out on his followers the Holy Spirit. Now Jesus' disciples were to take on the mission of proclaiming the kingdom of God. This is the Church – the people gathered by Christ and filled with the Holy Spirit, who now continue Christ's mission. Christ is present in the world through the Church. We are the body of Christ.

What is the mission of the Catholic Church?
The Church's mission is based on the life, death and resurrection of Jesus Christ. The Church proclaims Jesus Christ, worships Christ through the sacraments, forms a communion of people, gives witness to the gospel, and serves those in need.

What is the meaning of "sacred mysteries"?
The "sacred mysteries," or sacraments, are effective signs of God's saving actions in the world through the risen Lord, Christ Jesus. They have been instituted by Christ and entrusted to the Church. The purpose of the sacraments is to make us holy, to build up the body of Christ, and to give praise and worship to God.

Practical and Active

How does God work through us?
As we gather to celebrate the sacred mysteries in the liturgy, the Holy Spirit works through the gathering to reconcile us. Through the sacraments, Jesus Christ gives himself to the community. The Holy Spirit gives us the grace to live as Jesus lived, to serve as Jesus served, to love as Jesus loved. As we do so, the Holy Spirit shapes our community into the image and likeness of Christ.

As a member of the Catholic Church, what am I supposed to do?
Jesus says, "I am the true vine, and my father is the vinegrower… You are the branches. Those who abide in me and I in them bear much fruit, because apart from me you can do nothing." Each of us is called to communion with Christ, and to serve others according to what has been given us. We have been given different talents and gifts, so that all of us, by giving what we can of ourselves, "bear fruit."

How can the sacraments that I have celebrated become more meaningful for me?
The Catholic Church uses the word *mystagogy* to describe the time after receiving a sacrament. Basically, the word means "living with the mystery." The sacraments are special moments in the life of the Church in which we encounter Christ. The time after the celebration is for reflecting on what has taken place and "living our way" into the sacred mystery. It is important to reflect often on the meaning of the sacraments we have received.

Creative and Grateful

You can answer these questions for yourself. The answer is found in your relationship with God.

What difference does our participation in the Church make?

How does Jesus work through me and the Christian community?

How can we encounter God in the Church?

Unit 8

Relating to the world: Disciples and witnesses

Aim: to explore the call to bear witness to Christ in the world

Theme 23

Bearing witness to Christ

You never know how your actions and your presence will affect someone. For example, at one birthday celebration, the guests were invited to say a few words about what the person who was celebrating the birthday meant to them. The 18 guests each told a story of how this person affected their lives. They spoke of friendship, of healing and inspiration. They told funny stories and some heroic tales. Each one had been moved in some way by the life of this person. They could not have given a better birthday gift to their friend, since people aren't always aware of their impact on others.

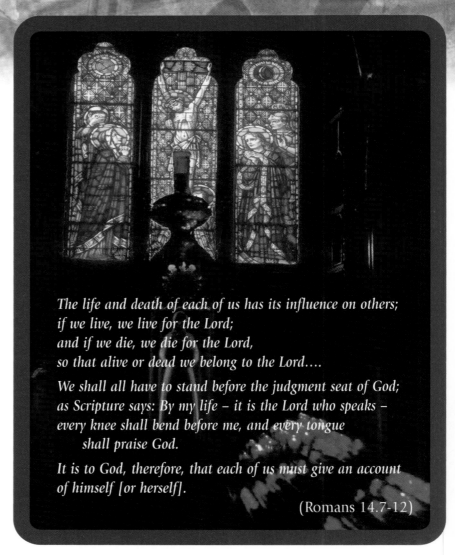

The life and death of each of us has its influence on others;
if we live, we live for the Lord;
and if we die, we die for the Lord,
so that alive or dead we belong to the Lord....

We shall all have to stand before the judgment seat of God;
as Scripture says: By my life – it is the Lord who speaks –
every knee shall bend before me, and every tongue
     shall praise God.

It is to God, therefore, that each of us must give an account
of himself [or herself].

(Romans 14.7-12)

If our lives can have such an effect on others, even when we may not be trying, just think of what is possible when we act intentionally! Christ calls us to follow him, just as he had called his disciples. Christ calls us into the world to be "salt of the earth, and light for the world." In this theme, you will explore what it means to "set the whole world ablaze" with the good news of God's kingdom.

Focus your learning

- **Aware and Informed**
  What is witness?

- **Practical and Active**
  How can I live my baptismal calling?

- **Creative and Grateful**
  How does God call out the best in each one of us?

Key terms

baptism, confirmation, Eucharist

communion of saints

witness

vocation

"I barely knew Marchelle, but when she noticed that I couldn't go to the school semi-formal because I couldn't afford a dress, she offered me one of her own. I was really touched. The fact that she cared enough to do that made me rethink how I judge others." – Samantha

"I changed my mind about my coach when he stopped by to see me when I was in a slump. I had thought that all he cared about was winning. I saw another side of him when he took the time to find out about the other things going on in my life." – Josh

"Going to World Youth Day in Rome was just the most amazing thing. Being in a crowd with two million other young Catholics for the closing Mass was a life-changing experience. I now realize that I am part of something huge. My faith connects me not only to God, but also to people all over the world." – Brittany

"The young people bring life to our parish. We need them and want them. When I see young people coming to Mass, doing the readings, and even just being there, this helps me to get over those days when my own faith gets a bit lukewarm and starts to falter." – George (a 72-year-old)

"When I see my parents kiss and make up after an argument, my respect for them grows. When I get married and have a family of my own, I hope that I can be as flexible and forgiving as they are." – Sophie

What do you think?

These people describe experiences from their lives that have made a difference to them. How have little things that others have done made a positive difference in your life?

George says that all that the young people have to do is show up, and that makes a big difference for him. Have you ever had the experience of someone telling you that something you did meant a whole lot to them, even if you could barely remember doing it?

Have you heard the expression, "You can talk the talk, but can you walk the talk?" What do you think it means for a Christian "to walk the talk"?

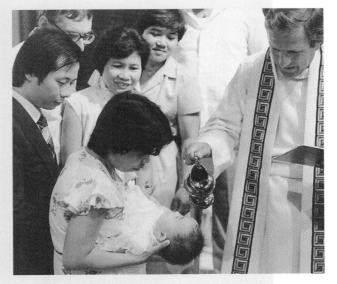

Called to bear witness to the truth

The sacraments of baptism, confirmation and Eucharist initiate us into a way of life. Through them, we are connected to Christ and are called, not just to believe the Truth (that is, Christ) in our hearts, but also to live out what we believe. Through these sacraments, we become what St. Paul calls a "new creation" (2 Corinthians 5.17). They transform us into "ambassadors" of Christ for our culture and the world.

Through the grace of baptism, each of us becomes "a new creature" – an adopted son or daughter of God, a member of Christ and a co-heir with him. We are freed from sin, and are enabled to believe in God, to hope in God, and to love God. We are given the power to live as children of God through the gifts of the Holy Spirit. And we are given the grace to grow in goodness and love as members of the body of Christ. (See *Catechism*, #1262-1270.)

In confirmation, we are anointed with sacred oil. This is a sign that we are sealed with the Holy Spirit. (A seal is a symbol of authenticity, of personal authority. For example, a passport carries an official seal, showing that this person is an authentic citizen of a country.) This seal of the Holy Spirit marks our total belonging to Christ and our enrolment in his service forever. It is also a promise that God will protect us and give us the strength we need to be faithful followers and witnesses of Christ. (See *Catechism*, #1293-1305.)

In the Eucharist, we share in the body and blood of Christ. Christ unites us with himself completely. He sustains us when we hunger for meaning, and nourishes us so that we have the strength and courage to remain faithful. Jesus offered his life on the cross; in the Eucharist we find the grace to offer our lives for what we believe in. Jesus promised to be with us always, and to never leave us

communion of saints:

The Church is the assembly of all the saints, both those living now and those who "sleep in the peace of Christ" (*Catechism*, #955). Christians form a body, a communion, around the person of Christ. There they receive the holy things of God. As the Eastern Church proclaims when the gifts of bread and wine are shown to the people: "God's holy gifts for God's holy people." Christians believe that all the living and the dead remain in this union with Christ.

alone. He sends the Holy Spirit to unite us as the body of Christ, the Church. In the celebration of the Eucharist, we are sent forth to serve the poor and to bear witness to Christ. (See *Catechism*, #1391-1398.)

Through these sacraments, we have been greatly blessed. But a blessing is not for putting away for safekeeping; it is for giving away so that it may bear fruit. Jesus used many images to teach about how God works in our lives: God's presence is like a seed that grows, like salt that gives things flavour, like a light on a stand that lights up the darkness, and like yeast that makes the entire loaf rise. We, in turn, are to be all of these things to others: We are called to be witness to Christ by bringing life to our culture and giving it flavour, by lighting up the darkness, and, like yeast, by enlivening those around us.

For your journal

To be a witness means getting involved. As Catholics, we are to bear witness to Jesus Christ within our culture. Sometimes this means challenging the values in our culture that harm people. Identify some aspects of culture that you feel ought to be supported or ones that ought to be challenged based on what Christ taught. What could be done about the aspects that need to be challenged?

On witnessing

A witness is someone who gives testimony about the truth. In court cases, we call on witnesses when evidence is needed. In matters of faith, where we do not see or have immediate evidence, a witness is someone who by his or her life gives testimony to their beliefs. In our culture, many people doubt the truth of Jesus Christ. Christians may feel quite lonely, and even be ridiculed or persecuted in trying to uphold what they believe.

We need witnesses of Jesus Christ in order to show to the world that faith is life-giving. How then can we be witnesses? A person who has suffered intensely can be a witness of the ultimate goodness and graciousness of life and the power of the suffering and death of Jesus. A mother or a father can be a witness of the truth of self-giving love, following the example of Jesus. A doctor can be a witness to the truth of the inviolable value of human life. And a Christian can be a witness, even in the most ordinary circumstances of life, to the truth of Jesus Christ. These people show by their lives that Christ is here. They are now the hands and feet of Christ, living out their conviction in what they do, in their outlook on life, in their hopes, and in their relationships. The more this faith takes hold, the more Christians become a living conviction, a living symbol of a gift. They become a sacrament of Christ, helping other people to encounter Christ in the most ordinary circumstances and events of daily life. For some, this witness to Christ in daily living is such an important truth that they are willing to give their very lives. Faith is of greater value than life itself. A martyr is such a witness of the truth and reality of God.

A cloud of witnesses

Dietrich Bonhoeffer was a passionate pastor in the Lutheran Church. He died in a German concentration camp in 1945, just before it was liberated. In his book *Life Together*, he wrote: "In a Christian community everything depends upon whether each individual is an indispensable link in a chain. Only when even the smallest link is securely interlocked is the chain unbreakable. Every Christian community must realize that not only do the weak need the strong, but also the strong cannot exist without the weak. The elimination of the weak is the death of fellowship."

We, as Church, are a community of the strong and the weak. We are a mosaic that needs the witness of all to be complete. Each individual Christian has something to add to the mosaic that no one else can. In the stories that follow, we turn to people whose actions were motivated by what they recognized as God's summons. They fulfilled what the Vatican Council said about holiness: "all the faithful of Christ of whatever rank or status are called to the fullness of the Christian life and to the perfection of charity. By this holiness a more human way of life is promoted." (Dogmatic Constitution on the Church, #40)

The Catholic Worker Movement was founded by Dorothy Day and Peter Maurin in 1933. It is grounded in a firm belief in the God-given dignity of every human person. Together, Dorothy and Peter published a newspaper, *The Catholic Worker*, and began a "house of hospitality," a place of welcome for the homeless. Today there are more than 175 Catholic Worker communities. They remain committed to non-violence, voluntary poverty, prayer, and hospitality for the homeless, the exiled, the hungry and the forsaken. Catholic Workers continue to protest injustice, war, racism and violence of all forms. This text is reprinted from *Dorothy Day Library on the Web* at URL www.catholicworker.org.

In the postscript to her autobiography, *The Long Loneliness*, Dorothy reflects on how the Catholic Worker movement grew:

Dorothy Day – The Postscript from *The Long Loneliness*

We were just sitting there talking when lines of people began to form, saying, "We need bread." We could not say, "Go, be thou filled." If there were six small loaves and a few fishes, we had to divide them. There was always bread.

We were just sitting there talking and people moved in on us. Let those who can take it, take it. Some moved out and that made room for more. And somehow the walls expanded.

We were just sitting there talking and someone said, "Let's all go live on a farm."

It was as casual as all that, I often think. It just came about. It just happened.

I found myself, a barren woman, the joyful mother of children. It is not easy always to be joyful, to keep in mind the duty of delight.

The most significant thing about *The Catholic Worker* is poverty, some say.

The most significant thing is community, others say. We are not alone any more.

But the final word is love. At times it has been, in the words of Father Zossima, a harsh and dreadful thing, and our very faith in love has been tried through fire.

We cannot love God unless we love each other, and to love we must know each other. We know Him in the breaking of bread, and we know each other in the breaking of bread, and we are not alone any more. Heaven is a banquet and life is a banquet, too, even with a crust, where there is companionship.

We have all known the long loneliness and we have learned that the only solution is love and that love comes in community.

It all happened while we sat there talking, and it is still going on.

Stanley Vishnewski, one of the early Catholic Workers in New York, recounts his first meeting with one of the founders of the Catholic Worker movement:

"The Day I Met Peter Maurin"

By Stanley Vishnewski

Taken from Wings of the Dawn *by Stanley Vishnewski and reprinted in* The Catholic Worker, *May 1976, pp.1,5. (www.catholicworker.org)*

The door opened. An old man came in. He wore a shabby, ill-fitting suit and heavy hobnailed shoes.[1] His pockets bulged with newspapers and pamphlets. I remember how the hobnails in his shoes clattered against the wooden floor, as he went past us without speaking. I had the impression that he did not see us.

"That's Peter Maurin," Mary Sheehan said. "He writes the Easy Essays for the paper. He lives up in Harlem."

I looked at the doorway through which the man had gone. I had thought that he was some "tramp" who had come in looking for something to eat.

Mary Sheehan must have sensed what I was thinking. "Peter doesn't care how he looks," she said. "He always has his nose stuck in a book. But what a brain he has. He knows everything about history. He could make a lot of money as a teacher."

"Where are you going?" Mary Sheehan asked.

"Home," I said.

She looked surprised. "Don't you want to eat with us? Its

___
[1] hobnail: a heavy-headed nail used for boot soles

almost five o'clock. Margaret expects you to stay for supper. We will be eating in a few minutes."

Peter Maurin was already sitting at the table. He was reading a pamphlet. Mary sat down next to him.

"Sit here," Margaret told me. "I'll put the food out." I noticed that there was an extra plate at the table. Margaret must have read my thoughts. "That's the Christ plate. We always set an extra place for anyone who comes."

I had not yet been introduced to Peter but he did not wait for an introduction. At that moment his face became alive and animated. He pointed his finger at me and said, "In the first centuries of Christianity the poor were fed, clothed and sheltered at a personal sacrifice and the Pagans said about the Christians: 'See how they love each other.'"

"Today," he continued, "the poor are fed, clothed and sheltered by the politicians at the expense of the taxpayers.

"And because the poor are no longer fed, clothed and sheltered at a personal sacrifice but at the expense of the taxpayers, Pagans say about the Christians: 'See how they pass the buck.'"

Peter spoke in a rhythmical sing-song. At that time I did not realize that he was reciting one of his own Easy Essays, but I had the feeling that he was quoting from something that had already been written. When he finished, he stared at me as if waiting for me to comment on what he had just said.

Margaret saved me from my embarrassment by asking Peter to say Grace. I bowed my head until it almost touched the plate. The meal consisted of meatballs, mashed potatoes, string beans, mushrooms, gravy, coffee, bread, butter and more slabs of apple pie.

"Someone gave us the food." Margaret said. "We have to finish everything up or else it will spoil."

Peter had moved his chair in order to be closer to me. Margaret and Mary cleared the table and began to wash the dishes. Peter talked as though addressing an audience. He raised his voice slightly. He mentioned names of saints I had never heard of before.

Peter said, "In the Catholic Worker we must try to have the voluntary poverty of St. Francis, the charity of St. Vincent de Paul, the intellectual approach of St. Dominic, the easy conversations about things that matter of St. Philip Neri, the manual labour of St. Benedict.'"

As Peter talked he rocked back and forth in his chair. Every once in a while, to emphasize a point, he would lean over and tap me on the knee. The wrinkles on his face seemed to move up and down as he kept talking. ➡

I finally asked the question that was on my mind. "What is the purpose of the Catholic Worker?"

To this day I do not know what colour his eyes were but I know that he looked at me more intently than anybody had ever looked at me before. Peter leaped up from his chair. He looked down at me.

"The purpose of the Catholic Worker," he said, "is to create a society where it will be easier for men to be good. A society where each person will consider himself to be his brother's keeper. A society where each one will try to serve. And to be the least. God wants us to be our brother's keeper. He wants us to feed the hungry at a personal sacrifice. He wants us to clothe the naked at a personal sacrifice. He wants us to shelter the homeless. To serve man for God's sake, that is what God wants us to do!"

"We need enthusiasm," Peter said. "Nothing can be accomplished in the work of social reconstruction without enthusiasm."

I was happy to hear Peter say this. I realized that the only talent I had to offer was enthusiasm, enthusiasm and still more enthusiasm!

- How did each of these individuals encounter Christ in the events of his or her particular life?
- What was remarkable about their lives?
- What did they contribute to the world?
- Can you imagine yourself in similar circumstances? What would you do?
- Why did they witness to Christ the way they did?

It's up to us

In his homily at the closing Mass of World Youth Day 2000 in Rome, Pope John Paul II said to the two million young people gathered there: "As I look at you now, at your young faces, at your genuine enthusiasm, from the depths of my heart I want to give thanks to God for the gift of youth, which continues to be present in the Church and in the world because of you....

"You will carry the proclamation of Christ into the new millennium. When you return home, do not grow lax. Reinforce and deepen your bond with the Christian communities to which you belong.... Paraphrasing Saint Catherine of Siena's words... 'If you are what you should be, you will set the whole world ablaze!'

"I look with confidence to this new humanity which you are now helping to prepare. I look to this Church which in every age is made youthful by the Spirit of Christ and today is made happy by your intentions and commitment...."

At the end of the gathering in Rome, Pope John Paul II announced that Toronto and the Church of Canada would welcome the young people of the world in 2002. As the theme for the event, he chose the text of Matthew 5.13-14: "You are salt of the earth..., you are light for the world." He made it clear that it is our task, with the help of the Holy Spirit, to bring Christ to our culture, and to set the world ablaze with the good news of God's kingdom.

"Last year our school built a team of students to work together in raising the awareness of social justice within our school community. In February, our team spent 10 eye-opening days in Nicaragua where we tried so hard to immerse ourselves in this new culture. I have been deeply blessed in my calling to be part of that team. There were two very important things that brought me to this involvement: first, my deep desire to empathize with others and second, my openness to hear Christ's voice in my life.

"I learned about love, charity, humility, faith and community. The poor people whom I met and lived with clearly illustrated the true meaning of community. The compassion and loving care they held for each other... was their strength. Each person we met welcomed us. My experience in Nicaragua not only opened my eyes, but warmed my heart. Mother Teresa said that good works are links that form a chain of love. This goal is one that we can realize in our everyday lives."

Amanda (Caledon East, Ontario)

"I have been part of and experienced many faith journeys of young people. The young people in St. Dominic's Youth Ministry continue to be part of regular Sunday Eucharist, not because they are forced, but because they want to. They know that they belong to a larger faith community. These young people are ministers of the word, ministers of hospitality; they witness at the confirmation programs, lead and go on retreats, work in the parish office, mow the church grounds, lead the children's Liturgy of the Word, and babysit during Mass. They play for the choir, sit on the Parish Pastoral Council, and are ministers of the Eucharist – in short, they serve. They dramatize the Good Friday stations of the cross, participate in justice and service projects, prepare school kits for the Free the Children organization, collect canned goods for the hungry, prepare and give out sandwiches to the homeless as part of a Street Patrol, etc. It is any one and all of these experiences that have allowed them to meet Jesus. Their Church experience has become meaningful and rich. In all that they do, they are great faith witnesses to the parish."

Dee

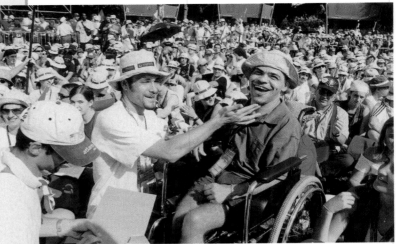

"I grew up Catholic. I went to a Catholic elementary school, a Catholic high school and even a Catholic university. Even though you might say that I was 'surrounded by my faith,' I struggled throughout the years (and even to this day) to try to understand what it meant to be 'Christian' and what role my Catholic faith played for me in my everyday life. Growing up I always felt that 'church' (the institution and its rules) was really empty. It just didn't speak to me as a young woman. In my mind, there had to be more to being Catholic than just attending Catholic institutions. If that was *all* that being Catholic meant, then I definitely didn't want to be Catholic or a Christian.

"This began to change when I graduated from university and worked at a place called Romero House. Romero House is an organization of lay persons who work and live with the needy/dependent of the community. It was here that I began to understand the true meaning of being Catholic and recognized what was missing from my experience of Christian Church. Although I had always been involved in social justice issues while growing up, it never occurred to me that God was directing my actions to do this type of work. It wasn't until I experienced a faith community of people who believed that part of being Christian was to actively live out their faith that I realized that God had a purpose for me too. This gave me much strength and courage. Working with refugees in a faith community made me *want* to be Catholic and to be part of a Christian experience."

Victoria

Supreme witness

Speaking to a group of more than a thousand young people packing a church in Rome during World Youth Day 2000, Bishop Diarmuid Martin of the Pontifical Council for Justice and Peace at the Vatican called on the young people to aspire to be martyrs. To be a martyr for Christ requires a lifelong commitment to be ready and willing to give of ourselves in love. Being a martyr is not a spur of the moment decision. It is an ability that is built up through daily prayer and a life of love. To be a martyr, in this sense, is to give oneself over completely in faith to Christ. For most people most of the time, this means living the life of a committed Christian. For some, it means having to choose between their faith and their life.

The *Catechism of the Catholic Church* describes martyrdom as the supreme witness given to the truth of the faith: it means continuing to bear witness even if the consequence is death. Martyrs bear witness to Christ who died and rose, and to the truth of the faith and of Christian doctrine. A martyr gives up his or her life rather than his or her faith. Faith is of greater value than life itself. (See *Catechism*, #2473.) ➔

Stop and reflect
- How are these young people responding to the call of the Church to witness within our culture?
- What contribution can you make?

Did you know?

…that the Vatican has documented 13,400 cases of Catholics who have given their lives for their faith in the twentieth century? Archbishop Michel Hrynchyshyn, chair of the Vatican Commission for New Martyrs said that the twentieth century will go down in history as "an era of martyrs."

At the World Youth Day vigil in Rome, where two million young people gathered to pray, the Holy Father said, "To believe in Jesus today… demands of us, just as it did in the past, that we take a stand for him, almost to the point at times of a new martyrdom: the martyrdom of those who, today as yesterday, are called to go against the tide in order to follow the divine Master…. Perhaps you will not have to shed your blood, but you will certainly be asked to be faithful to Christ! A faithfulness to be lived in the circumstances of everyday life."

Bishop Martin concluded his talk with a challenge to the young people: "When you go home, I hope that you can all say to your friends and families, 'I want to be a martyr' – a consummate witness to the love and mercy of God every day of your lives, a calling of great joy."

Giving supreme witness does not mean seeking death in order to give glory to God. Supreme witness means seeking life – for all people – to the full, in faith, hope and love, whatever the consequences.

Theme 24

Social witness in Canada

For several years running, the United Nations has named Canada as the best place in the world to live. (This is according to the UN human development index, which includes criteria such as life expectancy, level of education and standard of living.) Part of the reason that Canada has achieved this status is the involvement of its citizens in working for justice and human development within their communities. Even so, many Canadians continue to suffer the effects of poverty and discrimination. We are all called to do more.

In this theme, you will explore social issues in Canada that call for a response grounded in the kind of *agape*-love that Jesus talked about. It is a love that makes us present to those who suffer. It is a love that seeks to understand the causes of this suffering. It is a love that seeks to transform situations of injustice and conflict. It is a love that builds solidarity among us as members of society as we work to improve living conditions. It is a love that, in the end, Jesus will acknowledge: "Come, you that are blessed by my Father, inherit the kingdom prepared for you from the foundation of the world; for I was hungry and you gave me food, I was thirsty and you gave me something to drink, I was a stranger and you welcomed me…" (Matthew 25.34-35).

Focus your learning

- **Aware and Informed**
  What is social witness?

- **Practical and Active**
  How can I make a difference?

- **Creative and Grateful**
  How does the social action taken by others make my life better?

Key terms

social action	gospel value
social issue	common good
value	

24 hours to better the world

(by Paul Irish, reprinted with permission – Toronto Star Syndicate)

What a difference a day makes.

For 24 hours beginning at 9 a.m. today, 500 Catholic high school students will travel to 100 locations on 10 buses to tidy for the infirm, visit the elderly, feed the homeless and, hopefully, learn a bit about themselves and the people around them.

The program is called the 24 Hours of Service, and it's a non-stop, around-the-clock marathon that organizers say changes participants forever.

"When it's all over, the kids are exhausted, but they're happy and really feel they've learned something and contributed," says coordinator Neil MacCarthy of ShareLife, the charitable fundraising arm of the Toronto archdiocese which runs the event. "It's an experience they never forget."

The program started in 1999 with just three buses and 120 students, and has since mushroomed.

MacCarthy says the 24 Hours of Service emphasizes the ability of youth to make a positive contribution to the community.

"It's about helping one another and leadership," said MacCarthy, who said students were hand-picked from various schools, with the majority coming from the Toronto,

Dufferin-Peel and York boards. "The students will get a real hands-on experience."

This morning, students will leave Toronto's Cardinal Carter Academy…. They'll pick up trash in parks and beside roads, plant trees, clean and paint, sort clothing for the Salvation Army, and visit seniors and [people with disabilities].

"I'm pumped," said Cardinal Carter participant Mary Anne Afable, 19. "I'm already looking at it as a learning experience and a chance to help others." She said students aren't told exactly what their jobs will be until they arrive at an assignment, but the mystery adds an ingredient of excitement to the day.

Sarah Strathy, 18, also in OAC at Cardinal Carter, says she expects the day to open her eyes. "I think it's going to be great," she said. "I hear it's a lot of work, but I can tell we're all ready for the challenge."

MacCarthy said the students will be on the go all 24 hours, including providing food to the homeless. "Some of these kids may have never spoken with or met a person who lives on the street," MacCarthy said. "It's a first-hand opportunity to break a lot of stereotypes and for them to realize (that) a lot of times, misfortune can be blamed on various circumstances."

A highlight will be a 4:30 a.m. vigil to be held tomorrow at the corner of Yonge and Dundas Streets. The 500 students will fan out to sit silently on the sidewalk in solidarity with Toronto's homeless. "It will last about 20 minutes, and the students will be asked to contemplate what's happening in our society, and perhaps they can say a little prayer," he said. "I'm sure it will be quite a powerful scene." →

Organizers say the marathon ultimately helps participants think about helping the community. "If a student gets the opportunity to help at a food bank during the project, he or she may bring that idea back to his or her own school, and in turn may initiate their own food drive," he said.

"The 24 Hours of Service exposes the students to a lot of great ideas they can bring back to their own school and community."

What value does this kind of project have for the community? for the participants?

Although this even will last for only 24 hours, how do you think that it will affect the young people over the longer term?

Individually, sometimes we may feel that we don't have much to offer, or that we don't know how to participate in social action. How does working in a group help us to respond in an authentic way to Jesus' commandment, "love one another"?

Getting involved

Sometimes, getting involved is the result of our peer group or community drawing us along and supporting us in helping others, such as in the example of the 24 Hours of Service that we read about earlier. At other times, it's like something inside us spontaneously helps us to see the suffering of others, and that moves us to do something. This motivation can be a fleeting emotion. We may give some money and leave it at that – not quite satisfied that we have done enough, but enough to quiet our conscience. We know we can do more but we do not know how to do it. We are surrounded by so many needs that we feel overwhelmed, knowing that we cannot possibly contribute to all of them. So we do little bits here and there.

We may also become selective, focusing our energy into one cause. We support and get involved in areas that have the greatest impact on us or someone close to us. Sometimes this leads us to start something new because no one else has had the same experience as we have. Even then, we cannot do these things alone – we always need support from others. Most issues are too big and too complex for one person to tackle. In the case of many social issues, organizations already exist that have made it their mission to help others. There are local soup kitchens, parent-teacher associations, student unions, medical research societies, housing initiatives, ecological organizations, hospice movements, etc. These organizations allow us to channel our compassion and make it effective. They are a witness that we look after one another.

Our baptism and confirmation in Christ mark us as people who live for others. As Pope John Paul II said, "Solidarity... is not a feeling of vague compassion or shallow distress at the misfortunes of so many people.... It is a firm and persevering determination to commit oneself to the common good; that is to say to the good of all and to each individual... We are all really responsible for all" (*Sollicitudo rei socialis*, 1987, #38).

- Have you ever been involved in an organization or group with a mission to help others? What were your experiences?

- Have you ever wanted to do something but did not know how to go about it? Did you find the task too daunting? What do you think about it now?

- What is the meaning of Pope John Paul II's statement, "We are really responsible for all"? How are we responsible?

Highest quality of life, but not for everyone

Although the majority of people in Canada benefit from the highest quality of life in the world, "the social conditions facing Aboriginal people in Canada, taken by themselves, would place that population in sixty-third place among the nations of the world." ("Aboriginal Land Rights: A Jubilee Challenge Facing Canada," September 25, 2000, #5. For the full text of this letter by 12 of Canada's senior leaders of Christian churches, see the CCCB Web site: www.cccb.ca.)

- How should Christians act if not everyone is benefiting from this country's wealth?

Our call to be involved

One of the scribes came near and… asked him, "Which commandment is the first of all?" Jesus answered, "The first is, 'Hear, O Israel: the Lord our God, the Lord is one; you shall love the Lord your God with all your heart, and with all your soul, and with all your mind, and with all your strength.' The second is this, 'You shall love your neighbour as yourself.' There is no other commandment greater than these."

(Mark 12.28-31)

Democracy requires a system of common values

"Democracy is not a self-sufficient moral system. Democracy, if it is to be healthy, requires more than universal suffrage: it requires the presence of a system of common values.

"If democracy is not to become a democratic tyranny in which the majority oppresses the minority, it is necessary for the public to have an understanding of the common good and the concepts that underlie it."

("The Common Good and the Catholic Church's Social Teaching," Catholic Bishops' Conference of England and Wales, 1996, #34-35)

Civil Society Organizations (CSOs) help to protect the rights of individuals and minorities in a society. Otherwise, a majority may overlook these rights. Recall the definition of rights from Theme 17: *Rights are those things in society to which we are entitled. Some are legal rights (for example, laws that entitle us to a lawyer if we are arrested). Other entitlements are based on human dignity itself, such as people being entitled to food, shelter, work and security of person.* As you review the work that CSOs do in our society, try to identify which kind of rights they are concerned with. How are they contributing to a healthy democracy by promoting public "understanding of the common good and the concepts that underlie it"?

Civil Society Organizations

Civil Society Organizations (CSOs) are groups of citizens who have come together to deal with issues of national or global interest. Around the world, thousands of these CSOs deal with issues that governments are unable or unwilling to undertake. CSOs are now recognized as indispensable links between small communities and national or global communities. They bring to the fore all sorts of concerns: poverty, the environment, health, work, business and international aid. They work to protect human rights, women's rights, and the rights of youth, seniors, people with disabilities, and Indigenous peoples. In the past, these groups were often seen as working against government. Since the 1990s they have begun to be seen in a new light. They have become important groups through which governments are seeking to answer the needs of people. They can help governments increase and enrich the way they interact with citizens.

social action:

The first and greatest commandment is to love God and love your neighbour (Mark 12.28-31). *Social action* is doing things that contribute to the common good. It is concerned with the welfare of each individual. But it is also concerned with the social structures and conditions that affect our health and well-being. (See Principle #2 in Theme 2.)

Canadian social movements and their Civil Society Organizations

1. The Canadian social safety net

Ever since the Depression of the 1930s (and because of it) Canadians have pushed the government to bring in programs that provide the basics of food, shelter and clothing. Welfare, public housing, unemployment insurance, workers' compensation, old age pensions, and the Canada Pension Plan are all part of Canada's social safety net. Around the social safety net there have grown up all sorts of groups that promote, lobby for, and support these programs. Can you identify some?

2. The trade union movement

In the last century unions have dramatically changed the working conditions of the average citizen. They have fought for the 40-hour work week, minimum wages, sick leave, holiday pay, pensions, safety laws and standards, etc. Approximately one of every three workers in Canada belongs to a union. Can you name some unions?

3. Human rights

Canadian chapters of groups such as Amnesty International and Human Rights Watch work to protect human rights. Wherever human rights are threatened or not recognized, we find groups seeking to create awareness and further justice.

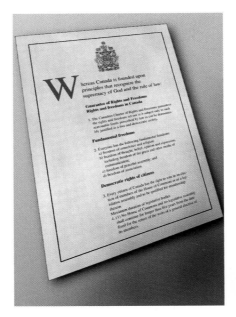

4. Canadian Charter of Rights and Freedoms

Canada has a Charter of Rights and Freedoms enshrined in its constitution. Many groups in Canada have seen new possibilities for justice through the Charter. They have found redress in the courts because of the Charter. Can you identify any such groups who have received compensation for a wrong?

5. Universal health care

Canada's universal health care system has evolved since the province of Saskatchewan established public, universal hospital insurance in 1947. In 1984, Parliament passed the Canada Health Act. It was to ensure that health care was publicly administered, comprehensive, universal and portable. Comprehensive, accessible health care is now considered the right of every Canadian. Today, health care is under pressure because of such things as political policy choices, trade agreements and globalization. Various groups are seeking ways to protect it. (Find the Catholic Health Association of Canada on the Internet: www.chac.ca.)

6. Public broadcasting

The Canadian Broadcasting Corporation was first established in 1936. Since then, Canadians have received government-funded radio and television broadcasting that provides a non-commercial, non-political Canadian perspective on news and culture.

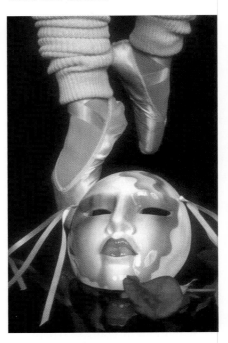

7. Canadian culture

Groups and individuals (including many artists) have been active in defending and promoting Canadian culture. Many CSOs work to enrich

Canada's mosaic of cultural expressions by supporting public broadcasting, Canadian magazines, theatre, dance, music, etc.

8. The ecumenical movement

Each of the Christian churches in Canada has made efforts to overcome the historical conflicts that have divided Christianity. Organizations like the Canadian Council of Churches have for many years promoted the dialogue between various Christian churches and among religions in Canada. (Look up Ten Days for Global Justice on the Internet: www.web.net/~tendays/.)

9. The right to life movement in Canada

A number of organizations, such as Campaign Life, seek to bring an end to abortion in Canada and defend the rights of the unborn.

10. Father Moses Coady and the Antigonish Movement

During the Depression of the 1930s, Fr. Moses Coady started

cooperatives to help people of the Maritimes survive. The cooperative movement has spread beyond the Maritimes to other countries in the world. They now include housing, food, agricultural, credit and buying cooperatives. (See Theme 6.)

11. Aboriginal rights groups

Many Aboriginal groups among the First Peoples in Canada have organized to seek redress for historical injustices. Land claims, rights to resources (fishing and logging) and the survival of Aboriginal languages and cultures are key issues.

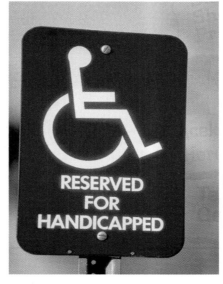

12. People with disabilities

A number of Canadian organizations promote the rights of people with all types of disabilities. Their work covers a range of issues, including accessibility of buildings, jobs, transportation, the Special Olympics, etc.

13. Canadian environmental movement (I)

Throughout Canada, well-organized environmental groups do work in many areas. The groups

covered by this category seek to protect the global environment. They do so by focusing on such things as resources, land use, protection of wildlife, the ozone layer, the preservation of rainforests, and the protection of the oceans against overfishing and pollution.

14. Canadian environmental movement (II)

These groups focus on changing consumer-oriented lifestyles. One major contribution of these groups has been to encourage recycling. Through their efforts, the three Rs – reduce, reuse, recycle – have become normal household practices. These groups also promote environmentally friendly or "green" products.

15. Canadian environmental movement (III)

Groups like the Canadian Environmental Law Association seek to enforce and strengthen existing laws governing our society's impact on the environment. ➔

16. Women's suffrage and women as persons movement

In the late nineteenth century and early twentieth century, women were organizing to get the right to vote. Later, the "Famous Five," whose

statues are found on Parliament Hill, worked for the legal recognition of women as "persons," who could therefore be appointed to the Senate. (See Theme 1.)

17. The women's movement

Even after women won the right to vote and to become senators, the feminist movement continued to struggle for social justice and equality for women. It still faces significant challenges. Today, it seeks reforms in politics, the media, law, health, education, the labour force and the home.

18. Pacifism

These groups are committed to a non-violent lifestyle. They seek

peaceful solutions to situations that could involve violence. They demonstrate against wars, refuse military service and respond to provocation without resorting to violence.

19. The peace movement (Canadian chapters)

This wide-ranging movement sometimes focuses on specific armed conflicts (for example, in Sudan, Tibet, or East Timor). It also addresses global concerns, such as the arms race, nuclear proliferation, etc. The peace movement takes to heart Isaiah's prophetic vision that "they shall beat their swords into ploughshares." (Log onto www.ploughshares.ca.)

20. Canadian anti-poverty groups

These groups work to give the poor a fairer share in the distribution of goods in Canada. They include groups seeking an end to child poverty (1.4 million Canadian children live in poverty), welfare reform, and a fairer distribution of wealth in Canada.

value:

A *value* is a good. Values refer to what is important. We do not create values; we discover them and are attracted to them. For example, we all want good health, a fulfilling life, meaningful employment, adequate food and appropriate housing. These five values exist and are important outside of any choice that we or society may make. If we make the wrong choices (that is, if we do not appreciate these goods or choose these values) then we suffer the consequences as a society. We pay the price in illness, high mortality, unemployment and homelessness.

moral value:

A *moral value* is a virtue. Honesty and tolerance are examples of moral values. When we choose to tell the truth, we develop the virtue of honesty. When we accept and respect others, we develop the virtue of tolerance. When we choose to incorporate positive values into our lives, we become virtuous.

gospel value:

A *gospel value* is a decision to act based on faith in the life, death and resurrection of Jesus. We learn about these values through the gospels and Church tradition. If we have been brought up as Catholics, we will have been taught these values by our parents and caregivers. As we mature, we consciously choose to make these values our own. Gospel values are also moral values. Jesus gives us the strength to choose them and to make them our own.

When I despair, I remember that all through history, the way of truth and love has always won. There have been tyrants and murderers and, for a time, they can seem invincible, but in the end they always fall. Think of it. Always.

(Mahatma K. Gandhi)

social issue:

A *social issue* is a situation of concern in society, brought about by suffering, need, injustice or neglect. Once we identify an issue, we often organize ourselves as individuals or groups to respond to it. Sometimes the issue is handled best by grassroots community organizations (who, for example, might establish a food bank, or work to improve safety in a neighbourhood). At other times the issues are larger, and governments and elected officials bear the responsibility to act (for example, in situations concerning transportation, health, the environment, or social housing). Sometimes we need to call governments to account for allowing injustices to occur – for neglecting those in society who have little economic or political clout.

common good:

The *common good* refers to all the social conditions that make human fulfillment possible. It is made up of three essential elements: (1) respect for the person; (2) the social well-being and development of the group as a whole; and (3) peace, i.e., the stability and security of a just order. (See Catechism, #1906-1909.) To this list, we could also add our responsibility to care for creation, since the health of our environment affects everyone. All Catholics have the mission to work for the common good of society. We do this by bringing gospel values to bear on social issues through social action.

Five steps to effective social action

In the document entitled *Ethical Choices and Political Challenges* (1983), the Canadian bishops introduced a method for helping Catholics fulfill their call to be responsible for others. This method expanded on one developed by Cardinal Joseph Cardijn a century ago for the Young Christian Workers movement. His method of Catholic social action was organized into three phases: see, judge and act. The Canadian bishops added two important steps, resulting in the following five steps:

1. Be present with and listen to the experiences of the poor, the marginalized, the oppressed in our society.

For the Canadian bishops, getting to know and listening to the poor was an essential first step. We need to be close to be able to act. We need to see the poor and the marginalized as more than just outsiders: they are excluded enough already. Solidarity begins by entering into their world.

2. Develop an understanding of the economic, political and social structures that cause human suffering.

This is the same as Catholic social action's "see." However, "seeing" means looking beneath the surface. To really see, we need to understand *why* the poor, the marginalized and the oppressed lack the means to support themselves, *why* they are excluded and *why* they have so little freedom. Much human suffering is not due to natural forces, but cultural ones. It stems from our social and environmental structures. Before we can act, we need to know why and how so many people have been left out.

3. Judge the situation in light of gospel principles and the social teachings of the Church.

Understand which social values and priorities are at stake. As Catholics we always need to bring the gospel of Jesus to bear on social issues. These gospel principles have been worked out in greater detail in the social teachings of the Church (see Theme 17). This is Catholic social action's second step: "judge."

4. Think and act creatively to come up with a different vision and model for social and economic development.

If we want to work toward a different world, we need to work with a vision of what a more just and fair world looks like. Here the gospel can be of great help, because it offers a vision of the kingdom of God. It offers hope. The gospel can help us to imagine a world that is different from the present one; for example, a world in which the poor are blessed.

5. Act in solidarity with those who are poor, oppressed or marginalized, and with other grassroots groups to transform economic, political and social situations that are unjust.

We can't transform the world alone. We need to work together with others. Find out whether others are already trying to change the situation that interests you. Always keep in mind your own Catholic roots and teachings in your social action. This is the third step of Catholic social action: "act."

The five steps of Catholic social action:

- Be *present* to the poor.
- *Understand* the causes of human suffering.
- *Judge* in the light of the gospel and Church teaching.
- *Think creatively*, guided by the vision of the kingdom of God.
- *Act together* to transform unjust situations.

Then the righteous will answer him, "Lord, when was it that we saw you hungry and gave you food, or thirsty and gave you something to drink? And when was it that we saw you a stranger and welcomed you, or naked and gave you clothing? And when was it that we saw you sick or in prison and visited you?" And the king will answer them, "Truly I tell you, just as you did it to one of the least of these who are members of my family, you did it to me"

(Matthew 25.37-40)

The *Catechism of the Catholic Church* and social issues

Respect for one another as persons comes out of looking at our neighbour (no matter who that person is) as "another self." Above all, we need to think about the other's life and the things he or she needs to live it with dignity. No laws could do away with the fears, prejudices, and attitudes of pride and selfishness that are obstacles to building true societies. We can overcome these barriers only through the kind of *agape*-love that finds in everyone a neighbour. The duty of being a neighbour to and serving others is even more urgent when it involves those who are disadvantaged, in whatever way. "As you did it to one of the least of these, you did it to me." (See #1931-1932.)

Theme 25

Social witness to the world

I n this theme you will read about coffee beans in Mexico and water pumps in Uganda, and how both of these things have something to do with our being witnesses to Christ in the world. When we read or hear about globalization in the news, it is often related to the world of business. We may be concerned with it because it affects how and what we study in school in order to get ready to compete and survive in the new global economy. The image of this emerging world in the media is one that we cannot ignore. We often hear the message, "Be ready, or be left behind!"

How should we get ready? What exactly are we getting ready for? Some say that we have to study math and science. Some say that we have to get connected through new information technologies. Others say that we need to encourage free trade, while still others say that we must oppose free trade. Through it all, we must not forget that Christ is the beginning and end of all things.

Focus your learning

● **Aware and Informed**
How does globalization affect people in different parts of the world?

● **Practical and Active**
How can we bear witness to Christ beyond our borders?

● **Creative and Grateful**
Who are the prophets today who challenge the world and give it hope?

For two thousand years since the birth of Jesus, the world has gone through some dramatic changes, and Christ has always been here, present through the Holy Spirit in the Church. This latest area of change is global in scope, and the way it proceeds can affect the life of the entire planet. While technology, economics and politics may all be very important, nothing can be more important than stopping to reflect on our core, our beginning, and our end – Jesus Christ.

Key terms

globalization

economic globalization

ecological globalization

political globalization

Padre Francesco

Meet Padre Francesco, a priest, theologian, activist and entrepreneur. Entrepreneur? That does not quite seem to fit together, does it? Well in his case it does. Padre Francesco's parish consists of more than 30 villages in the State of Oaxaca, Mexico, with mostly Aboriginal peoples. They are organic coffee growers, tending their crop under the shade of trees without chemical fertilizers. For years the coffee growers of the mountain villages had brought their few bags of

Padre Francesco (second from left) with UCIRI workers

coffee down to the valley and sold them to the state-run coffee cooperative. With the few extra pesos the farmers could buy clothing and household items, but little else. Padre Francesco had watched this annual ritual for some time. The people remained dirt poor; the small parcels of land that the villages owned communally provided their basic food, but there was no money for anything except the essentials. There was no way out of the cycle of poverty.

On a trip to Canada and Europe he noted the growing interest in organically grown food. The negative effects on the environment of the farming methods used by agribusiness were causing concern among consumers, and having an effect on the eating and drinking habits of the wealthy nations. People feared that genetically engineered foods, factory farms, and chemical fertilizers, pesticides and herbicides were leading to increased food allergies and illnesses. As a result, supermarkets and numerous smaller grocery stores began to promote ecologically sound products. On his trip, Padre Francesco met with members of Development and Peace, Caritas, Memisa and other Church organizations and came up with an action plan. What if he began a coffee cooperative with his coffee farmers and sold the organically grown coffee to Europe and North America? Thus was born UCIRI, a highly successful cooperative run by the Indigenous people themselves, using an ever growing network of people and organizations who are interested in organically grown coffee and in fair trade practices. In 1999 they produced 30,000 bags of coffee.

Did you know...

...that the Catholic Church teaches a "preferential option for the poor"? This means that the needs of the poor must take precedence over the wants of the wealthy. Globalization must not favour only the wealthy. On Judgment Day, as Pope John Paul II said in Edmonton on his trip to Canada, the poor nations will sit in judgment of the wealthy nations and ask them to give an account of their stewardship.

It did not end there. Through UCIRI, the villages in the mountains used their extra money to build a small agricultural school. They set up a coffee drying, roasting and packaging plant. They created an alternative market in Mexico, where they sold 1500 tons of coffee. Because of the NAFTA free trade agreement, however, many of the young people were leaving the villages to work in sweatshops along the US-Mexico border. So they set up their own blue jean factory to sell to high-end users in North America. Most interestingly, they →

realized the importance of an education program so that people from the villages could learn for themselves and also speak with people in North America and Europe. UCIRI is more than a business and cooperative – it is a way of life. In one of the annual general meetings the theme was *la mística de UCIRI* (the mysticism of UCIRI). They recognize that through their work, they are working to realize the kingdom of God in their own way. One of the coffee farmers' favourite scripture passages became the words of Jesus, rephrased in their own words: "Father, I thank you because you have shown ordinary people, the ones who are forgotten and are at the bottom, what you have kept hidden from the wise and the learned" (see Luke 10.21-24). They embodied part of this mystery. As UCIRI says in one of its slogans: "To fight for the earth is to fight for life."

> - How is the kingdom of God being realized, at least in some small way, among these people?
> - Do you know of any other person or group that does similar work to Padre Francesco?
> - How do religion and business become part of the same reality?
> - How does what happens in one part of the world make a difference in another part?

The whole world in my home

Around the World in Eighty Days was a popular movie in 1956. It was an adaptation of Jules Verne's book by the same name written in 1873. The book was a great success, as was the movie 80 years later, because the world seemed so big and travel seemed so slow. Only 50 years later, a movie about a race around the world in 80 days seems quaint. It is as if space and time have contracted. The world seems smaller. People who once seemed far away and exotic now appear regularly in our homes by way of television, video, radio, Internet, telephone, satellites, faxes, etc. Food products from around the world have become part of our daily cuisine. What used to be strange and foreign is now commonly found in our home or in our neighbourhood. In the 1960s the Canadian media guru, Marshall McLuhan, first coined the phrase, "the global village." The world has indeed become more like a village. We are no longer just local; we have become global. For the Church, which has always proclaimed itself to be catholic (universal), this has meant immense new possibilities. The sufferings and concerns of our fellow humans around the earth touch us as never before. We can no longer ignore the hunger, earthquakes, floods or wars of our global village. The celebration and joys of people halfway around the world are our joys and celebration as well. We have become catholic in a new way.

Globalization

Globalization has become a household word. But what has it meant to our daily lives? What difference has it made to the way we live in the world? Not so long ago it was unheard of to be able to send a message from Canada to another part of the world instantly and at a negligible cost. News about political events and natural disasters across the world would take days to reach Canadians. Today it is a matter of minutes. This apparent shrinking of distance and time has come to be called globalization.

What has happened to make the world seem like it has shrunk to a global village? Several factors have brought this about, but three key ones stand out: technology, economics and politics.

Technology

The technological revolution of the twentieth century has changed our understanding of time and space. The most drastic change occurred in the speed of communication. In a relatively short time span, people have invented the telegraph, radio, telephone, television, satellites, computers, cell phones, and the Internet, with new technologies emerging daily. In wealthy nations, nearly everyone is wired for communication. Today we expect communications to take place in seconds, rather than days, weeks or years.

Economics

Business has gone global. Although there are still many local companies that serve local needs, more and more companies have become international. Boundaries between countries, which in the past stopped trade, have been opened. Countries have banded together to form international free trade zones. Financial markets have been deregulated and function around the clock. Transnational companies see themselves as companies without borders. They move operations in accordance with what are called "market forces." Often this means finding the cheapest and least regulated locations to maximize their profits. Everyone has become an investor in the economy. The economy is the driving force behind globalization.

Politics

Until 1989 the world was dominated by two powerful groups who waged a sort of "cold war" against each other. On one side was the United States and Europe; on the other, Russia and its satellites. This world order broke down when the communist government in the former Soviet Union fell in 1989. Now you could say there is only one superpower: the United States. Economics and the "market" govern the new world order. Nation states such as Canada, Mexico, and the countries of the European Union have lost varying degrees of control over their own affairs because of technological and economic globalization. Since the "market" often responds only to economic forces, many people are concerned that democracy is at risk. The strong protest movements against globalization during the past years show that not everyone is happy with the new developments.

Students gather in Quebec City to demonstrate during a socio-economic summit of the Americas.

- What are the three factors fueling the move toward globalization?
- What are the advantages of globalization? What benefits has it brought to people's lives?
- What are the disadvantages of globalization? What dangers do you see for human life?
- What does globalization mean for social justice?

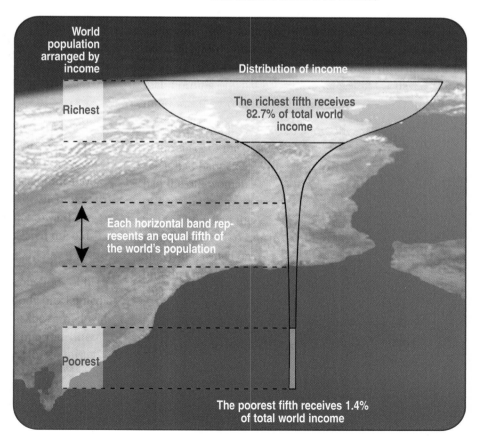

World population arranged by income

Distribution of income

Richest

The richest fifth receives 82.7% of total world income

Each horizontal band represents an equal fifth of the world's population

Poorest

The poorest fifth receives 1.4% of total world income

Globalization and its impact on ecosystems

As we move toward globalized economies, we have begun to ask, Will the earth be able to sustain the current rate of growth? The earth's non-renewable resources are limited. Wealthy nations are using up these non-renewable resources as if there were no tomorrow. If all the nations of the earth were as negligent as those in the North, the earth would soon be exhausted and unlivable. Driven by the economies of the wealthy nations, globalization has become something of a nightmare to the poorer nations. The process of globalization could, however, become the great equalizer for all the nations of the earth, giving poorer nations the chance at a just and equitable distribution of the world's wealth. Then it would be something to celebrate because it would stand as a symbol of justice. However, the distribution of the world's goods has become less rather than more equitable. As the gap between rich and poor grows, the poor often resort to desperate measures to survive.

What does this mean for the world's ecology? For the foreseeable future it means more pollution, more garbage, excessive energy consumption, increased international travel, and an even more inequitable distribution of larger and larger mountains of consumer goods. It means further depletion of the earth's resources and of the ozone layer, global warming, etc. The future of the planet is being placed at risk. So what is the solution?

- How should we reduce this spiralling growth in our consumption? By excluding developing countries from sharing in the consumer goods we enjoy? Surely the poor have just as much right to the earth's goods as the wealthy.
- Or does the challenge lie with the wealthy nations? Is it a matter of simplifying our lifestyle?
- Can we trust that technology will save us from the negative consequences of globalization?
- Do we have to come to a new understanding of global justice?

global warming:

Global warming refers to the worldwide increases in average temperature that are attributed to the warming effect of "greenhouse" gases, principally carbon dioxide. These gases trap heat within the atmosphere, much like glass and plastic trap heat in a greenhouse. The burning of fossil fuels, deforestation and other human activities are the main causes of the increase in greenhouse gas concentrations. In addition to climate change, global warming increases sea levels by melting polar ice caps.

ozone depletion:

Ozone depletion is the destruction of the stratospheric zone of the earth's atmosphere due to the release of chlorofluorocarbons, or CFCs, into the environment. CFCs, which come from such sources as coolants, cleaning solvents, plastics, aerosol propellants and foam insulation, eventually reach the upper atmosphere and act as catalysts that destroy ozone molecules. The ozone layer plays a crucial role in filtering out harmful ultraviolet radiation from the sun.

The Catholic Church and globalization

As with all other social issues, our reaction to globalization as Catholics is motivated by who we are – witnesses to Christ. The Church, through its teachings and its actions, bears witness to the fact that Jesus Christ is forever faithful to the poor. No matter how complex the issue of globalization, and whether or not it is good for humanity, the basis of our response must come from our relationship with Christ. Three fundamental aspects of the Church can help us answer the question of whether globalization is good or bad:

1. Unity among peoples

God is one and at the same time three persons. We call this the doctrine of the Trinity. As the world becomes increasingly one, it reflects the Trinity. As an image of the Trinity, however, the oneness of our world must respect the rich diversity of peoples and cultures. Jesus was looking for unity when he sent forth his disciples. He told them to go and "make disciples of all nations baptizing them in the name of the Father and of the Son and of the Holy Spirit" (Matthew 28.19). Through globalization the world can become a trace of God. As the Church we have a mission to ensure that our growing unity does not mean losing our rich diversity.

2. Formed in the image of Christ

In Christ, God began a new gathering of humanity. All of humanity was to be formed in the image of Christ. This process toward unity was set in motion in the incarnation. As we read in the Letter to the Ephesians, "God put this power to work in Christ when he raised him from the dead.... And [God] has made him the head over all things... the fullness of him who fills all in all" (Ephesians 1.20-13). Christ is cosmic: he is at work in everything, including the powers that are shaping our world into one, diversified whole.

3. Catholic

The Church's mission is to be "catholic." To be catholic means to be universal, that is, spread over the whole world. To be catholic means that no one is excluded. For the Church to be catholic means that each and everyone is necessary to make the body of Christ complete. It does not mean that one country or culture dominates the others. It means that everyone's witness must be heard. Unity needs diversity.

- How can globalization be a positive thing?
- How is Christ present in the process of globalization?
- What is the role of the Church in the process of globalization?

So how should the Church respond to globalization? There are basically two things we need to do:

- Welcome the growth toward unity that globalization is bringing about. The world is one and all human beings are one another's brothers and sisters. No one is to be left out. Support all genuine growth toward world unity.

- Respect the mosaic of culture and language of all the peoples of the earth. Don't try to homogenize all this diversity into one world culture. The model for Catholics lies in their understanding of the local Church, the diocese. The basic unit of the universal Church is the local Church, whether it is the Diocese of Hamilton, Regina or Beijing. Knowing who we are as a Church, we, the Catholic Church, bear witness actively to Jesus Christ, who is the "way, the truth and the life." Each local Church as a communion is an expression of the whole; it is not just a part of a whole. It is the whole Christ. Similarly, in each culture and language and people, all of humanity is present. Witnessing to Christ as a communion of peoples united in the same Lord is perhaps the greatest contribution that the Church can make to the creation of a global village.

Pursue a globalization based on sound ethical values

VATICAN CITY, MAY 17, 2001 (VIS) – The Holy Father this morning addressed three hundred participants in a meeting promoted by the Ethics and Economy Foundation of Bassano del Grappa, Italy. He focused his talk on the phenomenon of globalization, underlining that "the word 'global,' if understood coherently, must include everyone."

The Pope encouraged the members of this new foundation as they strive towards a "well-articulated reflection on globalization, solidarity and free economic initiatives based on solid ethical and spiritual values." He animated them "to pursue this work to insert into the economic field the expectations and indications of the Magisterium and Social Doctrine of the Church."

He said that globalization is "no doubt a phenomenon which allows for great possibilities for growth and producing riches," but "many also admit that per se it does not assure fair distribution of goods among the citizens of various countries. In reality, the wealth produced often remains in the hands of only a few, with a consequent further loss of sovereignty of national states, already rather weak in the area of development."

"The Church's doctrine," John Paul II affirmed, "teaches that economic growth must be integrated with high values, so as to become qualitative growth; therefore, fair, stable, respectful of cultural and social individuality, as well as ecologically sustainable."

He contended that "[humanity] must be the protagonist, not the slave, of the means of production... Globalization is... a phenomenon which is intrinsically ambivalent, halfway between a potential good for mankind and social damage with serious consequences."

"There must be," the Pope concluded, "intensified collaboration between politics and economy," especially to care for "those who could be victims of globalization on a worldwide scale. I am thinking, for example, of instruments which could alleviate the heavy burden of foreign debt of developing countries, or legislation which protects [children] from exploitation which occurs when children are sent to work."

Natural law

St. Thomas Aquinas, a member of the Dominican order, formulated the Catholic understanding of natural law. This law states that God created the universe and gave it a natural order. We are part of that order. We have been given the intelligence to be able to determine and uphold the laws of this natural order. All things in nature operate according to the laws that were implanted in them by God. Through the use of reason, we can study the natural order of the world and come to understand the way that God intended us to live. For example, we all understand that murder, lying and cheating are wrong. We recognize that, by their very nature, these actions are wrong. Aquinas believed that nature had the power to reveal divine order to the extent that human beings were able to understand. →

All Catholic social justice teachings are based on natural law theory. Any action or situation that is in conflict with natural law is seen as an injustice either to people or to the earth's natural resources, which sustain our existence.

- What do you think is meant by "order" and "natural law"?
- Can you give examples that support natural law theory?
- Can you think of an example of how natural law theory can apply to a particular social issue?

Who is a prophet anyway?

We hear many voices today speaking out on globalization and the resulting social issues. How can we begin to tell who may be a prophet in our time, and who is nothing more than a false prophet? Here are some criteria to help us distinguish the true from the false prophets:

True prophets

Do not attempt to call attention to their own person as much as their message

Often do not see themselves as worthy or capable of the missions God has given them to do and often ask not to be chosen

Although they may themselves be the centre of controversy, they promote unity, peace and justice

Willing to sacrifice their lives if necessary in order to be true to the message they proclaim

Are always concerned first about the welfare of others

False prophets

Often seek personal glory and praise, and perhaps material reward

Often create dissension for its own sake or to serve the goals of a very small, vested-interest group

Seldom "go the extra mile" if confronted by the threat of harm to their person

Despite their facade, will eventually come across as selfish or in serious error about the true nature of the human person

Ryan's well

by Ryan Hreljac, Ryan's Well Foundation

I am nine years old and I go to Holy Cross School in Kemptville, Ontario. I want to tell you about what one person can do to make the world a better place. Every eight seconds someone in this world dies because they don't have clean water. That makes me very sad.

I was in Grade 1 when I decided to build a well for the people in Africa. We were talking about people who didn't have toys or even clean water. Mrs. Prest, my teacher, told me how money that we raise could be used to help them. One cent was for a pencil. Two dollars was for a blanket. Five dollars was for five hot lunches. Then I heard Mrs. Prest say that $70 was for a water pump.

When I heard that people were dying because they didn't have clean water, I asked my Mom and Dad for →

the money. I begged and begged them. They told me that I could do extra chores to earn the money. I did lots of chores like vacuuming, washing windows, picking up brush from the ice storm and picking up pinecones for my Nana's crafts with my brothers Jordan and Keegan. When Mom and Dad gave me money for the work, I put it in a cookie tin up on the fridge, and that's how my well began.

After four months I saved my $70, and I took the money to WaterCan (a Canadian aid organization). When they told me that the $70 will buy a pump but that it was going to cost a lot more to build a well, I said I would just do more chores. My project got noticed by other people. Then lots of other people sent money. I can't believe I have my well now at Angolo Primary School in northern Uganda.

Next I worked for money for drilling equipment so there would be lots of wells. When you add CIDA's (Canadian International Development Agency) money in, I helped collect over $240,000 for water projects in Uganda.

Last summer I went to Africa to see my well and my new drilling rig. I went to Angolo Primary School to see my well. It was so cool. I drank from my well. It tasted so good! The school had a huge celebration. About five thousand people came. I also spent a day at the school. There were over one hundred kids in my class. We all sat on the ground. It was very crowded but I still had fun.

In Africa they say, "Water is life." Now I really understand what they mean. I dream of the day when everyone in Africa has clean water. That's a big dream. But I

learned that you can do anything, but only if you try really hard and you really want to. I want clean water for all of Africa so I know that I will need to help in other countries too. I will keep helping Uganda, but now I will help Tanzania too. Tanzania is one of the poorest countries in the whole world. They have a school in every village but they need help with wells and springs too, just like in Uganda.

I have a foundation called "Ryan's Well." My partners are WaterCan and CPAR (Canadian Physicians for Aid and Relief). This world belongs to all of us. I figure that if we all work together, we can make the whole world a great place for everyone!

- What moved Ryan to begin this project?
- What factors make his contribution to the world's poor so remarkable?
- Why do you think others became interested enough in Ryan's project to want to help him?
- How do you think Ryan's efforts have made a difference to the people of this small village in Uganda?
- Why do you think Ryan's parents thought it was important to take him to Uganda for the well-opening ceremonies?
- What do you think gave Ryan the courage to believe that he could raise so much money?

Journal reflection: Write about your reaction to the story of Ryan's well. What does this story confirm for you about the ability of young people to act on behalf of those in need?

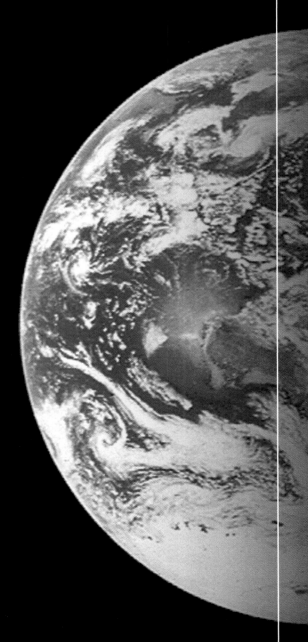

Then I saw a new heaven and a new
earth; for the first heaven and the first
earth had passed away, and the sea was
no more.... And I heard a loud voice
from the throne saying,

"See, the home of God is
    among mortals.
He will dwell with them as
    their God;
they will be his peoples,
and God himself will be with
them;
he will wipe every tear from
    their eyes.
Death will be no more;
mourning and crying and pain
    will be no more,
for the first things have
    passed away."

And the one who is seated on the throne
said, "See I am making all things new....
I am the Alpha and the Omega, the
beginning and the end."

(Revelation 21.1-6)

Unit 8 review

In this unit, you explored the call to bear witness to Christ in the world.

Aware and Informed

What is witness?

A witness is one who gives testimony about the truth. To be a witness for Christ is to be faithful to Christ in our daily lives, in what we say and do.

What is social witness?

Social witness is living according to the teachings of Jesus within the community, extending respect to all people. It means treating everyone as a neighbour. This is even more urgent in cases where people are suffering and disadvantaged. Jesus said, "As you did it to one of the least of these, you did it to me."

How does globalization affect people in different parts of the world?

Pope John Paul II said that globalization is "no doubt a phenomenon which allows for great possibilities for growth and producing riches" but "many also admit that per se it does not assure fair distribution of goods among the citizens of various countries. In reality, the wealth produced often remains in the hands of only a few, with a consequent further loss of sovereignty of national States, already rather weak in the area of development…. Economic growth must be integrated with high values, so as to become qualitative growth; therefore, fair, stable, respectful of cultural and social individuality, as well as ecologically sustainable."

Practical and Active

How can I live my baptismal calling?

My baptismal calling is to be faithful to Christ, to be a witness to the truth. To be a witness for Christ requires a lifelong commitment to be ready and willing to give of ourselves in love. Sometimes this calls us to go against the tide in order to follow Jesus. It means seeking life for all people to the full, in faith, hope and love.

How can I make a difference?

The Canadian bishops offer us a five-step method for making a difference in the world:

1. Be present to the poor, marginalized and oppressed, and listen to their experiences.

2. Understand the economic, political and social structures that cause human suffering.

3. Judge the situation in light of the gospel and the social teachings of the Church.

4. Think and act creatively to come up with a vision of the world more in keeping with the kingdom of God.

5. Act in solidarity with others who are working for justice.

How can we bear witness to Christ beyond our borders?

The Catholic Church teaches a "preferential option for the poor." This means that the needs of the poor must take precedence over the wants of the wealthy. Globalization must not become a process that favours only the wealthy. We must "think globally and act locally." Since our world is so interconnected and interdependent, our consumption habits have an impact beyond our borders. We must also share our wealth to meet the needs of people in developing countries.

Creative and Grateful

You can answer these questions for yourself. The answer is found in your relationship with God.

How does God call out the best in each one of us?

How does the social action of others make my life better?

Who are the prophets today who give the world hope?

Section III

Celebrating Christ in our Culture

Section aim: to pull together the year's work, and to celebrate Christ in our culture

Unit 9 Celebrating Christ in our culture

Aim: to celebrate Christ's promise in our lives

We are a eucharistic community

Focus your learning

- **Aware and Informed**

  How does our celebration of the Eucharist affect how we see the world?

- **Practical and Active**

  How can we look at life as people of the Eucharist?

- **Creative and Grateful**

  Can we be anything but thankful to God when we recognize how we have been blessed through Jesus Christ?

This theme is different from the others. At this point, you will have the opportunity to review all that you have covered this year from both a personal and an academic perspective. As part of that review, you are encouraged to put on a pair of "glasses" through which to view the entire course. Like sunglasses, these glasses filter the course material, and give it a certain shade. The "glasses" you will put on are the "glasses" of the Eucharist. More than anything else, our Catholic faith is shaped and nourished by the celebration of Eucharist. As a eucharistic people, we have a unique perspective to offer our culture.

We are a eucharistic people

At the start of the new millennium Pope John Paul II wrote: "Young people, whatever their possible ambiguities, have a profound longing for those genuine values which find their fullness in Christ. Is not Christ the secret of true freedom and profound joy of heart? Is not Christ the supreme friend and teacher of all friendship? If Christ is presented to young people as he really is, they experience him as an answer that is convincing and they can accept his message, even when it is demanding and bears the mark of the cross. For this reason, in response to their enthusiasm, I did not hesitate to ask them to make a radical choice of faith and life and present them with a stupendous task to become 'morning sentinels' (see Isaiah 21.11-12) at the dawn of the new millennium."

As you begin your review of all the work you have done this year, look at the "stupendous task" that the Pope says is yours. You are sentinels of the morning. You have the mission to announce where Christ is among us, in our culture. Since the beginning of Christianity, the Eucharist has been the source and summit of Christian life. We are a eucharistic people, and our fundamental attitude towards life is one of gratitude. We receive life from God with thanksgiving. St. Augustine, a bishop of the early Church, challenged his congregation at the end of Mass to "Go and become what you have received, the body of Christ." That is our challenge, too.

- What do you think St. Augustine meant by his challenge to his congregation?
- What does it mean to be eucharistic people?
- If this is to be the perspective of your review, what sorts of things do you think you will be focusing on in your review of the year?

Looking back: A personal review of *Christ and Culture*

Use these questions to guide your review of each theme:

- What did I think or feel about this theme when it was first introduced?
- What did I learn about this theme from the class activities?
- How has studying this theme affected my life, my relationships, my feelings, my actions and my values?
- How has this theme challenged or nurtured my relationship with Christ and the Church?

Select one of the following formats to record your reflections:

diary

book of reflections

prayer journal

word collage or art collage

poetry or prose

some other format (check with your teacher for approval)

Christ giver

He was old, tired, and sweaty, pushing his homemade cart down the alley,
    stopping now and then to poke around in somebody's garbage.
I wanted to tell him about Eucharist, but the look in his eyes, the despair
    on his face, the hopelessness of somebody else's life in his cart, told me
    to forget it.
So, I smiled, said "Hi!" – and gave him Eucharist.

She was cute, nice build, too much paint, a little wobbly on her feet as she
    slid from her barstool, and very definitely on the make.
"No thanks, not tonight," I said – and I gave her Eucharist.

She lived alone, her husband dead, her family gone. And she talked at you,
    not to you; words, endless words, spewed out.
So I listened – and gave her Eucharist.

Downtown is nice, lights change from red to green and back again,
Flashing blues, pinks, and oranges.
I gulped them in, said "Thank you, Father" – and made them Eucharist.

I laughed at myself, and told myself, "You, with all your sins, all your self-
    ishness,
I forgive you, I accept you, I love you."
It's nice – and so very necessary too – to give yourself Eucharist.

Tired, weary, disgusted, lonely. Go to your friends, open their door, say,
    "Look at me" – and receive their Eucharist.

My Father, when will we learn you cannot talk Eucharist,
cannot philosophize about it – you do it!

You don't dogmatize Eucharist; sometimes you laugh it, sometimes you cry
    it, often you sing it.
Sometimes it's a wild peace, then crying hurt, often humiliating, never
    deserved.
You see Eucharist in another's eyes, give it in another's hand held tight,
    squeeze it in an embrace.

You pause Eucharist in the middle of a busy day, speak Eucharist with a
    million things to do and a person who wants to talk.
For Eucharist is as simple as being on time, and as profound as sympathy.

I give you my supper, I give you my sustenance, I give you my life,
I give you me, I give to you Eucharist.

Excerpts from a homily given by Bishop Michael Malone, Catholic Bishop of the Maitland-Newcastle
Diocese, Australia, on the occasion of the Diocesan Jubilee Mass, Feast of Corpus Christi, 2000.

Jesus said to them, "I am the bread of life. Whoever comes to me will never be hungry, and whoever believes in me will never be thirsty.... Everything that the Father gives me will come to me, and anyone who comes to me I will never drive away; for I have come down from heaven, not to do my own will, but the will of him who sent me. And this is the will of him who sent me, that I should lose nothing of all that he has given me, but raise it up on the last day. This is indeed the will of my Father, that all who see the Son and believe in him may have eternal life; and I will raise them up on the last day."

(John 6.35, 37-40)

The *Catechism of the Catholic Church* and Eucharist

The Eucharist is the source and summit of the Christian life. All of the other sacraments, and the work and life of the Church, are bound up with the Eucharist and are oriented towards it, because Christ himself is present in the Eucharist. (See #1324.)

Theme 27

We celebrate Christ's promise in our lives

This seems like an ending, but in many ways it is also just the beginning. Life is like a spiral – most things go around and around through the cycles of our days, weeks and years. While many things change, many more things seem to remain constant, except that we go deeper and deeper each time around. We get a fuller sense of life the more we experience it.

You now have the experience of another religion course behind you. A cycle of that spiral has come full circle. That means that you are setting out on another cycle where you will experience new things, and see old things in a new way. You are bringing with you insights and experiences that you did not have before. You will change the world through your thoughts and actions. Be faithful to Jesus, and through the power of the Holy Spirit working in you, you will bring Christ to your culture. But for now, hold everything! It's time to celebrate!

Focus your learning

● **Aware and Informed**
How has God blessed you?

● **Practical and Active**
How do we receive what God wants to give us?

● **Creative and Grateful**
How can we best give thanks to God?

"Go forth to love and serve the Lord."

[Christ] is the image of the invisible God,
the firstborn of all creation;
for in him all things in heaven and on earth were created,
things visible and invisible...
– all things have been created through him and for him.
He himself is before all things,
and in him all things hold together.
He is the head of the body, the church;
he is the beginning, the firstborn from the dead,
so that he might come to have first place in everything.
For in him all the fullness of God was pleased to dwell,
and through him God was pleased to reconcile to himself all things,
whether on earth or in heaven,
by making peace through the blood of his cross.

(Colossians 1.15-20)

Acknowledgements

Christ and Culture, Student Text, is the Grade 10 catechetical resource of the *We Are Strong Together* © series, written and produced by the National Office of Religious Education of the Canadian Conference of Catholic Bishops, Ottawa, Canada.

Approved by
The Episcopal Commission for Christian Education, Canadian Conference of Catholic Bishops, Accompanying Bishop: Most Rev. Richard Grecco.

Project Specialist, Youth Portfolio
Jonas Abromaitis

Editing and Writing Specialist
Alan Born

Resource Development Group
Jonas Abromaitis, Marchelle Ball, Chris Brochu Soentgerath, Joanne Chafe, Bob Gagnon, Most Rev. Richard Grecco, Lynn Haley, Frank Kewin, Sharron McKeever, John van den Hengel

We acknowledge with gratitude the work of Heather Reid and Myrtle Power in guiding the development of the liturgical and prayer resources of this program.

We also thank Hans Posthuma and Nancy Keyes for their assistance in editing and proofreading the text.

Finally, we thank the pilot teachers, co-ordinators, consultants, school boards, dioceses and others throughout Canada who contributed to the development of this resource.

Citations and Text References
The Scripture quotations contained herein are from the New Revised Standard Version of the Bible, copyrighted 1989 by the Division of Christian Education of the National Council of the Churches of Christ in the United States of America, and are used by permission. All rights reserved.

Excerpts from THE JERUSALEM BIBLE, copyright © 1966 by Doubleday, a division of Bantam Doubleday Dell Publishing Group, Inc. and Darton, Longman and Todd, Ltd. Reprinted by permission of the publisher.

Excerpts and logo from the *Catechism of the Catholic Church* – Copyright © Concacan, Inc. – LIBRERIA EDITRICE VATICANA, 1999, for the English translation in Canada.

Excerpts from the *General Directory for Catechesis* – Copyright © Concacan, Inc., 1997. All rights reserved.

Excerpts from the English translation of *Rite of Holy Week* © 1972, International Committee on English in the Liturgy, Inc. (ICEL); excerpts from the English translation of *The Roman Missal* © 1973, ICEL; excerpts from the English translation of *Rite of Christian Initiation of Adults* © 1985, ICEL. All rights reserved.

The English translation of *The Lord's Prayer*, prepared by the English Language Liturgical Consultation (ELLC), 1988.

Art and Design
Creative Art & Design, CCCB Publications Service

Cover Art: Ron Tourangeau

Illustrations: Nora Brown, Ron Tourangeau

Photos
Berkeley Studios - United Church of Canada – 105C; www.catholicworker.org - 204, 205; Cartolibreria Salbaroli – 60, 65, 67C, 71; CCCB – 46, 74CL, 75C, 216CL; CCCB/Ron Tourangeau – 11 All; Corel Corporation – 41, 43 All, 51; Corbis International – 13; CP Picture Archive – 24/Thaksina Khaikaew, 25BR, 26/Craig Douce, 28, 237BR/Chuck Stoody Pool, 66CR/Brian Hendler, 146/Jacques Brinon, 223CR/Jacques Boissinot; Fr. Andrew Shim – 191CL(b); Instituto Geografico De Agostini/William Morrow: New York - 89; The Jerusalem Post/Ariel Jerozolimski – 66BL; Joyce Harpell – 44, 202T, 202C, 232, 238TL; L'Arche Cape Breton – 18CR; Lifetouch Canada Inc. – 123; Magnum Photos, Inc/Micha Bar'Am – 58; Marta Braiterman Tanenbaum – 62BR, 62TR; NASA – Cover and inside background, 139C, 223BR, 229, Unit Titles; National Conservation Training Centre – USFWS/Canada Geese by Wyman Meinzer – 17; National Oceanographic and Atmospheric Administration/NOAA – 22/Commander John Bortniak, 40TR/The magical power of that morning cup of coffee/OAR/ERL/NSSL; Nova Development Corporation – Cover and inside background, 10, 12, 27, 29, 32-33 All except TLa, TLe, TLg, BLb, 37, 42 All, 49CL, 49CR, 63, 64, 68, 73, 76-77 All except 77CR, 79TR, 79CR, 85CR, 87TR, 91, 94, 96, 98, 101, 103, 104-105 All except 105C, 106, 107, 111, 117, 120, 121, 124, 125, 126, 128, 129TL, 129TC, 131TL, 131BL, 132, 138TR, 138CL, 138C, 139TL, 147, 151TL, 151 All, 151BL, 152TR, 154, 165, 176, 176, 178, 178, 185 All, 197, 200, 214BR, 214TL, 215 All, 216CR, 216TC, 219 All, 222, 234-35 All, 238TR, Unit Titles; Courtesy of Odessa Filmworks – 152C; Pam Driedger – 180BL; Library of Parliament of Canada – 35BL, 164; Pèlerinage sainte Thérèse de Lisieux – 100; Philip J. Horrigan – 82TR; PhotoDisc, Inc. – 36TR; Photos To Go – 8TR; Planet Art – 59, 69, 97, 114-115, 157; Pontificio Consiglio per i Laici – 53 All, 199, 206CR, 207 All, 208, 209 All, 226TR, 238CR, 238BR; Ron Tourangeau – Good Shepherd cover and inside, 92, 182; Servizio Fotografico de "L'O.R." – 55, 83, 172, 231, 233, 239; ShareLife/Henry Lam – 211 All, 212; Sister Servants of Mary Immaculate – 74TR; image: size-isnt-everything.co.uk – 93, 114-115TL, 116, 137, 138TR, 138BC, 139TC, 149TR, 160, 223TL; Skjold Photographs – Cover BRa,b,c, 5, 6, 7, 13C, 14, 16, 18TC, 23, 31, 32-33 TLa, TLe, TLg, BLb, 36TC, 38, 39, 54, 61, 62BC, 62BL, 77CR, 79CR, 81CR, 81BR, 86, 90, 112, 113, 118, 119, 122BC, 122BL, 122BR, 122TC, 122TL, 128CR, 129BL, 129C, 129CL, 129TR, 135CR, 136, 144, 156, 161, 169, 184, 188, 191CLc, 237BR, 237C, 237TL, 237TR, 239C, 239TC, 239TL; Susan Hreljac, Ryan's Well Foundation – 227, 228 All; Tom Hocker/Tree of Life Imports – 57, 82BR, 167, 238C; Union of Indigenous Communities in the Istmo Region (UCIRI) – 220, 221 All; W.P. Wittman Photography Limited – Cover BRd, 25TR, 35TR, 79CR, 79BR, 80, 81TL, 122TR, 133, 142 All, 143, 158, 170, 177, 178, 178, 186, 187, 189, 191BR, 191BC, 191BL, 191TL, 191CLd, 192, 202BL, 210, 238CL, 238BL.

Printed and Bound in Canada by
Transcontinental Printing

Published by
Publications Service, Canadian Conference of Catholic Bishops, 2500 Don Reid Drive, Ottawa, Ontario, Canada K1H 2J2
Tel.: 1-800-769-1147
www.cccbpublications.ca

Christ and Culture, Student Text, Copyright © Concacan, Inc., 2001. All rights reserved.

Reprinted in 2002, 2005 and 2009.

ISBN 978-0-88997-457-9

Legal Deposit
National Library of Canada, Ottawa, Ontario

CCCB Publication Code: 183-285